THE GRAIN OF WHEAT

THE
GRAIN OF WHEAT

FRANK PAKENHAM
EARL OF LONGFORD

> 'Except a grain of wheat falls into the
> earth and dies, it abideth by itself.
> But if it dies, it beareth much fruit.'

COLLINS
ST JAMES'S PLACE, LONDON

William Collins Sons & Co Ltd
London · Glasgow · Sydney · Auckland
Toronto · Johannesburg

First published March 1974
Reprinted March 1974
© The Earl of Longford 1974

ISBN 0 00 216263 6

Set in Monotype Fontana
Made and printed in Great Britain by
William Collins Sons & Co Ltd Glasgow

TO ELIZABETH

Contents

List of Illustrations   *page* 7
ACKNOWLEDGMENTS   9
INTO POSITION   11

PART ONE

POLITICS
   I A Gilded Seat   27
  II Man Proposes   43
 III Resignation   62

PART TWO

IRELAND
   I A Dual Allegiance   81
  II The Dormant Years   90
 III The Sleeper Stirs   97
 IV The Reckoning   107

PART THREE

PRISONERS
   I Punishment and After   119
  II A Life Sentence   140
AT THE SIDE OF YOUTH   153

PART FOUR

THE PERMISSIVE SOCIETY   177

PORNOGRAPHY
   I A Moral Imperative   186
  II 'Straight Ahead, of course'   197
 III Questions and Answers   208
 IV Cheers and Hisses   219

PART FIVE

BOOKS IN MY WORLD   233
CLOSE AT HOME   248
TO LIVE IS TO SUFFER   261
A SINGLE THREAD   271
INDEX   281

Illustrations

Between pages 104-5
The Pakenham Family, 1948
The author with Eamon de Valera (Lensmen)
The Wilson Cabinet, 1964
Melting Pot Foundation, Brixton (Brian Moody)

Between pages 200-201
'Lord Porn' Cartoons
    (*Evening Standard* and John Murray)
Some members of the Pornography Committee
    (*The Times*)
A new beginning (*Allan Warren*)

Acknowledgments

I am deeply grateful to all those who have in any way helped with this book. My Personal Assistant, Gwen Keeble, has been more concerned with it than anyone. She and Barbara Winch typed the manuscript. Marigold Johnson, the 'scribe' of our Pornography Report, has again been invaluable. Molly Barger, John McBennett, Father Cronin and Basil Rooke-Ley have helped me at various stages. The members of my family have never failed in benevolent criticism. Judith has been kind enough to prepare the Index; may it be the other way round next time! Elizabeth has fostered in me yet once more 'the impossible dream' of living up to her standard.

The text was completed by the end of April 1973. The proofs were handed in finally at the end of October. Many things have occurred in the great world and on my little stage in the interval. The Irish situation has moved on, as have the various organisations I have been concerned with and the individuals I care for. Roy Robertson remains in charge at the New Bridge; David Turner has succeeded Jon Snow at New Horizon. I have made as few changes as possible. It seemed best to finish the story at a definite moment.

London
October 1973

Into Position

'The blackbird says to him, "brother, brother,
If this be the last song you shall sing,
Sing well, for you may not sing another.
Brother, sing!"'

JULIAN GRENFELL
Into Battle

For the third time I am writing memoirs.

'Three times is a lot,' wrote Sir Winston Churchill in connection with alleged failures at the Battle of Jutland. I can fairly claim that a lot has happened to me since my previous autobiographies *Born to Believe* and *Five Lives* were published in 1953 and 1964. Among other things, I have sat in, and resigned from, a Cabinet, led the House of Lords, founded with friends and presided over a novel form of youth centre, written alone or jointly more than one book, entered publishing as the chairman of an old-established firm, initiated and chaired an Inquiry whose fame or notoriety became worldwide, and been mixed up throughout with Irish affairs and prisoners.

The most celebrated autobiographies, those, for example, of Saint Augustine, Rousseau, Cardinal Newman and Benvenuto Cellini, have usually been compressed into a single book. Casanova illustrates the opposite practice and so, more happily, do Sir Osbert Sitwell and, through his *Diaries*, Sir Harold Nicolson. Evelyn Waugh was generous to his friends, but caustic about their memoirs. His own first volume left him in his early twenties, so that much more was reasonably expected. No man, as Parnell might have said, can say to the autobiographer, 'thus far shalt thou go and no farther'. In my case, if anyone asks me 'do you think that three volumes have really been necessary?' I must leave the public to answer. What follows is, broadly speaking, the history of my last ten years. But I am assuming that many will not have come across the earlier volumes or, if they have, will not remember them.

When I was asked in 1936 on joining the Labour Party what made me a Socialist, I am on record as replying: 'A study of the Gospels and the influence of my wife.' That still seems to me the essential truth. But two other factors cannot be passed over. There were my family circumstances and my special kind of brain, painfully limited in the sphere of the arts and natural sciences, well above average in literature and very strongly developed for any logical purpose. But in terms of career, nothing would have happened to me without my wife. I can conceive of myself as marrying no one else, and I sometimes think I would otherwise have finished as a lay brother in a monastery - possibly as their public relations officer, or keeping the books not very accurately.

My family background cannot entirely be dismissed with a single word 'aristocratic'. The Irish aristocracy making their lives in England have always been to some extent princes in exile, rather than fully self-assured members of the ruling class. Maybe they exaggerate the distinction. A friend of mine has a landlady who said to him recently: 'I am so glad you are lunching with the Duke of Longford.' 'He is not a duke,' he told her, 'he is only an earl.' 'Any English lord is all right by me. I can't stand those foreign counts.' 'But Lord Longford,' he felt bound to tell her, 'is an Irish earl.' 'Part and parcel,' she replied, 'part and parcel.'

I was a younger son in a family where, financially speaking, the eldest son received an income of many thousands and the younger children a few hundreds each. It was assumed that I would have to make my way in the world but it was doubtful whether I would be able to afford to marry, unless and until a benevolent great-aunt died. In fact, she died when I was 32 and left me my present home, Bernhurst, at Hurst Green in East Sussex. My father was killed at Gallipoli, my widowed mother lived very quietly on our large estate in Ireland and our smaller place in Oxfordshire. Outside my family, I hardly knew an adult male in the holidays and was infinitely far removed from the *haut monde*.

If the atmosphere of my upbringing was highly 'conservative', this was implied and not explicit. The ethos did not remotely resemble that which Lord Butler has described so tellingly in his case. It was not till long after I grew up that I learned that one of my grandfathers was Sir Robert Peel, or that the Duke of Wellington had married my great-great-aunt. Coming from Eton, however, I simply assumed that one was a Conservative in politics just as one left undone the bottom button of one's waistcoat. Early in my time at New College, Evan Durbin from Taunton School, son of a nonconformist minister, and soon to be one of my dearest friends, faced me on our staircase with the question: 'Man, have you ever been hungry?' and insisted that no one of conscience could be other than Socialist. I answered inflexibly, even arrogantly on Conservative lines, but looking back I can see that I simply rationalised a posture that I had assumed automatically. Yet I was always ready to accept a Christian framework for the argument, so that my fine air of obduracy was a good deal more vulnerable than I allowed to appear to Evan or myself.

When I am asked occasionally at meetings whether it is right to indoctrinate small children with Christianity before they can speak for themselves, I answer this question more confidently than most others. I was taught Christianity in the home literally at my mother's knee, and from the earliest days therefore I said my prayers night and morning, though our home was not overtly religious. In years to come, throughout my twenties, in the decade or more before I turned to Roman Catholicism, I underwent many doubts and uncertainties. My church-going lapsed almost totally. But some life of prayer persisted in the background, some minimal attachment to Jesus Christ through the Gospels. When I became a Socialist in 1936 I was not very close to religion except in the sense just explained. Nevertheless, I was entitled to claim that the Gospels did indeed play a large part in my political conversion. But it was a rather complicated story.

I left Oxford in 1928 with a first class degree in Philosophy, Politics and Economics (Modern Greats), strong and growing political interests, much stimulated by recent contact with the super-star Lord Birkenhead and his enchanting family, and with no money to speak of but a promising if humble position on the foothills of political society. Eight years later all that was over except the friendships which have never failed with the Birkenheads, Astors and quite a few others less famous. Short of a change of sex, my life could hardly have been altered more radically. But I began by taking one step backward. From 1930-2 I worked in the newly formed Conservative Research Department sharing a room with the present Lord Brooke of Cumnor. For him I forecast a big career of public service though not (so I wrongly supposed) in politics. Our Chairman, of whom I saw little, was Mr Neville Chamberlain. I had some slight contact with Mr Baldwin at grand weekend parties. Both men, so unlike in almost everything, won my genuine respect. Neither was in the slightest interested in the theoretical approach to politics of a young man full of his recent success in the schools.

Just before I joined the Conservative Research Department I had spent a few months in the Potteries as a lecturer for the Workers' Educational Association teaching in state schools during the day. I continued lecturing for them once a week while involved in Conservative research, riding two horses which carried me emotionally in sharply opposed directions. In theory the W.E.A. was politically neutral, but virtually all my students in the Potteries were ardent Socialists. The deprivation and human waste were unmistakable. My personal devotion to them affected me at all levels. However, I continued for a while to adjust it to my Conservative philosophy and prospects.

Far more influential than all other events was my marriage to Elizabeth on 3rd November, 1931. I had fallen in love with her at first sight at four in the morning in Hugh Gaitskell's rooms in New College after a Commemoration dance. I woke up from slumber to find her bending over me. I have always assumed since that I look my best asleep. I lost contact with her thereafter while I worked in London and she completed a glamorous career at Oxford. But I reappeared in her life impelled by a dream, almost a vision, and obtained for her also work in the W.E.A. in the Potteries. We became engaged to be married in the station waiting-room at Stoke-on-Trent, waiting for the 1.45 a.m. to take us back to London. We had been evicted from the North Staffs Hotel by the manager when the light was switched off at midnight and we continued our dalliance.

Elizabeth was and is a radical reformer. There were, and still more there are, many other aspects of her personality. The world is by now well aware of her creativity in literature and more recently in history. Her devoted motherhood and her love of children goes even deeper. Creativity in this case reaches heroic dimensions, but her instinct for all things living carries her far beyond her own children and grandchildren. Her radiance has been famous since her Oxford days. Her unself-conscious appeal never, in my experience, fails ('No one so successful was ever so unself-important,' Lady Diana Cooper once said to me). Her public speaking and political capacity led Hugh Dalton to insist that he could have worked her on to the National Executive of the Labour Party in the thirties. Without question she would have been Labour M.P. for Kings Norton in 1945 if she had not abandoned her political career in the interests of myself and the children. (The majority of my friend, and her successor in the seat, Raymond Blackburn, was, in the event, 12,000.)

When we moved down the aisle together at St Margaret's, Westminster, I was still, to the outward eye, a young Honourable with a good future in Conservative politics. I still saw myself in some such light. But I am sure now that once I fell in love with her and we married, my career as a Conservative was over. Not that she made that at any time a stipulation. Yeats says that in his youth he hated Maud Gonne's politics as his only visible rival. That was never our situation. The truth was expressed, if not very politely, at some kind of conference on social affairs in the early thirties where I was supposed to represent the Party. 'You're only a dud Conservative,' I was brutally told. Whoever said that was just about right.

My Conservative position was never soundly based. I had never attained it through family associations such as those of Quintin Hogg, or hard intellectual slog such as that of Henry Brooke (which is not to imply that Quintin's Conservatism has ever lacked intellectual content). My experiences in Stoke-on-Trent had set on foot more disquiet than I liked to acknowledge. I had no integrated political convictions to match those of a radical reformer like Elizabeth, or of anyone whose head and heart were at one.

Within a few months of my marriage, early, that is to say, in 1932, I met Mr de Valera, of whom more anon. After forty years I still regard him as a unique politician among those whom I have personally encountered. If I desire to assert that now, it can be assumed that his early impact on me was traumatic, although it could not affect my English politics immediately. By 1935 I had published my *Peace by Ordeal*, still the standard book on the Anglo-Irish Treaty of 1931. As with the W.E.A., so here. In theory I could have remained a Conservative while becoming an Irish nationalist, and indeed did so for a time. In each case, however, leaving out emotion altogether, my mind was opened to values hitherto undetected by me and undetectable, so it seemed, by Conservative politicians.

It must be realised that since my First in Modern Greats I prided myself, in spite of my lingering Christianity, on being a rational theorist. Evan Durbin and I actually started a society called 'The Theorists', but we got so much pleasure from blackballing our contemporaries that the society never grew beyond our two selves. I saw myself, in other words, as one who applied reason to all things, very much including politics. By this time the Conservative record in Ireland and contemporary approach to Ireland made no sense at all. And if this were so in Ireland, could it be that the same intellectual defects might invalidate its other traditions? The Irish question, therefore, contributed to my move leftwards.

In years to come I would summarise my reasons for leaving the Conservatives and joining the Socialists in an affirmation of human equality. Once only in my recollection I failed to speak clearly in this way. That was when King George VI asked me on my becoming his Lord-in-Waiting, 'Why did you join them?' And out of deference to a revered monarch, I gave an evasive reply. Every human being, I have said a hundred or perhaps a thousand times, is of equal and infinite importance in the sight of God and should be treated accordingly in the government of man. I said this very thing not many months ago in a debate at the Oxford Union (result in our favour 496-234) and was indignantly interrupted and denounced by a high-minded young Conservative minister.

I cannot remember now exactly when I accepted this explicitly as a guiding clue. In my last days as a Conservative I clung to the distinction between what was ideal and what was practical. The Socialists had come to represent the nobler aspiration, but the Conservatives still offered a better chance of actual prosperity for all. I consoled myself for quite a while with a leading article in *The Times*. 'Unfortunately wealth is like heat. It is only when it is unequally distributed that it performs what the physicists call work.' But then the strain of inner conflict was telling. On the one hand were my Conservative background, my career prospects, almost all my friends, and some rather fragile economic reasoning; on the other, a dormant Christianity restlessly stirring on social questions under the impact of the Potteries - and Elizabeth.

I did not cross my political Rubicon rapidly. The process took about four years (1932-6). It is open to anyone to say that once I left the Conservative Party, being married to a Labour wife, enormously interested in politics, and perhaps more ambitious than I admitted to myself, I was bound to finish up as a Labour politician. It certainly looks plausible now. But I must emphasise how much I still belonged in the early thirties to the Conservative side in life-style and friendships, not least as a tutor of Christ Church, Oxford, from 1932 onwards. Christ Church, among many claims to fame, gave Britain nine prime ministers in the nineteenth century. It may or may not have been, as seemed to many of us, the most delightful, but it was certainly the most aristocratic college in the world.

Again my vaunted rationality refused to let me become an easy convert to a political party whose recent performance in office had left on me, as on so many others, such a deplorable impression. Like Cardinal Newman, I hovered for an unconscionable time before taking the final leap. A Fascist meeting in the summer of 1936, when I sustained concussion and other minor injuries (whether or not undeservedly), precipitated action. But by that time I had already just about reached the conclusion that, in the world of the mid-nineteen thirties, with crisis and conflict round every corner, it was a cowardly dereliction of duty not to take sides and that the progressive side was the only one possible for me. I duly joined the Labour Party in Cowley, beginning work as an assistant agent in the local elections, and from then till the war functioning intensively among the grass roots. In 1936 the idea of getting into Parliament, or indeed getting anywhere in that sense, did not figure consciously. A general election had been held not long before and the Conservatives had won another large, though reduced, majority. Ambition must be thought to have figured ater but not at the moment of choice.

Rather more than three years further on (January 1940) I was received into the Catholic Church, a possibility which had certainly never crossed my mind till early 1938. A religious conversion of this kind is obviously far more profound than a political switch of allegiance. In an external sense, however, it must have seemed less surprising. Religious conversions, after all, are taking place daily. A political conversion like mine from the Canning Club and Conservative Research to (eventually) a Socialist ministry cannot easily be paralleled except in the story of Sir Oswald Mosley.

So many psychological explanations are customarily offered for Catholic conversions that I leave that side of it to others. A deep yearning for security may have been present, but it could be just as possible to claim that supernatural grace operated mysteriously. A factor I ignored in my *Born to Believe* was my special Irishness. Catholicism outside the north-east corner of Ireland is manifestly the religion of the country and readily associated with Irish sentiment on all sorts of emotional levels. Membership of the so-called ascendency has, of course, not infrequently worked the other way. In some parts of Southern Ireland our Protestant family might have been cut off from their Catholic neighbours or feared them or despised them. The opposite was the case with us. Of our few land-owning neighbours the majority were Catholics. Such Irish influences, however, were not present to my conscious mind when I was moving or being moved into the Catholic Church in 1940, except that the congregation attending the local Catholic Church on the Iffley Road were almost all of Irish origin.

Consciously a serious systematic search for religious truth began in early 1938. I realised suddenly and poignantly that without much more religious certainty there was little meaning in the life on which I was set, with all its absorbing public interests and its no less absorbing ambitions. More specifically from then on I threw myself into a search for Christ on whom I had brooded for so long but so half-heartedly. 'Lord, I believe. Help Thou my unbelief' was my consistent cry, and Father D'Arcy, the Master of Campion Hall, a stone's throw from Christ Church, my infinitely gentle mentor.

Why did I select him rather than any of the benevolent and learned Anglicans in whom Oxford was so rich? Partly, no doubt, it was a question of sheer personal devotion. Partly, and more fundamentally, because from casual conversations over the years I had become convinced that he would help me to find a coherent religion if anyone living could. I was a young don seeking faith desperately but determined, from professional self-respect, to face every conceivable intellectual difficulty whether emanating from Gibbon, Renan, Karl Marx, in whom I was versed for other reasons, Bertrand Russell, or my new friend and colleague Freddy Ayer, emerging as the hero of the young. What books did I read? What books did I not read during those years of overpowering anguish and excitement! A few books I mentioned in *Born to Believe*, those of Arnold Lunn rightly among them. But now I feel that Grand Maison's three volumes on Jesus Christ answered my deepest needs more than any other book. It became clearer and clearer that my life had to be built anew on a belief in the reality of Jesus Christ, or not reconstructed at all.

I was soon convinced that if I really believed the Gospel story, I would believe that Christ founded a Church and the Catholic Church was that Church. But still I hesitated and fretted. The one thing that Father D'Arcy did not do was to try to expedite my reception. When at the outbreak of war he left for service in America, I had still failed to commit myself. Then things happened quickly. It was understood that my regiment would soon be going abroad. Evelyn Waugh, closer to me than any other Catholic layman, wrote me a telling exhortation. One morning I woke with the conviction clear at last that the Catholic Church was indeed the Church of Christ and that I was defying the truth if I stayed outside.

The next moment, or so it seemed, I was undergoing a rapid emergency instruction from priests whom I already knew quite well from my attendance at their church. Then came the reception itself at the Greyfriars, Iffley Road, the one event in my life apart from my marriage which contained no imperfection and could never conceivably be regretted.

The years sped past, but at first not gloriously for me. I came of a long line of soldiers, not to mention a few sailors. My great-great-uncle, Sir Edward Pakenham, Kitty Wellington's brother, had been killed as he led his men to an inevitable defeat at New Orleans in 1815, unaware that peace had been declared. My father had been killed in similar fashion in 1915, leading his brigade at Gallipoli. His standard of courage dominated my youthful imagination. As far as I can judge, I am neither braver nor more timorous than the average, but I have always been apprehensive by nature and the effort to live up to a heroic standard landed me in many predicaments.

In my own circles, which by this time were mostly academic or socialist, I was more or less first in (of those who joined up), and first out, of the army. I joined the Territorials in the summer of 1939, as a private soldier - received a commission in the Infantry at the outbreak of war, and by May 1940 had been invalided out with a nervous breakdown, mercifully finding a patriotic outlet as a company commander in the Home Guard. Here, indeed, was absolute failure. For five years I suffered the anguish of a civilian status, while the young men I had been teaching and the vast concourse of the nation's manhood underwent such suffering and achieved such incomparable things.

Today I can feel, though I never glimpsed it then, that the compensations derived from my poor war record have been more than sufficient. With prisoners, ex-prisoners, outcasts generally and all those who hesitate to show their faces abroad, I have had one unfailing and unforeseen point of contact. I can say and mean and be believed - 'I also have been humiliated.' The gulf is bridged as if by magic. If my sense of compassion has been strengthened and activated from any human experience, it is from my own infirmities and the indignities I have myself undergone.

Three years, 1941-4, as personal assistant to Sir William Beveridge, placed me close to the crucial preparations for the Welfare State. Then came six years in the Attlee Government, starting as a political Lord-in-Waiting - the lowest thing in ministerial life - and finishing as First Lord of the Admiralty, one place outside the Cabinet, which I frequently attended. Here I recall that when the end came, Lord Attlee, meticulous as always, wrote to thank me for my services. Clearly what he valued was my spokesmanship in the Lords, where I represented the Government at one time or another on almost every topic. (Between 1945 and 1968 I inhabited the Government or Opposition Front Bench in the House of Lords, uninterruptedly - in its own way a record.) In my own eyes, any small glory I had earned lay elsewhere. From 1947-8 I was Minister for the British Zones of Germany and Austria where, in those days, we maintained a civilian staff of close on 30,000. From my first excited visit to the British Zone, I proclaimed the doctrine of ardent friendship for the Germans, insisting that this was the only approach conceivable to Christians.

I told the near-starving population, 'You are absolutely right to be proud of being German' - an unpopular sentiment in allied countries. I created the impression that better times, freedom and equality were on the way. And in the event I was not far wrong. But by that time I had been 'kicked upstairs' to become Minister of Civil Aviation and to enjoy myself among the people more than the aeroplanes. I still pride myself on having been well ahead of public opinion on Germany, but I never stopped asking myself whether it would not have been more edifying and less misleading to resign. This lingering self-criticism may have helped to speed my departure from a later Government.

The thirteen 'wasted years' between 1951 and 1964 saw me fully occupied. For eight years I was chairman of the National Bank, departing, according to *The Economist*, as an enormously successful amateur banker and acquiring a great *tendresse* for the staff in Ireland and in England. Four books, two autobiographical, two concerned with crime and punishment, were the literary output. And of course there were various committee chairmanships, and endless speaking in the House of Lords where I opened debates, for example, on youth, universities, the economic situation, homosexuality, and prisons (more than once).

Prisoners and ex-prisoners were my biggest new departure outside banking, though I had been an official prison visitor just before and just after the war, in Oxford. With my books *Causes of Crime* and *The Idea of Punishment* and the speeches in the Lords went the formation of the New Bridge, a society for ex-prisoners which I touch on later. In one way or another, I came to know many prisoners intimately, male and female, some of them convicted of the gravest crimes. Whatever the effect of our friendships on them, my own social outlook was transformed. By 1964 I was already making plans for a kind of junior New Bridge for helping young delinquents, if Labour should lose the election, or if I were not asked to serve in a Labour cabinet.

But what of politics? If a politician announces that he has no political ambitions, I automatically distrust him. I had never renounced the aspiration of serving in a Labour Cabinet and, whatever the cynics might say, continued to see in that my best opportunity of service. I was only 45 when the Attlee Government ended, and after steady promotion was one place outside the charmed circle. I had deliberately resigned from the chairmanship of the National Bank to be available for Cabinet service without, of course, any guarantees. I had strong claims on Cabinet office, which meant in practice on the leadership of the Lords, the only post likely to be going. But the appointment was by no means a walk-over. Lord Alexander of Hillsborough had proved a doughty and, on the whole, an effective Leader of the Opposition Peers. He had been awarded, and had earned, an earldom and the Garter for his exertions. Admittedly he was approaching 80, but he was determined to set aside age and infirmity. I think that he was fond of me, as I certainly was of him, but his attitude to the Catholic Church and to Anglicans who were too soft towards it was one of frenzied suspicion. He was the only speaker in the whole House who opposed the Archbishop of Canterbury's visit to Rome.

Curious peers sometimes ask me what Albert and I used to argue about so strenuously on the front bench. Once at least he was interpreting for me the Epistles to the Hebrews. 'There you are, Frank,' he cried triumphantly, 'read what it says - a sacrifice not to be repeated, *not* to be repeated.' The Catholic view of the daily Mass seemed to him finally overthrown. Every now and then his ultimate fairness took over. I overheard him saying to Lord Lawson while a Roman Catholic peer was preaching morality: 'You know, Jack, these fellows are the only Nonconformists left.' His piety, which expressed what the Bishop of Leicester once called 'the simple religion of the people' was indubitable, as was his textual knowledge of the Bible. But my situation was awkward. My prospects were then not exactly assisted. For one reason or another, I was pin-pointed as a Catholic par excellence.

And then, early in 1963, Hugh Gaitskell died - Mr Valiant-for-Truth as I called him in an article in *The Observer*.

He used to refer to me as his oldest friend, though several others were closer to him, if only through membership of the House of Commons. It is possible, though far from certain, that if he had lived, I would have become a member of that House. It would have needed an amendment to the Bill under which Lord Home and Lord Hailsham renounced their peerages. I had not only inherited a peerage in 1961, but been awarded one in 1945, and this latter one was the obstacle. Esmond Warner, *my* oldest friend, used to tell me that I was far too old to entertain so youthful a fantasy. (I was just under 60 when the Labour Government was formed.) Hugh was tremendously pleased when I raised the idea with him. Pleased and surprised, 'You really mean you'd give it up?' he said to me. I think he thought some family loyalty would prevent me. but he seemed confident that the change could be brought about.

When Hugh died, Harold Wilson was sympathetic, but could not be expected to take the same amount of interest.

Soon after Hugh died, Harold Wilson told Elizabeth at a dinner that he hoped to see me Lord President of the Council. But life was still very uncertain for me, as for many others, by the time of the general election.

PART ONE

Politics (I)

A GILDED SEAT

By the late afternoon of Friday, 16th October, 1964, it was
known to all who followed television that Labour had won
the general election by a small majority, and that Harold
Wilson had set off for the Palace. Like a considerable number of
others, I was now in a fine old state of excitement and anxiety.
My life for the next few years was clearly going to be dominated
by a decision of Harold Wilson's in the next twenty-four hours.
At such a moment, a politician of reasonable public spirit will
rejoice in the victory of his party to the benefit, he sincerely
believes, of his country. But it would be hypocrisy not to admit
that his own future looms very large. Elizabeth and I were at
Bernhurst, fifty-odd miles from London. We awaited news with
what restraint we could muster. The news when it came was,
from our point of view, neither one thing nor the other. Half a
dozen Cabinet appointments were announced, but there was
no reference to the Leadership of the House of Lords, so that in
a personal sense I was no wiser.

Now arose a ludicrous dilemma, which even in retrospect
puzzles me, as it has puzzled many others. One knew - I think
it was announced - that the rest of the Cabinet would be
published by the following evening. It was surely inconceivable
that Cabinet Ministers would be invited on the telephone,
whatever might happen to smaller fry. If I did not go up to
London, therefore, and sit about in our Chelsea flat, awaiting
the summons from Downing Street, how would I ever get
appointed at all? On the other hand, to make my way to London
quite gratuitously on a Saturday morning would be a humili-
ating operation and would in any case, to be effective, involve
a message to Number Ten, to let them know where I was.

Six years later, when Mr Heath was forming his Cabinet, I
happened to meet a potential member in our newsagents on

the Saturday morning. 'It must be an anxious day for you,' I suggested. 'Not at all,' said the potential one, 'I am not the sort who hangs about round the telephone.' 'Quite,' I went on, a shade insensitively, 'but I have been through all this myself, and one has to be accessible, if you are wanted.' The future Cabinet minister melted slightly. 'Oh! that's an easy one. You get someone else to sit by the telephone!' Margaret Thatcher - for it was she - endeared herself to me at that moment.

In the event I repaired to London and awaited my destiny. It was some time in coming. One of the children was ill which complicated the suspense for Elizabeth in the country, and myself. My daughter Antonia was as resolute as ever. Her husband, Hugh Fraser, had just lost his job as Air Minister with the fall of the Tory Government and she was expecting another child at any moment. But she came round to Chesil Court, answered all telephone calls, and generally bolstered my morale. When the telephone rang it could have been the hospital or No. 10. In fact it was the latter. In a flash it seemed I was seated at the Cabinet table, with Harold Wilson in the chair from which Lord Attlee had often received me. 'I want you to be Leader of the House of Lords,' said he, without any beating about the bush, 'and Lord Privy Seal. It ought really to be Lord President of the Council but they said that Bert Bowden (the new Leader of the House of Commons) ought to hold that position.' He went on to say that there were those who had not favoured me for this job, 'but I consulted Clem Attlee; he had no doubt at all. He said, "It must be Frank." ' Harold Wilson feared that Lord Alexander (Leader of the Opposition Peers at that time) would be upset, but after all Albert Alexander was close on 80. He had had a lot of bad health recently. It was possible to give that as a reason for not selecting him. This, in fact, had been done. He ended the brief interview with the words: 'We should have a lot of fun together.' I found him a more inspiring figure than on any previous occasion, but in the circumstances that was explicable.

I have never learnt the nature or source of the opposition to my appointment. Some months later our Chief Whip, Malcolm Shepherd, told me, with obvious sincerity, that he felt that I was proving a most successful Leader of the House of Lords and that he had not expected it. About that time, when one or two journalists were already beginning to suggest that I would disappear before long, he referred to my 'great leadership' at a party of Labour peers, in front of Harold Wilson. I fear that Albert Alexander himself must have been bitterly disappointed, but he behaved with true dignity towards me until his death, which occurred not long after the Government was formed. I recall that Clem Attlee, who went down to the funeral with me in my official car, was the only mourner wearing a top hat. As he often said of himself, he was a true Victorian.

So there I was, my worldly objective at last attained. I knew that I could go no higher. Years before, Hugh Gaitskell, a closer friend than anyone else who was ever likely to be Prime Minister, had made it plain that, apart from the Lord Chancellor, there would never be more than one peer in the Labour Cabinet. He obviously had not visualised such a one holding a department. It was not likely that Harold Wilson would be more generous to the Lords, or go farther out of his way on my behalf. What I had not grasped, however, in spite of my supposed experience, was that the strength of the Labour Leader of the House of Lords would depend so completely on the Prime Minister.

*

In well-informed discussion of Cabinet organisation it is usually assumed that the non-departmental ministers (Lord President of the Council, Lord Privy Seal - my appointment - Chancellor of the Duchy, etc.) would exercise co-ordinating functions. The Lord President of the Council and the Chancellor of the Duchy did so in the Wilson administration. But no such opportunity was afforded me nor, for that matter, my successor, Eddy Shackleton (who, however, was made Minister for the Civil Service and was conspicuously successful in that role as in others). I cannot emphasise this point too strongly. If I had been, as I expected, Chairman of an important Cabinet sub-Committee with other Cabinet Ministers serving under me in that connection, my whole status and influence in the Cabinet would have been transformed. There was a moment when, with some support from the Prime Minister, I was seeking the right to investigate the overall services provided for youth – a right grudgingly and partially accorded. Roy Jenkins, as Home Secretary, was one of the Ministers opposing my interference on departmental grounds. 'Of course,' he said, 'you ought to have been Chairman of the Social Services sub-Committee.' Never at any time did I feel that personal animus came in here. Rather do I feel sure that Harold had no intention of allowing any Leader of the Lords to occupy the position of senior Counsellor held by Addison in the Attlee Government. From the word go, my position was to be kept low on the list, sixteenth out of twenty-three, at the time of appointment. Ministers came and went, but my placing remained the same (virtually). When Eddy Shackleton followed me, he was listed last but one, which showed that the Prime Minister's unflattering attitude was directed towards the Second Chamber itself rather than towards its Leader of the time.

When people ask me, therefore, what it is like to be Leader of the House of Lords, I must begin by distinguishing between a Conservative and a Labour Government. Being Leader of the House of Lords, even in a Conservative Government, is not what it was when I first joined the House in 1945, or for some years afterwards. Even after the days of Addison and Salisbury, Quintin Hogg used the position to great effect in the country, when combining it with the Chairmanship of the Conservative Party. Today the House is much stronger intellectually than it used to be, and there are many topics outside Party controversy where its expertness gives it greater influence than ever before. (The Social Services are a large example.) But in regard to the great issues of Party controversy, its role is much diminished. Even so, in a period of Conservative rule, its leading figures are likely to be much more revered in their own Party than are their Socialist equivalents when it comes to their turn.

The only two Cabinet ministers in the House of Lords were the Lord Chancellor and the Leader of the House of Lords – myself from October 1964 to January 1968, and Eddy Shackleton from January 1968 till June 1970. No one could have been a better comrade than the Lord Chancellor, Gerald Gardiner. When it was clear that I seemed likely to resign, he alone made strenuous efforts to dissuade me, although Tony Greenwood

sent me a much-valued letter, and Bob Mellish, learning about
it at the last minute, begged me not to proceed. If I did, he
assured me with heartfelt simplicity, I should 'cease to exist'.
I tell the story later of Gerald's intervention to illustrate the
strength and subtlety of his friendship.

In the Cabinet Gerald Gardiner had immense and well-
deserved prestige with Harold Wilson whom he knew intimately and, in some measure, with all other members. On his
own subjects (hanging was the supreme example) he was
adamant and profoundly influential, but on most topics he
took the line that he was not a politician and, like some other
Lord Chancellors, was therefore slightly outside the decision-
making process.

There was a sense, therefore, in which I was, from first to
last, a solitary figure in the Cabinet, vulnerable for more reasons
than one, most of all because I had no real backing in public
opinion. I had no constituency; I had not been elected by anyone. Not only that, the other members lived a life together;
they shared the triumphs and disasters of the House of Commons; they had far more opportunities of talking to one
another informally than could ever come my way. They were
very nice to me; in a certain sense all the nicer because I was
not in direct competition. There was not a single one of them
with whom I had, then or later, any personal trouble. Yet I
remained an outsider.

It was no great surprise to me that when I resigned I did not
receive a single letter of regret from Cabinet colleagues, though
Gerald Gardiner and my successor, Eddy Shackleton, went out
of their way to pay most handsome tributes in the House of
Lords. Roy Jenkins, seeing me some months later at an official
function, came across to apologise for not writing. He con-
fessed to having been indignant at my attitude towards another
aspect of his economy package. 'I very nearly wrote,' he added.
My reply was not very Christian: 'I am told that a lot of
colleagues very nearly wrote.' Roy, I should add, though much
younger than myself, has for many years been a personal, not
merely a political, friend of Elizabeth and myself. The word
'friend' in politics carries so many meanings as to have lost
its significance. One enjoys, if one is lucky and reasonably

good-tempered, friendly relations with large numbers of colleagues. By such a test, the atmosphere in the Cabinet during my time was friendly and fraternal, for which Harold Wilson, the chairman, deserves the major credit.

One further point I should add in describing the weakness of my position. Reputations on the top political level were made and sustained by performances in the House of Commons, as Roy Jenkins and Tony Crosland rapidly proved. When my deeply valued friend, Patrick Gordon Walker, ceased to be Foreign Secretary through no fault of his own or, for that matter, Harold Wilson's, Michael Stewart had just won a Parliamentary triumph with a speech on comprehensive school education and was forthwith appointed to the Foreign Office - cause and effect, so it seemed. The straightforward way of improving my position was closed to me through my incarceration in the Lords. It was surprising how seldom our achievements, including my most crucial orations, were known to my Cabinet colleagues. They seemed to have enough on their own plates without reading our Hansards. But there were exceptions to this rule. I replied to a testing debate on Rhodesia at the time of the Unilateral Declaration of Independence. It was vital that the measures should go through that night, and Harold Wilson and other leaders crowded in to listen. Next day, Harold Wilson congratulated me in front of the Cabinet on my effective control of the House. I think that it came as a real surprise to him.

Meanwhile, I had to perform in public as Leader of the House. When I resigned I was overwhelmed with letters, including many from members of the House, who referred in glowing terms to my Leadership. But Joe Champion, Deputy Leader of the House of Lords during my first two years, told me that he himself had received 250 letters of sympathy and esteem, which he certainly deserved. So I must not exaggerate my success. In *Five Lives* I referred to the House of Lords as being kind to leaders. There is a tremendous desire to make the place work, not to mention a deep-rooted courtesy to those in positions of temporary authority. So one is left quite uncertain whether one was more or less effective than one's predecessors and successors. To those who do not know the House of Lords,

I must explain that the Leader of the House has more responsibility for the flow of debate and for orderly questioning than anyone else; much more than the lord Chancellor who is nominally the Speaker, but he is on no account allowed to interfere. He has no power to tell anybody to do anything. He certainly cannot call anyone to order, except by means of tactful suggestion. If a peer persists in asking supplementary questions, for example, the Leader will choose a moment when the House, as a whole, is clearly restless and then suggest that it is time to move on. But if the peer is absolutely obdurate, there is nothing that the Leader can do about it except move that the noble lord be no longer heard. In my time I have seen this happen only once, when Viscount Stansgate more or less forced Quintin Hogg, then Leader, to adopt this extreme remedy. In a minor sense, I found this task of curtailing tedious supplementaries particularly irksome. My successor, Eddy Shackleton, and his Tory replacements, George Jellicoe and David Windlesham, strike me as better suited to it, but perhaps they have not really enjoyed it any more than I did.

The saddest feature of my role as Leader of the House of Lords was the little scope it gave to my reforming passion. Years ago I remember that master stylist, Evelyn Waugh, saying to me, whilst severely criticising my first volume of autobiography: 'I can't see a man painting a gate without wanting to tell him how to paint it better.' For myself, I can't imagine being placed in charge of an institution without wishing to improve it, in other words to alter it substantially. Shortly before the Wilson Government was formed, I had presided over a very strong committee set up by Harold Wilson to draw up plans for the prevention and treatment of crime. Half a dozen members of the committee, from Gerald Gardiner downwards, were now members of the Government and, in one way or another, the main proposals moved forward towards the Statute Book. Here and elsewhere I could indeed lend my support and in Cabinet supply my vote, but if there was to be a creative outlet, it could only be in my own department - the House of Lords itself. I was convinced that the House of Lords was full of anomalies (it still is) and should be radically reformed. The idea of reducing its *powers* was, in a vague kind of way, official Labour policy. What I was primarily concerned with, however, was to place its *composition* on a rational footing. Such a project, one might think, would commend itself to all Liberals and Socialists, if it involved eliminating or at least much reducing the hereditary element. One might assume that large numbers of Conservatives would be opposed to reform for this very reason. In fact, the position was, from the beginning and throughout, much more complex.

More or less by accident, I had taken part in more discussions of the reform of the House of Lords than anyone alive except my companion and inspiration in the talks, Commander Henry Burrows, Clerk assistant in the Lords (No. 2 at the 'Table'). Henry, a gallant naval officer in two wars, had ferried me in his car to Rye Golf Club every weekend from 1951 onwards. It would be an exaggeration to say that we never talked about anything except reform of the House of Lords. Henry has many interests, falconry not least, but no weekend passed without our discussing Henry's special plan for reforming the House of Lords, the two-writ scheme, as he called it. The only time I became exasperated was just after I had missed a short putt in a high wind on a tricky green - the seventh at Rye. Henry approached me, shouting through the hurricane: 'You do believe in the two-writ scheme, don't you?' Mercifully the wind carried away my furious answer. In fact, I did believe in it. I still believe in it, though I do not expect to see it now introduced in my lifetime. But it very nearly, in a somewhat modified form, became the law of England.

Briefly, under the two-writ plan, all existing members of the House of Lords would continue to be allowed to come there and *speak*, but only those who were created peers, either before or after the introduction of the scheme, would be allowed to *vote*. Hereditary peers as such would therefore lose the vote, although distinguished hereditary figures such as Lord Carrington and Lord Jellicoe, on the Conservative side, or Lord Listowel or Lord Shepherd across the gangway, would obviously be given voting peerages and thus maintain their voting rights. At present whoever has won the debate, the Conservatives triumph in the voting lobby by virtue of the hereditary block. This domination would be broken with the disappearance of the hereditary peers as voters. From a democratic point of view, in the second half of the twentieth century, the main anachronism would disappear, which one might think (though one would be wrong) would appeal to all honest radicals.

Why, then, retain the right of the existing peers (though not their children) to continue attending and speaking in the House? In the first place there was an argument from the best sort of expediency. I hoped (and I don't think I was wrong) that, the antagonism of the hereditary peers and the Conservative Party as a whole would be much mitigated if the hereditary peers were treated courteously and were allowed to disappear gradually in a dignified manner. But also, I had satisfied myself after many years of active service in the House of Lords that the House stood for certain values in human behaviour which were different from those of the House of Commons, and should not be brutally liquidated. I conceded, of course, that if one were starting afresh in the 1960s, one would establish a second chamber with no hereditary element. Taking things as they were, I believe that a gradual transition - in regard to speaking as distinct from voting - would help the House prestige. I lay emphasis on that word 'prestige'. I was aware that by this time the *powers* of the Lords must be minimal. Nothing else would be acceptable, nor indeed justifiable in principle. The will of the democratic House must prevail in a democratic age. But I believed, and still believe, that a second chamber can have great influence for good. For this purpose it must have prestige, and with this in mind some continuity is essential.

By the time I became Leader of the House of Lords, Henry Burrows had retired. But our games of golf continued. He spurred me on more zealously than ever. In fact, I needed no goading. A time came when I raised the whole issue of reforming the composition of the House of Lords in front of the Cabinet. Nothing could have been less successful. I was laughed to scorn. Gerald Gardiner alone supported me. He had shared in producing our paper for the Cabinet. There had been a long, somewhat acrimonious, dispute over the previous item. When it came to our turn, Harold Wilson remarked genially, 'Whatever may be said about the last topic, I can imagine nothing quite so divisive as an attempt to reform the House of Lords.' A sentiment which won general approval. I talked angrily of not being happy to stay in a Cabinet where this was the attitude. I meant it. I don't think, however, that most members took my words very seriously. That sort of thing is said a shade too often without being followed up. In any case the Lords as a topic was always regarded as light relief, except when their immediate approval was required for emergency measures. Perhaps this should not have happened, but with twenty-one from the Commons and two from the Lords, happen it did.

I had no intention of leaving the matter there and a new personality soon appeared on my side, operating much more powerfully than I could. Dick Crossman had joined actively in the frivolous reception of my reform proposal. But by the autumn of 1966 he had become Leader of the House of Commons and was displaying his fine imaginative grasp of comprehensive parliamentary reform. He was quick to realise that it was impossible to make sense of the House of Commons while leaving the House of Lords fundamentally anomalous. He became converted in principle to something like the two-writ plan for the Lords. From that moment onwards, its chances of success rose and fell or moved sideways with him.

When Dick Crossman was a young don at New College, Oxford, in the 1930s, he was a phenomenon, more continually argued about than anyone else of his period. Oscar Wilde said to Yeats about W. E. Henley: 'I had to strain every nerve to equal that man at all.' Many of us have never quite lost that feeling about Dick Crossman. His mental prowess was incontestable. He left an indelible mark on his pupils in the university and his adult education classes. He might be reckoned the greatest adult education tutor of all time. His public lectures on Nazi Germany filled the examination schools; his broadcasts on *Plato Today* were a sizzling tour de force. H. A. L. Fisher, Warden of his College, ex-Cabinet Minister and renowned historian, referred to him in my hearing as a 'fine, bustling fellow'. 'Dick,' he said to me, 'has just discovered Bismarck and thinks that I might like to know about him.' But Fisher in fact had a tremendous belief in Dick's future.

Meanwhile, as captain of Aylesbury rugby XV, I welcomed Dick to a place beside me in the second row of the scrum. He and Patrick Gordon Walker, who also played for us, were Greyhounds (University 2nd XV). When called on to lead the pack, Dick, surprisingly fast for a man of such powerful build, transformed it instantly.

By the time Harold Wilson formed his Cabinet, Dick was 56. He had never held any government office, even the most trivial. He had dented the national scene at quite a few points, but in terms of career things had gone wrong for him alike through his strengths and his weaknesses. Ernest Bevin told a friend of mine in 1945 that he had his eye on two young men particularly - Dick in the first place, myself in the second. Dick quarrelled with him over Palestine and I over Germany. Each of us reacted in character. Dick denounced Bevin up hill and down dale, I allowed myself to be steered upwards into a less significant ministry. To adapt some lines from the Greek anthology:

> 'Both perished;
> Which the nobler part only the great gods know.'

By 1964 Dick had for long been identified with the Left and associated with Wilson as opposed to Gaitskell.

Wilson's rise to the leadership had at last given Dick a long-denied chance to use his splendid talents of brain and energy and, when he employs it, charm. He had become as amusing as any man in politics. He had known tragedy, but by this time had found a deep peace with his wife and children in the tranquillity (at weekends) of a farming life.

Successively Minister of Housing, Leader of the House of Commons, and Minister for Health and Social Security, he could point by the end of the Government to a departmental record that was second to none. In Cabinet he often showed flair and prescience; his dialectics were a joy to the impartial observer, less so to his opponents. Yet he has never escaped a certain question mark among those he has worked with. The old jibe was that, whatever he said today, he would say the opposite tomorrow - though this is far too crude a comment in the light of his successful administration. He would not be himself if he did not remain the most unpredictable of the leading figures in politics. Partly this is because his particular integrity compels him to speak his mind wherever the argument leads him, and sometimes without overmuch forethought; partly because his sheer intellectuality inclines him to novel ideas as such. But truth compels one to mention a less pleasing side of his character, which causes him to ignore human feelings to the point occasionally of downright bullying. A shrewd ambassador said to me the other day, after watching some of his television programmes: 'I suppose you could call him a great human being.' I demurred, somewhat uncharitably, while agreeing that Dick is immensely human and has revealed elements of greatness. I cannot forget the occasions when he has literally reduced men and women to tears without, I am sure, intending to, through sheer insensitivity. His bulky frame, mass of untidy grey hair, firm blue eyes behind thick-rimmed glasses, can inspire trepidation. My wife, who has always admired him and is very fond of him, supplies an image - a mace of polished steel. He has been weak on the religious side hitherto. 'No one,' he is reported to have said to the Cabinet, 'can call me a Christian,' when he was, in fact, propounding a Christian thesis.

When he was gravely ill during the war he decided, so it is said, to give Christianity a chance, and asked for a New Testament. It was opened for him, by accident or design, at the Epistle to the Galatians. He studied it intently for a while, then hurled it across the room: 'What rot it all is,' he exclaimed, and decided to die unshriven. But he has so much personal warmth, he is capable of feeling and promoting so much enthusiasm that one does not despair of what will happen if, next time, someone offers him the New Testament while he is in full health and he opens it at a passage closer to the spirit of his life-long master, Socrates.

*

Journalists tell me that Lord Carrington, Leader of the Opposition in the House of Lords at the time, a man of what Sir Winston Churchill would have called 'mark and merit', began to work for Lords Reform about the same time as I did. I did not realise that he began quite so early, but at any rate it was not long before we were in touch and clearly thinking along similar lines. I brought Peter Carrington and Dick Crossman together at dinner. I would not ordinarily think of them as soul-mates, but they are both brilliantly realistic and large-minded when it comes to action. They were soon working hand-in-glove. Eddy Shackleton at the beginning of 1967 became Deputy Leader of the House of Lords. Six years younger than myself, he was obviously destined to succeed me, but apart from a magnificent effort in Aden, where he was said to have talked the insurgent leaders into the ground, he was not very heavily employed that year. Along with George Jellicoe and, in a different capacity, Gerald Gardiner, he did an immense amount of detailed work on the reform package and, if the plan had succeeded, would have deserved as much credit as anyone. Meanwhile, Dick Crossman sold the conception to Harold Wilson, to the Cabinet and to a not very enthusiastic Parliamentary Labour Party. When I resigned from the Cabinet in January 1968, it certainly seemed that the House of Lords would be reformed and that in essentials the dream of Henry Burrows would be realised.

Dis aliter visum. A strange combination led by my beloved son-in-law, Hugh Fraser, and Enoch Powell, on the one side, and Michael Foot on the other, fought a long delaying action in the House of Commons. There was clearly no great enthusiasm in the later stages among M.P.s and the whole idea was dropped, it may well be for many years. By that time Dick Crossman had ceased to be Leader of the House of Commons, a more significant event than my disappearance from the Lords' leadership; my successor, Eddy, was, after all, no less keen than I was, though entitled to feel a less absolute personal commitment. Standing back from the episode for a moment, one is bound to ask why the enthusiasm in Labour circles was so limited. I am sure that no other plan would have been more popular. The truth is that the Labour Party has for many years been completely schizophrenic on the issue. Harold Wilson saw this clearly enough when he referred at the earliest moment to its divisive character.

Conservative peers of the wiser sort, led by Peter Carrington, wanted the House of Lords to have a positive and unmistakable influence. Like Peter they were sick of the irrationality of its constitution which deprived them of all standing in the public eye. In the last resort, it forced them to give way to every Socialist proposal, however far-fetched, for fear of themselves being abolished. But, correspondingly, Labour politicians, unless they were forced to think with special clarity by the nature of their work, were unable to make up their minds whether they wanted the House of Lords to be rational or irrational in composition, to be taken seriously or laughed at. So long as it remained irrational, it remained futile, or at least impotent, and many of them preferred it that way. I do not think that we would have got very far if I, an academic who was quite ready to resign on this issue, had not happened to coincide with Dick Crossman, also a political theorist, who was profoundly committed to a total reform of Parliament. It might easily have come off, but it didn't.

Some comment on my general performance in the Lords must be offered. I set myself from the beginning to 'get the Government business through', including, of course, much controversial legislation. Anthony Howard told me some time before the Labour Government was formed that Harold Wilson believed that I could be particularly useful in this sense. I am not sure whether my aristocratic connections and my remote Conservative past were, on balance, helpful. I would think that Joe Champion, a former railwayman, would have been just as effective, not to mention Eddy Shackleton, with his fine record in the air force. Be that as it may, no one could dispute the smoothness with which the Government business went through, but it was possible to feel that this was because the Conservatives were too circumspect to interfere with it. I used to ask myself occasionally whether indeed I was doing the job in the way required of me. Would it not have suited Harold Wilson better to have been given an excuse for a series of rows with the Lords, which would have given him a scapegoat in the country? He never said anything remotely resembling this to me, but the thought flitted more than once through my mind. Meanwhile I plodded on diplomatically and, according to my own ideas, successfully. When I resigned eventually, I could say with sincerity that what I would miss most was the chance of showing kindness to numerous members of the House and of the public. Every Leader has his own method here. Lord Salisbury, Leader of the Opposition from 1945 to 1951 but always socially dominant in the House, performed a special role in making the small Labour Party feel at home. No one, I am sure, could have been more accessible or happier than I was in this part of my work.

The Abortion Bill of summer 1967 presented me with the sharpest moral issue. It was a Private Member's Bill which, as all the world now knows, has greatly facilitated abortion. Nothing that we said at the time against it has proved to be exaggerated. Euthanasia has not yet followed it. Can one be sure that it will not? The Parliamentary Labour Party had been well softened up on abortion. I do not question the sincerity of its champions, which often became fanatical. In the Cabinet the fiction was still maintained that the Government was neutral. Recent revelations by supporters of the Bill have made this look highly misleading, but from the point of view of myself, the only Catholic in the Cabinet, it was a vital point that I was not being asked to share the responsibility for the measure. If it had been a Government Bill, I would have resigned within the hour.

My acute problem was how to conduct myself when the Bill reached the Lords, I being Leader of the House at the time. Eddy Shackleton told me then, and has repeated it since, that I would have done better to speak against it, if that was my conviction, from my place in the middle of the front bench. He may have been right, but the Labour peers as a whole were very much against my attitude to abortion. I shrank from even seeming to commit them to my vehement opposition. Rightly or wrongly, I adjourned to a bench behind the bishops and denounced the Bill from there.

My posture on this occasion was, as far as I can make out, unique in the history of the House of Lords. In 1961, Lord Alexander of Hillsborough, Leader of the Opposition, and I had left the front bench together and spoken on Lord Arran's motion on Christian Unity from the rear - he against it, I for it. But I can't find that a Leader of the House had ever previously done what I did. It could hardly be done more than once, if a Leader wished to continue to retain the allegiance of his followers. I was aware that I was running a certain risk of this kind in making my demonstration. I certainly did not seek any opportunity of confrontation. Whatever my relations with the Prime Minister or the Government collectively, I deeply valued a sense of fraternity with our Labour peers, which I would never gratuitously imperil. Fortunately in a sense I had no dilemma, because no option. In the last resort it did not much matter which quarter of the House I spoke from.

Politics (II)

MAN PROPOSES

Was the Labour Government in 1964-70 more of a success or a failure? History will not settle the matter decisively. We can still claim if we wish that the Liberal Government of 1906-14 was the greatest of modern times, or contrariwise that it brought us to the verge of civil war over Ireland and landed us in an actual war with Germany. Taking the six years as a whole, I would personally say that the Wilson achievements were inferior to those of the Attlee period. But the last year of Attlee, after the collapse of Bevin and Cripps and in spite of the emergence of Hugh Gaitskell, was one of disintegration, leaving a fine old mess in the end. Wilson, on the other hand, inherited a fine old mess, and he, Roy Jenkins and the Cabinet had pulled the balance of payments round before they departed, though like all our other post-war governments, they left the problem of inflation unsolved. Probably the record fell below the expectations of most of their supporters and, indeed, their own. But that was because after thirteen years of Opposition, and a good deal of self-intoxicating propaganda, the hopes were pitched impossibly high.

What, if anything, went seriously wrong? In the course of six years so many decisions were taken by a government or on its behalf that one cannot begin to examine them in detail. The main mistakes of commission seemed to have been two: the failure to devalue soon enough and the obstinate retention of our position East of Suez.

But the moral arguments for the course actually followed should not be neglected. They illustrate the inextricable blending of moral and technical considerations in nearly all major decisions. It is impossible to exaggerate the decisive influence of the predicament of sterling on every aspect, great and small, of our activities. It was not until long afterwards

43

that I, and no doubt many others, learned that on the very first Saturday, while I was wondering whether or not I would be summoned to Downing Street, the crucial decisions were being taken by Harold Wilson, George Brown and Jim Callaghan, with Harold Wilson the predominant partner. By the time the Cabinet first met on the Tuesday, we were not asked to confirm the decision to maintain the existing fixed value for sterling. We didn't even know - most of us, anyway - that there had been a decision. We were asked to take the existing value of sterling for granted, and duly did so. But I vividly remember that at the end of that afternoon's Cabinet, Jim Callaghan received a message from somewhere, and reported with satisfaction that sterling had had a good day. We were entering on matrimony, therefore, as it were with a beloved wife whose heart was liable to give trouble at any moment, and might 'conk out' entirely unless most sensitively handled. The sheer precariousness of our position, as it was or as we felt it to be, must be allowed for in every controversial decision we embarked on, certainly during the three and a quarter years while I was a member of the Cabinet.

It is easy to say it now, and the fact of our tiny majority must never be forgotten, but all of us were obviously far too readily intimidated by what can only be called orthodox Treasury and City opinion. Perhaps for the first few months this deference was inevitable, but if we really, as we believed, understood economics as well as they did, we should have shaken ourselves clear much sooner and not waited for disastrous events to do it for us.

George Brown's National Plan was excellent, so were his and others' ideas of growth, but all in the event were undermined by the balance of payments, and the decision, made and adhered to, to treat devaluation as the unmentionable thing. Quite literally we were imbued with the idea that even to talk about the possibility was not dissimilar to discussing the possibility of defeat by Hitler during the war.

I must now trace briefly my own impingement on the devaluation crisis of July 1966. It chanced that on the crucial Monday, I travelled up to London with my old friend of the

National Bank, Norman Biggs, now chairman of Williams & Glyns Bank. Incidentally, one of my biggest mistakes while in Government was to fail to take advantage of friendships of this kind acquired during my eight years in the City, and of similar friendships among academic economists. I was so obsessed with the duty of discretion that I sterilised myself as a useful contributor in the economic field. Be that as it may, I derived from Norman a more burning sense of crisis than had come my way up till then.

Very unusually for me, I telephoned Jim Callaghan, the Chancellor of the Exchequer, on arrival at Whitehall, and asked for an urgent interview. I propounded my own measures, including a prices and wages freeze, etc. but saw at once that things were even graver than I had supposed. Jim was resolute as always, but very conscious of implications only half grasped by me. He told me disarmingly, 'You know, Frank, I was brought up to say my prayers regularly. I have just started again this week.' He made it plain that devaluation was, whether one liked it or not, an issue with which the Cabinet was going to be immediately confronted. George Brown, Deputy Prime Minister, would push it for all he was worth and was not likely to continue in the Cabinet if he were defeated. Jim did not wish to press me to back him up in defending the exchange rate, out of personal loyalty. He was grateful to me for having stuck by him on many occasions in the Cabinet when he was in danger of being left alone. He arranged for me to talk to an economic adviser, but this utterly disinterested man left me at the end completely uncertain whether he was for or against devaluation. Jim, I think it was, who suggested that I should talk next to George Brown himself. I duly did so; everyone, it will be noticed, behaving with edifying, almost too edifying, correctness. George in turn arranged for me to talk to one of *his* economic advisers. Here there was no dubiety or beating about the bush. I left him more or less under the impression that the Treasury was against devaluation and the Department of Economic Affairs in favour of it. It only remained to have dinner with Douglas Jay, President of the Board of Trade. He convinced me that the economic arguments were balanced and that the moral arguments brought one down heavily against devaluation because of the repudiation involved.

I hesitate to claim that if, as nearly happened, I had joined the devaluation group of ministers (whose existence, I may say, was up till then unknown to me), I might have swayed the issue. After the debate which followed in the Cabinet, Tony Crosland, sitting next to me, remarked: 'All the intellectuals except you supported devaluation,' so perhaps for once I was something of a marginal man. When it came to the vote, devaluation was defeated easily. Yet few members can have felt that they knew enough for a valuable judgment.

I have reported this sequence of events as an example primarily of how one cannot expel a moral element from even the most technical decision. On a different plane, it may strike students of government as rather peculiar that it needed a chance meeting with an old City friend to alert me to the gravity of the crisis. It will be noticed also that it was only in these very exceptional circumstances, with an immediate confrontation awaiting us in the Cabinet, that I received any expert economic advice at all. During the remaining eighteen months I stayed in the Cabinet, I tried to learn from this experience, and on occasion with considerable difficulty obtained some expert assessment. But the experts in question were not only very hard to get hold of, being in any case much over-worked; it never seemed to me that they were ready to speak with complete candour. They would seldom give a personal opinion which contradicted the existing policy of their own minister, or if they came from the Cabinet Office, the official line.

The other great mistake of the Wilson Government, in my view, was its obstinate refusal to abandon positions East of Suez; but here again there were moral arguments both ways. It may be that in the public consciousness and the fighting services there was a residue of old-fashioned imperialist feeling. As a high Treasury official said to me soon after our Government was formed: 'We seem likely to be haunted by the ghost of Empire.' But it was not that kind of sentiment which weighed with me and, I should imagine, most of us. When Harold Wilson said, in a dangerous sentence: 'Our frontier is on the Himalayas,' he was not suggesting that we should exercise dominion over anybody. My point of view - it may well have been his - was much closer to the collective security that we aspired to in pre-war years as essential to the philosophy of the League of Nations. It was our duty, somehow or other, to play our part in resisting aggression wherever it happened in the world.

I turn aside to record my own greatest disappointment during the Wilson period - our failure to make any progress at all towards World Government. But there at least we could not be blamed. Hugh Foot (now Lord Caradon) was an inspired appointment at the United Nations. Whether there was much point in calling him a Minister of Cabinet rank is rather more arguable. It produced a few minor problems for me, as Leader of the House of Lords, but my admiration for him and his work never wavered. In the early sixties I had done a lot of work on plans for an international peace force and generally for movement in a World Government direction. I had presided over two representative committees.

It had been a special joy to be associated in this new form of international vision with Clem Attlee, who at the age of 80 carried the banner of World Government all over America and elsewhere. But when the time came, the opposition of Soviet Russia - she was not the only obscurantist, but the main one - nullified all immediate hope of major progress. At the beginning of our Government I saw Anglo-American resistance to aggression as the only substitute available for genuine collective security, although it could be no more than an interim method. In other words, the withdrawal from East of Suez seemed to me and to most of us an abdication of duty, if humanly speaking it could be avoided.

As time went on, it became obvious that it was economically impossible to play the part we had assigned to ourselves, and more and more doubtful whether those we were seeking to defend could benefit from our assistance. And so I changed my whole approach to the issue. But if anyone asks the question, how far governments are influenced by moral considerations, this part of the story illustrates the fact that they always should be, but that moral considerations may point in more directions than one. They can never be obeyed in total abstraction from economic realities.

On the home front, I suppose that something of a moral dilemma arose every time a desirable social objective was postponed or cancelled for shortage of funds. The debate on the postponement of the raising of the school-leaving age, of which more farther on, or, for that matter, on the imposition of prescription charges, provides an example. Internationally, the issue which arose at the end of 1967 of whether to send arms to South Africa aroused more internal passion than anything else in my time. It was the only period, mercifully, when the atmosphere in the Cabinet room was positively unpleasant, and the attitude of one or two senior Ministers towards the Prime Minister most unattractive. Taking his premiership as a whole, he was wonderfully good at maintaining an amicable and, indeed, entertaining atmosphere within the Cabinet room, but during this short period his magic was insufficient. Various accounts have been given of what occurred. There has been some disposition to question the straight-forwardness of the Prime Minister's conduct. From anything I saw in the crucial Overseas and Defence Committee, and in the Cabinet itself, there is no justification for this whatever.

The issue at stake was one on which honourable and enlightened men could reasonably differ. At that time, the end of 1971, stringent economies were being called for at home. It was natural that every nerve should be strained to improve our balance of payments. Arms to South Africa were an obvious expedient. Much trouble was taken to persuade us that the arms could never be used to suppress rebellious Africans. Naturally enough, the Department of Economic Affairs, the Board of Trade, and the Ministry of Defence were strenuously in favour of selling the arms in question. Their Ministers were powerful figures and put the case with force and logic, in the Defence and Overseas Committee. Harold Wilson, for the only time in my experience, seemed almost isolated. Then Dick Crossman and Michael Stewart took his side; but he was still in a minority. My own status on this Committee was a shade ambiguous. I had originally got myself invited as the top spokesman on these issues in the House of Lords. By now I was a constant attender, though never quite sure whether I had or had not a vote. There was no doubt about it on this question. I was sure that the matter must at least be held up, in view of the Prime Minister's opposition. He had warned us of the very deep feeling that was already stirring in the Party. To say the least it would be monstrous, I felt, to ride rough-shod over it, without notice or warning.

My vote levelled the score in the Committee, so the issue was postponed for the moment. Misunderstanding soon raised an ugly head. By a complete coincidence, Jim Callaghan, who was unavoidably absent from the Committee, made some remark at a back-bench dinner, which created the impression that the adversaries of the Prime Minister were working overtime against him. Others who sympathised with the P.M. and were in any case horrified by the very idea of selling arms to South Africa, organised themselves actively. The antagonisms in the Cabinet were really painful. I need not spell out the story further. There came a moment when the newspapers were expecting a decision from the Cabinet. It was not forthcoming, and the anti-Wilson elements spread their own tale all too zealously. They were hoist with their own petard and the Prime Minister emerged triumphantly. The sale of arms to South Africa was flatly rejected and the Ministers who had been involved in the proposition were left far out, on a very unpopular limb. No one in my view had behaved discreditably, yet a member of the Cabinet told a friend of mine that 'he had never known how dirty politics was until this episode'. So each side thought that the other had tried to take an illegitimate advantage. The immediate result was a horrifying growth of mutual suspicion. I disappeared from the scene soon after. So I gather did the suspicion. (The two things were not connected!)

If one is interested in the moral factor in politics, one is left asking oneself whether a moral outcry among back-benchers is an indication that the ethics of the Government are 'deteriorating' under economic or such-like pressures. It may be so, perhaps was so on this occasion, but back-bench emotion and certainly public emotion are not necessarily a criterion of integrity. Casting our minds on a few years, we find Mr

Heath's Government confronted with the expulsion of British Asians from Uganda, by the tyrannical edict of General Amin. A Public Opinion poll at that time indicated that the vast majority of the population were against the acceptance of the expelled Asians into this country. But Mr Heath, the Home Secretary Mr Carr, and their colleagues, to their eternal credit, defied public opinion and accepted the moral obligation. The leaders of the Labour Party did likewise, if perhaps a shade belatedly. No one knows what back-bench opinion would have amounted to on this occasion. I am merely pointing to the distinction between the responsibilities of those who rule as compared with the attitudes of the general public. The latter are not bound by circumstances to take all factors into account and, for that very reason, retain a simplicity which may be purer, but may just as easily be cruder or more selfish.

The attitude of the Wilson Government towards South Africa was always uneasy. Obviously we all detested apartheid, but for that matter we heartily disliked a large number of other systems. Few of us, I suppose, would have admitted to any sympathy with what was going on in Soviet Russia or Eastern Europe generally, or had a good word to say for Franco's Spain, where three million British tourists, we are told, are happy to spend their holidays. The racialism of South Africa struck a special chord of horror, yet not such a chord as to rule out economic relations. I was heart and soul behind the Wilson Government's policy towards Rhodesia, but logically we should have been ready to recommend and implement sanctions against South Africa once it was plain that South Africa was stultifying the whole conception of bringing Rhodesia to book. But there was never much likelihood of our doing so for unashamed economic reasons.

I could not fault Harold Wilson's handling of the Rhodesian question. As always, he *said* some things in his natural exuberance which made his policy look much less sensible than it was. His remark early on that, 'the problem would be solved in weeks, rather than months,' was particularly unfortunate. But the whole Cabinet was agreed that strong measures had to be taken. The idea of using force, i.e. of invading Rhodesia, was carefully examined by the Defence experts but was never a serious likelihood. So a persistent, if unheroic, course of economic sanctions was the only procedure remaining.

The Prime Minister's meeting with Ian Smith on the *Tiger* brought me for once into the very centre of operations. On the Monday afternoon, after returning from the *Tiger* visit, he was waiting in No. 10 Downing Street for the news from Salisbury as to whether the Smith Cabinet had accepted the terms. When their decision was known, a comprehensive statement would be expected in the House of Commons, and I should be called on to repeat it simultaneously in the House of Lords. Incidentally, this was one of the least attractive chores attaching to my office. Reading someone else's statement has a peculiarly chilling effect on reader and audience, and I used to become more and more frozen as I proceeded. I have noticed the same in many others, but I suspect that I was one of the worst offenders, and Wilson's were some of the longest statements. The reading finished, one was immediately interrogated, frequently with no opportunity of providing oneself with supplementary replies. The whole thing was apt to be a bit of a nightmare.

Be that as it may, my surrogate role on this occasion gave me an exciting time of it. I suppose that I was in the Cabinet room at No. 10 for a couple of hours. My mind inevitably went back to midnight or thereabouts on 5th December, 1921, the British Ministers waited in that very room while the Irish delegates fought out their last bitter arguments at their headquarters in Hans Place. Lloyd George had issued the ultimatum earlier in the evening that, unless the Irish signed the Treaty in front of them, they would undergo the horrors of 'immediate and terrible war'. Austen Chamberlain recalled that, in spite of or because of the strain they were all undergoing, the room rang with happy laughter.

I cannot remember any noisy laughter on this latter-day occasion, but Harold Wilson's greatest quality has always been his cheerfulness in difficult moments, and we were quite a happy party as we sat and waited. Whisky and soda was served, at perhaps six o'clock. I am not a whisky drinker myself, except under strain. This time I yielded. As far as I can remember, everybody imbibed moderately, with the whole exception of the Prime Minister, who seemed to need neither stimulus nor tranquilliser. The party consisted of himself, two Ministers who had been intimately involved in the *Tiger* talks, and a handful of key officials. Much of the time was spent by the Prime Minister in dictating the factual report of recent happenings, craftily prepared to serve as a basis whether the answer from Smith was 'yes' or 'no'. Suddenly news began to come through, but confusingly and unofficially. There was some Reuters' flash that the Rhodesian Cabinet had rejected the plan; some I.T.N. message that it had been accepted. Harold Wilson, optimistic to the end, reflected briefly on the extraordinary accuracy of I.T.N. reports. But then a shorthand-typist came in with irrefutable evidence. She had just taken down a full message from Our Man in Salisbury, and there was no doubt whatever that it amounted to total rejection. Harold Wilson called for another shorthand-typist and set to work. With lowered head and bowed shoulders, striding up and down the Cabinet room, he looked more and more like Winston Churchill in bulldog mood.

As he proceeded, a vague disquiet assailed me. Surely he was overdoing things a bit? We should soon have a reference to 'a fight on the beaches' and the long hand of retributory justice reaching out to grab the evil man. I tried to pluck up courage to intervene, but faltered. I muttered something to a high Civil Servant beside me. He murmured back blandly, 'No good doing anything while he's on the up and up. We wait to catch him on the down swing.' But I was conscious that in a short while I would be delivering these extreme pronouncements to a restless House of Lords, already irritated by waiting over-long. Mercifully Harold Wilson had an additional thought. 'Call in Gerald and Marcia,' he said crisply. And in came Gerald Kaufmann and Marcia Williams by a door at the far end of the Cabinet room that I had never seen made use of. Marcia Williams soon won my undying respect. While I was too craven to intervene and the rest of the company kept silent for their own reasons, she spoke out boldly: 'You can't say that,'

she said at a certain moment. Then I, too, found my tongue
and the speech was suitably adjusted. In all the circumstances,
it seemed to me a very good effort.

One of the most gratifying developments in our Cabinet life
was our conversion by a large majority to the idea of going
into Europe, though this looks ironical now. We were certainly
not a pro-European Cabinet when we started, although George
Brown, Roy Jenkins and Tony Crosland (the last two not
initially in the Cabinet) were doughty European champions,
and they were not alone. It fell to my lot, as H. A. L. Fisher
used to say in his Cabinet reminiscences, to handle various
international debates in the House of Lords. I had all along
been openly favourable to the European cause, though never in
any very glorious or compelling fashion, and I was naturally
anxious to emphasise any governmental leanings of that kind.
I soon became aware that nothing that I could say in favour of
Europe would be too strong for the various Foreign Office
officials who provided me with briefs. In an important sense,
therefore, the powerful drive towards Europe came quite
constitutionally from the Foreign Office officials. Michael
Stewart was Foreign Secretary, March 1965 to July 1966, and -
as far as I could judge - was helping things along. He has always
been a dedicated but cool and rational Socialist. Also, incidentally, a fine public speaker. In social gatherings he was even
more unobtrusive than Lord Attlee, which is saying much.

I had happened to sit next to Michael at the Labour Party
Conference in Brighton in 1962, when Hugh Gaitskell delivered
an 80-minute oration - one of the most powerful ever heard
at the Conference - and, whatever the verbal balance, swept the
far from reluctant delegates into a frenzy of opposition to the
Market, Michael clapped courteously, but no more. I asked him
curiously how he felt. 'I agree with him on the whole, but I
thought he rather over-stated the case.' If anyone could be
relied upon to be dispassionate about the issue, it would be
him. At some point he seemed to come down on the side of
Europe.

Nevertheless, I shall always believe that it was the coming of
George Brown to the Foreign Office which tipped the scales in

favour of a European policy. Without him, I doubt whether
the Prime Minister would have been won over, and until that
happened the majority were always adverse. The elaborate
democratic procedures adopted for the Cabinet discussions
have been fully set out by Harold Wilson in his book. Speaking
in shorthand, I would say that this was a good example, not of
how a Prime Minister cannot dictate to colleagues, but of how -
if he plays his cards right - he is worth at least half a dozen
votes in the Cabinet. There is nothing extraordinary or sinister
in this. The chairman of any large committee possesses the
same sort of influence if he is worth his salt. At any rate a
majority gradually emerged of slightly more than two to one
in favour of entry. It is true that the decision was, strictly
speaking, one of only agreeing to entry if the terms were right,
but no one - winners or losers - after the crucial vote at
Chequers had any doubt as to which way it had gone. Douglas
Jay, whose devotion to the anti-Market cause compelled my
admiration even though I disagreed with him, motored back
to London with me afterwards. He asked me whether I thought
he ought to resign. I begged him not to. I suppose out of
personal friendship. I still don't know whether I gave him the
right advice or whether it had anything to do with his staying
on in the Cabinet.

In terms of concrete achievement this, in my eyes, was George
Brown's finest hour. I speak as a pro-European. The long-run
influence of the Labour decision to seek entry was incalculable.
Without that, it is difficult to believe that we should in fact be
entering Europe - a big credit therefore to George Brown!
Something more perhaps must be attempted at this point
regarding that extraordinary character. I like very much the
last lines of his autobiography, where he tells us that as he goes
up and down the country he is still given a heart-warming
reception among ordinary people who do not believe that
getting into office and clinging on to office are the be-all and
end-all of existence. There is an awareness here of part of his
own strength. He has a fine natural brain, undisturbed by
formal education; he has the indefinable power of communi-
cating in conversation or public speech with all sorts and conditions of men, including the real proletarians. In others,

this last quality seems to atrophy too often, as the politician settles down to a middle-class existence.

In the same book he is very frank about his weaknesses, though I am still not sure whether he appreciates their least attractive element. I saw him mainly at Cabinet meetings, where he was extremely impressive, very succinct when called upon, perfectly ready to hold his peace for long periods, always expressing genuine convictions, even where they might not always be congenial to the Cabinet, yet making every allowance for the views of others. Hardly more than once did I see him unduly excited, though one was aware that such outbursts occurred. In such company I naturally did not see him take advantage of his position to speak rudely to those who could not easily strike back. Yet it was this last type of weakness that suggests an insecurity which, in retrospect, can be seen to have disqualified him from the premiership. Being a peer, I had no vote for the election of the Leader in 1963. I think that I would have voted for George Brown - I am sure that I would have been wrong, but he remains one of the few men on any side of politics who arouses warm feelings among millions of electors. Not just because of his eccentricities, possibly in spite of them, but because he seems to be the kind of patriot with whom millions of people identify easily - a man whose heart is stirred by all sides of the national life; a man who speaks his mind and at his best speaks instinctively for his countrymen. A Britisher, but not just a Britisher. You have only got to see him at an Irish Club dinner on St Patrick's Day and listen to him singing rebel songs to recognise his love for Ireland in general, and Cork in particular, where he is proud that his family came from. He is himself a serious Anglo-Catholic.

George Brown looks like being one of the last working-class figures to reach the top in politics. The coming of popular education and the vast extension of higher education have made it less and less likely that a man like Ernest Bevin or Herbert Morrison would today leave school uneducated. Yet the Labour Party originated in the protest of the industrial masses against the savage injustices of their lives. When I myself joined the Labour Party in 1936, it was still possible to treat it as part of the working-class movement, though there was always the tension between the demands of a single class, admittedly the majority, and the dictates of universal justice. When Harold Wilson's Government was formed, there were half a dozen members who might be called working class, although obviously by the time a man becomes a Cabinet Minister he is not exactly a typical proletarian. George Brown, Frank Cousins, Tom Fraser, Arthur Bottomley, Ray Gunter could, at any rate, describe themselves as working class without absurdity. All these had passed away by the end of the Wilson Government. Roy Mason might be regarded as their sole replacement. Yet the power of the organised working class is at least as great today in its impact on Labour policy as ever it was. The, to me, forbidding figures of Messrs Jones and Scanlon (against whom I have nothing personally) exemplify the point. How the working-class leaders in that sense are to combine in the future with the leaders of the Labour Cabinet remains to be seen. In regard to his own Government, Harold Wilson had the right idea, but it did not work out. Is it intellectually snobbish to suggest that a first class degree equips you to make your point more briefly than a training in the mine or at the bench, although the latter produces sometimes richer experience and a riper wisdom?

I always remember that on one occasion when we tried something like a filibuster in the House of Lords in resisting the destruction of the L.C.C., the dons were no good at all. The most brilliantly concise speaker in either House, Barbara Wootton, would have found the whole operation intolerable. Other academics like myself were unimpressive. Whereas an old friend of mine, a former railway clerk, felt liberated and talked on happily for hours. Whatever the reason, the working-class element had more or less been eroded from the Wilson Government by the time it came to an end. Incidentally, the old Etonians and such-like had also by and large disappeared. Three old Etonians were members of the Attlee Cabinet - Hugh Dalton, Lord Pethick-Lawrence, and Lord Listowel. In the Wilson Cabinet I was the only one, and I had fallen by the wayside halfway through. A similar process can be distinguished in regard to the other top public schools. It is true that Dick Crossman - Winchester - and Gerald Gardiner - Harrow - were still there at the finish, but we must assume that if Labour wins next time they will not be *in situ*. The general drift is clear. I say it without enthusiasm, bitterness or cynicism. The representative Labour politician is more and more a grammar school man or woman, with the public school class and the working classes occupying fringe positions. Is the same process at work in the Tory Party? Is the change permanent from Sir Alec Home and the magic circle to Ted Heath and Broadstairs man?

How far did religion impinge on the performance of the Labour Government? Not much on the face of it, but perhaps it was too much to expect that it should. On one occasion, Tony Crosland, sitting next to me in Cabinet, took up a point with me, *sotto voce*. It arose from a speech I was to deliver that afternoon on Education, he being Minister of Education at the time. 'Can you really justify your statement,' he asked me, 'that we are a Christian Cabinet?' I did a quick count round the room, though much of it was inevitably guess-work. 'I make it eleven Christians, beginning with the top three - Harold Wilson, George Brown and Jim Callaghan - six non- or anti-Christians, and four don't knows. I don't know what they think about religion and I surmise that they don't.' 'Which am I?' he asked me. 'I've put you down as a don't know,' I replied. I never discovered how far he thought I was right in regard to himself, or the others. At any rate he made no objection to my proposed formulation.

It is often said that the Labour Party owes more to Methodism than Marx. That is clearly true without signifying much, except very indirectly. The real comparison would be with the works of the Fabians. The works of Marx have had a negligible effect on the Labour movement in Britain, as compared with the Continent, for example. Historically no one can question the tremendous influence of the nonconformist tradition, still exemplified today by families like the Greenwoods and Hendersons, not to mention a prophetic leader like Donald Soper. But the Church of England has contributed George Lansbury, Stafford Cripps and Trevor Huddleston, among many others. Services are held before the party conferences in which the leaders always participate even when, like Hugh Gaitskell, they would not describe themselves as practising Christians. When the Government was re-formed after the election of 1966, a moving service was conducted for its members by Donald Soper and Mervyn Stockwood.

But what difference did all this make in practice? Not surprisingly, there was never a division in the Cabinet where Christians were on one side and non-Christians on the other. So the Christian leaven had to do its work unannounced.

Harold Wilson enjoyed and cultivated excellent relations with all the religious leaders, particularly perhaps with Cardinal Heenan, an old friend from Liverpool. Tony Crosland, on becoming Minister of Education, told me that Harold Wilson had enjoined on him the necessity for friendly relations with the Cardinal. One can assume that religious interests were as well looked after during the Wilson period as was expected by anyone.

But another class of ideology, far closer to Humanism than Christianity in its inspiration, was very influential during these years, particularly among the younger Labour M.P.s. Mr David McKie has contributed a fascinating chapter on the quality of life to a book called *The Decade of Disillusion - British Politics in the Sixties*, of which he was one of the editors. I pass over the important sections devoted to the physical environment and deal below with the personal and moral issues in the chapter on *The Permissive Society*. But Mr McKie mentions that an essential signal for reform was the arrival at the Home Office of 'that most rational and civilised of politicians, Roy Jenkins'. He, with Tony Crosland, had been propounding ideas of this kind for quite a few years.

It is quite likely that Harold Wilson will remain Leader of the Labour Party during the foreseeable future, but in any ordinary sense, Roy Jenkins is the one immediate alternative. I will end this chapter by trying to set him in a wider and more up-to-date context.

He takes criticism very well. When he was asked whether he minded the derisive label of 'smoothy chops', he replied urbanely: 'It was not precisely the soubriquet I would have chosen, but it does not cut very deep.' In my eyes he deserves a more interesting title than 'rational and civilised'. He has been a late developer, not outstandingly academic. He has emerged as a political writer of striking perceptiveness and of ever-growing literary accomplishment. He is the first and only Chancellor of the Exchequer since the war to put our balance of payments right. A great deal of economic comprehension went into that and a great deal of moral stamina. He took up the cause of Europe, when to do so was utterly opposed to his interests and embroiled him with his great friend Hugh Gaitskell, on whom his career apparently depended. Day in, day out, he has prosecuted that cause, making the odd mistake, so it would seem, here and there, but setting it inflexibly before his personal interests. How can I tell what impression his personality makes on the general public? Bright-eyed behind his spectacles, a little over-weight, perhaps, but full of animation and physical energy both on the tennis court and elsewhere, a man of the twentieth century to his fingertips, yet carrying somewhere within his personality an earlier South Wales background.

He likes a battle in spite of his rather mild appearance, though he looks tougher now than he did a few years ago. I said to him that someone else was more aggressive than he looked. 'Do you think,' he asked me, 'that I am more aggressive than I look?' When I told him that he was, he seemed highly satisfied. Going into the Cabinet one day, he showed me the draft of a letter he intended to write to the Prime Minister. 'Since you ask me,' I told him, 'this will lead to a row.' His eyes gleamed pleasantly. 'I should rather welcome a row,' he replied. He, if anyone at the top of the Labour Party at the moment, can be rated a man of principle. But as soon as one pays him that compliment a cry of protest breaks out from other notables. Immediately after his speech at Oxford on 10th March, 1973, Barbara Castle indignantly denied his special claim to integrity. I have already discussed the difficulty of defining principle in politics. What meaning am I to attach to it here?

In Roy's case we cannot ignore his professional success as a biographer of Dilke, Asquith and certain contemporaries. Alone among his contemporaries on the front benches, he has

provided for himself an alternative career to politics. (I am
excluding complimentary directorships.) He is said to have been
offered the editorship of *The Economist* before the Labour
Government was formed. He told me once that if you are
Chancellor of the Exchequer in your forties, you are able to
take a tranquil view of lesser positions that might or might
not be offered you; but that, of course, is only true if you fulfil
yourself outside politics. He is in a position, in other words,
to take a big view, a situation which has its strength and weakness. There are the accusations of indifference to the more
humdrum colleagues in the Smoking Room, and if this is true
it is a political deficiency. As against that, he has the detach-
ment and perspective to enable him to assess the events of
today against the backcloth of history. But his historical and
literary talents have a deeper significance.

If one may compare him, as is done so often, with his
brilliant contemporary Tony Crosland, one questions whether
Roy's initial intelligence, however measured, is greater than
Tony's. The latter delves more deeply into particular social and
economic questions and expresses himself concerning them
more incisively than any politician I know. But Roy stands a
little farther back and is somewhat better equipped of the two
to attain a wide and just perspective. As a result, in my eyes,
and in those of many well-informed judges, he comes before
us now as a remarkably consistent figure. No doubt discrep-
ancies in his record can be dredged up by adversaries, but his
career has steadily unrolled itself in a fashion that we can all
understand, as we understand the careers of Asquith or
Campbell-Bannerman or Attlee. Europe is only one example,
though the most striking. Against the flexibility of Wilson and
the rigidity of Heath (till forced by unexpected events to
change), I would attribute to Roy Jenkins the kind of inner
political coherence that comes out well in history if the hero
survives at all. Repeating that last qualification, I cannot fail
to describe him as a statesman.

But quite apart from Harold Wilson's immovability, it is
highly doubtful whether Roy Jenkins will ever be leader of the
Labour Party. The fact that *The Times* and so many eminent
Liberal persons support him so devoutly, suggests that emo-

tional liaison between him and the Socialist multitudes is unlikely to be warm or intimate. He has a unique power of revivifying the worn-out terminology of political discussion with many fresh turns of phrase. In his articles and his reported speeches, he communicates superbly with the educated classes and dominates the House of Commons when he extends himself. But will the working masses, still neglected by politicians at their peril, ever identify with Roy Jenkins sufficiently to make him their leader? The European issue will pass. On Income and Prices he has preserved a less than heroic posture up till now, but in a Party sense seems to have left his hands fairly free. Will he convince the Labour Party as a whole that he is a genuine Radical, a Socialist indeed in some sense at least; an egalitarian as the editor of *The Times* and the leader of the Liberal Party are not?

Even among the Party faithful, certainly within the House of Commons, there are large numbers of good Socialists who have seen him as the largest hope of countering the left-wing militancy under whose influence, for the time being, the Party has fallen. It may be that he will personally triumph; at the moment it does not seem very likely. One earnestly hopes that for many years yet he will never be far from the leadership.

Politics (III)

RESIGNATION

Nothing in my membership of the Wilson Government became me so well - it was said at the time - as the manner of my leaving it. Be that true or not true, no incident illustrated better my relationship with that Government than my decision to resign because the promised raising of the school-leaving age had been postponed. But it must not be thought that I was the only resigner. We as a Cabinet were described on occasion as 'not the resigning type', but statistically that is quite incorrect. Besides myself, Frank Cousins, George Brown and Ray Gunter resigned from the Government - Chris Mayhew and Margaret Herbison from important positions outside. This would appear to be a record of its kind. In the thirteen years of Tory rule only Bobbity Salisbury and Peter Thorneycroft resigned from the Cabinet. In the six years of Attlee government there were no resignations from the Cabinet till those of Aneurin Bevan and Harold Wilson near the end, and so on if one looks into history.

There is ample scope for a treatise on resignations. I must curtail my reflections here. Of all the deeply appreciated letters I received, perhaps the one I treasure most is that from Bobbity Salisbury. He wrote, as he himself said, from 'some small experience of resignation'. In fact, he was the only politician living to have resigned from two governments (Chamberlain's 1938 and Macmillan's 1957). 'People will always say,' he wrote, 'that it is the wrong time and the wrong issue. It will never be the right time and the right issue. But when you reach the point when you know in your heart that it is impossible for you not to resign, then if you do resign you will never regret it.' I have certainly found that his words were true in my case. Everyone who resigns comes to it in his own fashion. I would venture the general opinion that the Prime Minister of the day is usually relieved when it happens, even though he may not have wished it to happen in quite that way.

The first thing to say about my resignation is that it was a genuine and not a phoney resignation. I was just 62 at the time (January 1968). Harold Wilson had made it plain that Ministers over 60 were not required for ever, although in such cases he was always anxious to be helpful and provide alternative occupation. In the autumn of 1967 I had agreed to stay on until the reform of the House of Lords, as expected, became law. In other words, for another year or so. I would certainly not have felt justified in flouncing out without grave cause.

In my letter of resignation, I wrote:

'The postponement is apparently condemned by those educationalists whose opinion I value most. It is sharply opposed to the long-term policy and fundamental ideals of our Party and to pledges we gave as recently as last September. It is inconceivable that I should commend it to the House of Lords.' It had been a much-appreciated honour, I went on, to lead the House of Lords during such a fruitful period. 'After twenty-two years on one front bench or another, I take my place with zest on the back benches, among our devoted Labour peers . . . It will always be a source of pride to myself and my family that you should have chosen me for such high offices in your Government from whom I have received nothing but kindness, to whom I wish nothing but good.'

It will be noticed that I lay deep emphasis not only on the wrong involved in the postponement itself, but in the breach of an undertaking recently given. More than once during the crucial discussions about the so-called 'cuts' to follow devaluation, Harold Wilson had used the phrase 'there must be no sacred cows'. Indeed, he had used it some months earlier when the postponement of the raising of the school-leaving age had with difficulty been beaten off by the efforts of Tony Crosland, then Minister of Education, and supporting Ministers like myself. But by the end of 1967 I had become convinced that no commitment would be safe if the slogan of 'no sacred cows' were to be applied remorselessly. I feel entitled to accept congratulations from time to time for having resigned on an educational issue. But in a wider sense I was leaving a Cabinet where the sanctity of promises seemed to be on the point of losing its significance. This question of whether a government is ever entitled to abandon a commitment is full of difficulties. At that very moment we were, in fact, with my hearty approval, abandoning our main positions East of Suez. I should not like to go to the stake, therefore, for too rigid an interpretation of the rule that a government's undertakings must be kept in all circumstances to the letter. Nevertheless, in the case of raising the school-leaving age, the economic advantages of the postponement seemed so trivial, the moral commitment so recent and so glaring, the educational issue so obvious, that I never had any doubts that it was a resigning matter as soon as I realised that postponement was on the way.

As already indicated my experiences in the Attlee Government come in here. I had been desperately unhappy when I was Minister for Germany (and later) at our failure to apply what I believed were Christian and Socialist principles to the Germans. A little later we applied them, but under diplomatic rather than moral pressures, as the Russian threat developed. More than once I had tried to resign and been held off in masterly style by Clem Attlee. I still treasure more than one of his letters running like this: 'My dear Frank, I will look into the point you mention as soon as possible. Yours ever, Clem.' Which left me floundering. Once when I indicated my desire to resign immediately, he managed to avoid seeing me until the situation had taken some new turn which provided a further excuse for postponement. I made up my mind in the long intervening period that if ever I wanted to resign, I would issue what would amount to an ultimatum and act on it unless it was complied with.

Over 1968, I must be fair to all concerned, particularly Patrick Gordon Walker, my closest friend in the Cabinet, and Minister for Education at the time. I must recall why, by the end of 1967, the Labour Government was on the point of postponing the raising of the school-leaving age, which it had reaffirmed as a policy as late as the previous September. The £ was devalued, Roy Jenkins came in as Chancellor. Everyone understood that cuts of some kind were necessary. I cannot blame him for adopting the obvious tactic and calling for approximately equal reductions from all the relevant departments. In the case of education the postponement of the raising of the school-leaving age was an inevitable candidate. Patrick Gordon Walker thought that any other educational cut would be worse. There was never any reason whatever why he himself should resign on this issue. No politician has ever been so cruelly treated by fate. His good temper and serenity in the face of political misfortunes, and later ill-health, showed how much the Cabinet lost when they were deprived of his services.

But every man is the keeper of his own conscience. When I thought of the 15-year-olds who were to be deprived by the Government's proposal of a year's education, I said to myself - not for the first time but more urgently than ever - that this was the section of the population most neglected by the community. I would never look myself in the face again after all my fine talk about my dedication to youth if I betrayed them now. But my concern, as already explained, was wider.

I felt that a Labour Government that gave way here would have no binding commitments left. At an early moment I wrote a private letter to the Prime Minister to warn him of what my attitude would be if the proposal went through. It became more and more likely that this would happen. The battle was not yet lost. About a week before the final decision there was a crucial debate in the Cabinet. Two categories of Ministers were specially vehement against the proposal. George Brown, Jim Callaghan and Ray Gunter expressed their heartfelt regret that their own schooling had been cut short so soon, while former Ministers of Education, Michael Stewart and Tony Crosland, spoke incisively from their expert knowledge of the educational system. I let the Cabinet know quite clearly that I should be leaving them if the raising of the age were postponed. George Brown - Foreign Minister - had to leave the Cabinet Room for a diplomatic encounter. On the way he passed my chair and said in my ear: 'I think I'll go out on this one, but keep in touch with me.' Alas! that did not prove possible. In the ensuing week he circled the globe in efforts, on the whole successful, to explain to our Allies the impending changes in our Foreign and Defence policies. I gained the impression from George's *Memoirs* that he wished afterwards that he had in fact 'gone out' on this issue which was certainly intelligible to everyone. If the Deputy Prime Minister had, in fact, resigned, or been on the point of resigning a week before the decision, what might not have happened at that convulsive moment?

By the end of the afternoon it seemed almost inevitable that the postponement would go through and my resignation take effect, but on the Sunday between this debate and the final one, Gerald Gardiner paid me a surprise call at our flat in Chelsea. He said that he understood that I was resigning on a point of principle, namely the deferment for two years of the raising of the school-leaving age. But at what point did the principle begin to operate? Supposing the deferment were only for one year, would that be a point of principle? And the greatest cross-examiner of the day raked my innermost conscience with his friendly but inflexible light blue eyes. I am still not quite sure what impression I conveyed in my reply. Certainly he made a gallant attempt when the time came to raise the compromise of a single year's deferment. Mercifully for my conscience the battle lines were by that time drawn and he found no supporters. The battle of the previous week was re-fought as ardently as before - George Brown and others fighting to the end - but no one modified his position. My side, though I was by no means the leader of it, was defeated in the event by twelve votes to nine.

There were one or two odd little proprieties to be observed. It appeared that my letter of resignation addressed to Harold Wilson had to be sent down physically to the Queen at Sandringham before it could take effect. Her confirmation could be and was received by telephone. Next morning, a Tuesday, I went in to see Harold Wilson in his room at the House of Commons for the last time. As always, I admired him in moments of tension. The cuts were being announced that afternoon. He did not know whether other Ministers were resigning as well as myself. The prescription charges had brought much distress, especially to Jennie Lee, his dear friend and universally popular Minister for the Arts. Her husband, Aneurin Bevan, had resigned on a similar issue with Harold Wilson in 1951. The loss of her would be altogether more severe than my disappearance. But he remained cool. His opening, 'But Frank, I am sorry that it should have come to this,' could not be complained of. He did not reproach me, though he expressed a fear that I might have put Patrick Gordon Walker in a difficult position. We parted certainly not as enemies but rather as strangers. That was how we remained on the few occasions we ran into each other till August 1969, when my daughter Catherine was tragically killed. On that occasion he wrote me a very warm-hearted letter. I replied. He alone of all our many correspondents wrote again. That, I like to think, is the real man. It is certainly an important part of him.

And so, for the first time after so many years in the House, I found myself on the back benches, sitting between my oldest friend in the Lords, Will Henderson, and Harry Walston - so generous to all, but not generously treated in the Government. George (Viscount) Gage, Father of the House on my reckoning, wrote to me at the time I resigned: 'When I looked at you sitting there as Leader of the House, I wondered. You did it very well, of course, but the House of Lords' leadership is such an Establishment thing, that I wondered . . .' So perhaps I had found my true level at last.

Nora Phillips was the first though not the only member of our front bench to welcome me in my reduced capacity. But for quite a while mutual embarrassment persisted. It always does. How far, I asked myself, had I kept contact with Chris Mayhew after his brave resignation from the Government? One lunch at the time. But after that as long as I remained a member of the Cabinet? It was not till we were both 'outside' that once again we drew together.

I was surprised and inexpressibly touched when the Labour peers presented me with a bust of myself, sculptured by Judith Bluck, of our own neighbourhood, who won a bronze medal with it in Paris. Eddy Shackleton spoke, as always, gracefully. I replied with a quotation from the end of Cronin's book, *The Stars Look Down*: 'Though he had failed to lead the van in battle, at least he was marching with the men.'

I made a firm resolve under no circumstances to embarrass the Government - and within a few weeks had broken it. I found it impossible not to vote against the Government on the question of the entry into this country of the Kenyan Asians after the speeches of Fenner Brockway and John Hunt, two of my chief heroes in the House. Violet Bonham-Carter was all the dearer to her friends because she never let them off lightly. 'Surely,' she said to me in a high state of indignation, 'you are going to resign over this?' For once I had the last word with her. 'Resignation is the one thing you can't do twice running!'

*

This seems to be the place to try to analyse my dissatisfaction with the Wilson Government. Obviously, as I explained earlier, I did not feel that I myself was adequately catered for. After all, I was one of the handful of members at the beginning who had had considerable experience in the Attlee period. In 1964 Harold Wilson, Patrick Gordon Walker and Jim Griffiths were the only three members of the new Cabinet with previous Cabinet experience. I had had three years as Minister of Civil Aviation and in 1951 had been promoted to being First Lord of the Admiralty. In the intervening years I had been chairman of a clearing bank for eight years and I assumed (quite wrongly as it turned out) that use would be made of the kind of experience seldom if ever acquired by Socialists. I felt, and still feel, that I was largely wasted in the Cabinet.

Suppose Hugh Gaitskell had lived? Whether I had been in the Commons or the Lords, I am not sure how it would have worked out for me in the Cabinet. Hugh would have made a much more masterful Prime Minister than Harold Wilson; he held such passionate convictions on so many things. When I saw an old film the other day of him speaking at the time of Suez, I could only rub my eyes and say to myself: 'They don't make men who care like that nowadays.' If he had found me a dissident or a passenger, he would not have long retained me. In that respect he would have been less indulgent than Harold Wilson. But at least I would have had an opportunity to display my powers to the full and to offer counsel to one who would have thought it worthwhile to listen to me.

Trying to set aside grievances and frustrations, I still draw a distinction between Harold Wilson and myself in our understanding of principle in politics. There is no doubt that the whole atmosphere of the Government was coloured by his approach. But what do I mean when I talk about principle or, for that matter, morality in politics? I am not referring to the morality of private life, in which Harold Wilson and his Ministers would in any case be above reproach.

In a human sense Harold Wilson's virtues, some of them already touched on, are far more visible than his defects. When my daughter Rachel was married to Kevin Billington in December 1967, Harold Wilson came to the wedding at considerable personal inconvenience. It was about the worst moment of his premiership; there was real hostility to him in the Cabinet over arms for South Africa. But he soon became the life and soul of the party, and if anyone tells me that all politicians are good at that sort of thing, and that it means nothing, I don't agree in this case. Clem Attlee was just as friendly in attitude but nothing like so articulate.

Harold Wilson made instant friends with our housekeeper who had come up from the country, also with Mrs Motteram, a blind old lady who had been my secretary. When he at last had to go, he refused to do so without saying goodbye to Mrs Motteram. He was equally at home with Rachel and Kevin, with Kevin's parents who came from Warrington, not so very far from his constituency, and of course Cardinal Heenan, his friend for a good many years. Few prime ministers, one would think, have excelled him in general benevolence towards all sorts and conditions of men.

But when politicians are denounced as insufficiently moral it is not this kind of virtue that is questioned, although in fact a political hostility tends to produce a personal denigration. The public are entitled to ask questions about what might be called the public spirit of their public men. There again, I would be slow to criticise Harold Wilson or the other colleagues I sat with. Comparisons are presumably impossible, but after a long period in Opposition this Cabinet, relatively young in years and full of intellectual ability, revealed an insatiable appetite for work, with the Prime Minister setting a supreme example. In *Five Lives*, published in 1964, I defended him against a charge of deviousness. I would defend him still against that particular charge, though perhaps not quite so wholeheartedly. His worst fault, which for all I know I share, and which is certainly very human, is or was a desire to impress those he was with, particularly journalists. At the very least he allowed his intimates to talk to journalists about his colleagues, which led to suspicion all round. Cecil King, in his book of Memoirs, records Harold Wilson in July 1965 as saying of myself: 'Frank Longford quite useless. Mental age of twelve.' In retrospect this does not upset me, as I thought the complaint was that my mental age was 112! I must take it that, whether or not those were the exact words, some such message was conveyed to this eminent newspaper proprietor. A Lobby journalist showed me an actual transcript of a press conference in which Harold Wilson had referred to speculation about a change in the Leadership of the Lords, in such a fashion as to confirm the impression that it was on the way. This at a time when I happened to know from him that my position was secure. If and when he is Prime Minister again, I am sure that he will avoid such indiscretions. Of course I was not the only one to receive such treatment.

Politicians are supposed to be dominated by their love of power, and certainly no one has ever achieved supreme power or remained in it very long by accident. Real statesmen, said Prince von Bülow, the German Chancellor, are governed by two forces - love of country and love of power. Or in other terms, ambition and public spirit. I believe there to be a vital truth here. Half the arguments that take place about statesmen, past and present, derive from the uncertainty as to which aspect we are looking at of what is inevitably a dual character.

By the time one reaches a position at the very top one is concerned not only with one's own fortunes, but with those of one's Party. Since he has been in Opposition, Harold Wilson has been belaboured from many quarters for his attitude to the Common Market, but the course he has pursued has caused me no surprise. I would assume that the unity of the Party he led would rank at the top of his priorities (not that he would ever, even for that purpose, take a step which he believed to be opposed to the interests of the country). Most of Wilson's critics still entertain the highest regard for Lord Attlee's standards. It is worth asking, therefore, in passing whether Lord Attlee himself, during his twenty years of leading the Labour Party, did not attach as much importance as Harold Wilson to Party unity? Did he not himself consider that if he had not been laid up in hospital at the time, he would have found a way of averting the resignations of Aneurin Bevan, Harold Wilson and John Freeman?

But to return to my alleged distinction between Harold Wilson's approach to principle in politics and that of someone like myself. Second-liners such as I must be chary of implying that their own methods and criteria would have worked well on the highest level, given the chance. Not long ago I gave up my seat on the train from Etchingham to Charing Cross to a young middle-aged lady. When she thanked me at the end of the journey, she told me: 'It's an honour to be given his seat by a man of principle.' No doubt she had my so-called campaign against pornography in mind. I am sure that far more people have told Enoch Powell that he is a man of principle than have ever said the same to me. At the end of 1972, he emerged I am told as a radio Man of the Year, with over 500 votes, while Ted Heath got 200. I was fifth with 21, and Harold Wilson got 18. So I am not implying that someone who is called a man of principle is superior to one who isn't. I am just saying that he is different. He may be simply a man whose form of conscience makes it difficult for him to work indefinitely with colleagues. This might be said of me, and indeed of some of the House of Cecil. But that is not, I feel, the end of the story.

What the public looks for is strength of personal conviction, and this is often judged in terms of consistency. But the test of consistency is not itself consistently applied. Winston Churchill till 1939 would hardly have been described as a man of consistent convictions. Yet within a few months of becoming Prime Minister he established himself for all time in the public mind as the greatest of British champions. Ted Heath would probably be regarded as a man of principle by almost all fair-minded persons. The consistency with which he has pursued his European ideal through good times and bad has sufficed to provide him with a permanent aura of integrity. He has, since becoming Prime Minister, made at least three drastic departures from anything expected of him: in regard to Northern Ireland, the treatment of lame-duck businesses, and general attitude to trade unions. Yet intelligent critics would still be more inclined to refer to him as rather too rigid than too flexible, whereas with Harold Wilson the opposite impression was created throughout his period.

With hindsight one can see that the Labour Government should have devalued the £ at the outset, or as soon as possible afterwards. One can see that the withdrawal from the whole East of Suez commitment should have come much sooner than 1968. As regards the first point, I was never in advance of the actual policy. As regards the second, I saw the light halfway through. The point I am making here is that Harold Wilson and his Cabinet as a whole, much influenced of course by him, can be blamed today for rigidity rather than flexibility. If Harold Wilson has given an impression of lacking political conviction, the record does not at first sight support the criticism.

A good deal of the impression has been derived from his words rather than his deeds. Take the devaluation of 1967, for example. No one could have hung on more tenaciously if his life had been at stake than Harold Wilson to the value of sterling. But when he was overpowered by circumstances and devaluation followed, he made his famous broadcast in which he reassured the public about the £ in their pockets. Whatever the precise semantics of the speech, and the subsequent explanations, this passage did not ring true at the time or since. Again, long after I had left the Cabinet, he fought valiantly for Barbara Castle's Trade Union policy. The moment came when he was left alone in the Cabinet and was compelled to surrender. Not, I would say, ingloriously. I would certainly never suggest that in the circumstances he ought to have resigned. But at once he was putting a bright face on the turnabout and adding to the impression that he did not mean what he said; or that if he did mean it at that time, he couldn't have meant it before. To put the matter crudely, his instinct to act as a public relations officer for his own Government has, in the long run, cost him dear.

Or has it? As I write these words, he has now been Leader

of the Labour Party for ten years, six of them as Prime Minister. There is no apparent likelihood of his being supplanted in the foreseeable future. I and others who criticise him are unable to point to anyone who could have performed his task better, since the tragic death of Hugh Gaitskell. What I call his exaggerated public relations technique is repugnant to many and, on occasion, to myself. But in so far as it represents an optimism, a buoyancy, a resilience, and is closely linked with his underlying fortitude, it has proved serviceable to himself and, it may be, to the country. However, it is deeds that count in the end.

One or two variegated thoughts about life in the Wilson Cabinet. Being a Minister, of course, was nothing new to me. Starting as a Lord-in-Waiting, I had been successively Under-Secretary for War, Minister for Germany and Austria, Minister of Civil Aviation, and First Lord of the Admiralty in the Attlee Government. When that Government came to an end and I disappeared along with it, I wrote an emotional and quite eloquent piece in the *Observer* about my return to normal existence. When I resigned from the Wilson Cabinet, I wrote an article in the *New Statesman* in which I quoted the earlier article, rather surprised it would seem at its portentousness, considering that I had not even been in the Cabinet. But a common thread runs through both these farewell messages - a sense of shared fraternity and comradeship lost to me. In my 1968 article, I asked: 'What of the emotions of the act of resignation itself?' and I gave this answer:

Let us assume that the rational conscience has firmly put money, glory and power in their proper place, and that the arguments for 'going' are coercive. Yet it can never be, perhaps never should be, as easy as that makes it sound. To leave a government at a time of grave difficulty like the present is equivalent to leaving the front line in war, or at least it feels like that. It needs much internal justification and is hardly credible without distress. Who can be sure that his emotions will operate obediently as the docile servants of a rational choice?

Five years later, I cannot quite recapture that intense feeling which must have been more subconscious than conscious. In the critical economic situation of early 1968, I did not exactly feel that I was leaving them in the lurch, but certainly on their behalf retained profound anxieties. It is perhaps not unduly modest or facetious to suggest that their last two years, the years without me, were even more successful than when I was present. Intellectually they were a remarkable crew. Eight of them had first class degrees from Oxford – Harold Wilson, Dick Crossman, Douglas Jay, Denis Healey, Roy Jenkins, Tony Crosland, Michael Stewart (and myself). This must be easily a record. The standard of debate was very high. Jim Callaghan, the most fluent speaker I have ever listened to, George Brown, with his effortless power to arrest attention, Barbara Castle, with her instant eloquence on behalf of her particular department – though sometimes she went on too long – these three were in a broad sense equal to the alpha men just mentioned.

Merit judged by Cabinet performance made its way to the top. In 1964 Roy Jenkins and Tony Crosland were still outside the Cabinet, but Harold Wilson, much to his credit (for they were supposed to be hostile to him), gave them full opportunities which they amply exploited. Barbara Castle was ranked twenty-three out of twenty-three at the beginning, but she and Dick Crossman – a somewhat suppressed figure as Minister of Housing early on – were right at the top before the finish. Harold Wilson himself was on fairly weak ground at the outset, hardly a quarter of the members would have voted for him when he became Leader. It was a very different thing by the end.

Yet even the Prime Minister in full plenitude could not get the Cabinet to accept Barbara Castle's policy for industrial relations. The Prime Minister possesses enormous powers; unlike the chairman of any other large organisation, he has the power to hire and fire his Ministers and, just as important, he can switch them round at a moment's notice. But in another sense he is one man against a score of others, most of whom believe they could suitably occupy his position. The price of his supremacy is unwearying vigilance and unremitting tact. These last qualities Harold Wilson indubitably exhibited, along with benevolence at all times, astuteness when it was not always necessary, and courage in the darkest moments.

*

There will be some disposition, not only among Socialists, to judge the integrity of the Wilson Government by its fidelity to Socialist principles. This is no place to attempt even the most cursory summary of the economic and social achievements of that Government or assess them in the light of history. Were our social policies different in degree or only in kind from those which would have been pursued by a Tory Government?

Can we claim that our approach to an Income and Prices Policy was wider? The real confrontation with the trade unions had not taken place during my time in the Cabinet, though it was already casting its shadow. Barabara Castle, then Minister of Transport, had formulated the dilemma: 'Should we face a political crisis now, rather than an economic one later?' And I, like all or nearly all the intellectuals in the Cabinet at that moment, was favourable to the bolder course.

Can we claim that our record on Overseas Aid was better than a hypothetical Tory performance?

At the end of it all, how much redistribution of wealth had actually been effected? How did the really poor emerge relatively and absolutely? On all these points controversy has raged fiercely since the Government fell. A few very broad observations must be ventured. When the election came there were many excellent points to be made by Party spokesmen. Roy Jenkins, Chancellor of the Exchequer for the last half of the period, gives us perhaps as good a perspective as anyone. He insists that the Wilson Government had much to be proud of in its social record, but that we certainly could have done better and certainly must do better next time.

He recognises, of course, the persistent trouble with the balance of payments and partly due to that our failure to achieve economic growth. But he refuses to accept either of these factors as an adequate excuse for our failure to reduce poverty far more drastically. He concludes that we are never likely to be able to eradicate it except as part of wider policies for social equality.

Not long ago a Socialist expert, never far from the formulation of Party policy, admitted to me that the redistribution of wealth in favour of the poor had indeed been disappointing, but 'we were running up a descending escalator'. In other words, the natural bias of a market economy - even a mixed one like ours - would be in favour, left to itself, of increased *inequality*. We had at least counteracted that tendency. This conclusion fits in with Roy Jenkins's argument that in a future Labour Government we must set out to reverse such a trend much more deliberately and systematically. With all of which I agree.

But to leave it there is to lay myself open, not for the first time, to the accusation of carrying Party loyalty to the verge of the deceptive. My dear friend Dora Gaitskell tells me that my surplus of literary goodwill 'obscures the bones of an argument'. No doubt an 'old pals' presentation of the Cabinet is of little service even to old pals themselves. Let me attempt therefore a note of unusual candour. In my view there was an underlying weakness in the Labour Government on a level which meant more to me than that of economics or diplomacy. There was what I can only call a shortage of radical passion. It was not that the Labour Cabinet lacked sincerity in their desire to help the poor or underprivileged in this country, or the underdeveloped peoples overseas. But they lacked any fire in their belly remotely comparable to that of - shall we say - Lloyd George (by no means my hero) in his Radical days; or of some of Attlee's Cabinet. When the crunch came they succumbed to what they considered the 'facts' of the situation; the economic realities. When Margaret Herbison, Minister of Pensions, staunchest of Socialists, resigned from the Government she murmured as she left the Cabinet Room almost in tears: 'They don't care for the old people any more.' She did not mean it literally any more than I meant it literally when I said the same privately about their attitude to the young at the time of my own resignation. But she meant (I would assume), and certainly I meant, that they lacked the inflexible spirit that prompted Beveridge whenever he was asked whether we could afford to abolish want. He invariably replied, 'We can't not afford to abolish it.'

Thirteen years in the wilderness had branded the harsher

realities of political power and impotence too deeply on my colleagues' minds. On some subconscious plane the idea of losing an election had become associated with shame, humiliation and disgrace. For my part I believe that every Cabinet should start by realising that the loss of an election is as inevitable as death for the individual. It will come sometime. Next time, perhaps, or the time after. Sometime assuredly. In the meantime, while the light lasts, all that matters is to find and follow the path of conscience and duty. Here lay the real source in my own eyes at least of my difference with my colleagues collectively, though there was not one whose serious purpose I would wish to disparage. It was so much easier for me to feel these things seated at the margin than for those who carried supremely the hopes of millions and the main responsibility for the future of the nation.

PART TWO

Ireland (I)

A DUAL ALLEGIANCE

'I die full of intense love for Ireland . . . I die loving England, and passionately praying that she may change completely and finally towards Ireland.' (Erskine Childers, Nov. 1922, shortly before execution.)

There has never been a time, I have said and written more than once, when I was not proud to call myself an Irishman. But I cannot object when the label 'Anglo-Irish' is applied to me. Terence de Vere White has written a striking book about this latter category. Literature in the English language is rich in Anglo-Irish names. But if one is asked how many Anglo-Irishmen have been British Cabinet Ministers, one starts off gaily with the Duke of Wellington and Lord Castlereagh, then comes more or less to a stop. Irish property, such as that possessed by the Dukes of Devonshire and the Marquesses of Lansdowne, would not by itself be a sufficient qualification, nor would Irish extraction, whether from the North (Bonar Law, Hailsham) or the South (Brown, Callaghan, Healey). It would be difficult to exclude Carson and Brendan Bracken, though neither would leap into the mind as Anglo-Irish in the conventional sense.

In any case a distinction must clearly be drawn before and after the Free State came into being in 1922. Until then, an Irishman could be just as unselfconsciously British as Sir Alec Home from Scotland, or Lloyd George from Wales. But for the last fifty years it has been possible (it has been and is frequently done) to hold both an Irish and a British passport, which is certainly not true of the Scottish or Welsh. I have held both at different times. When I paid repeated visits to Germany as British Minister in 1947-8, I operated at first on an Irish passport, until it became rather embarrassing to my staff who had to justify it.

There are advantages and disadvantages in possessing an emotional national allegiance to a country other than the one where one builds one's career.

The schizophrenia was at its most acute at the beginning of the war. With intense thankfulness, I allowed myself to be briefly extracted from the Infantry to become the Irish expert in the Ministry of Information. One visit (in civilian clothes, of course) to Ireland was enough to bring home to me the ambiguity of my position. I returned to the army with positive relief though not, as explained elsewhere, for very long. I persuade myself, however, that understanding so thoroughly the point of view of one other country has helped me in international relations and elsewhere. When I proclaimed all over a stricken Germany a Christian message which I claimed was official British policy, Sir Winston Churchill, meeting me at a Buckingham Palace garden party, spelt out slowly the gratifying words, 'I am glad that there is one English mind suffering for the miseries of Germany.' But Mr de Valera, with greater awareness of my Irishness, said to Lord Moyne: 'I am glad that they have sent Lord Pakenham to Germany; he is the one man who might understand.' So there may have been assets, as well as liabilities, in my complicated loyalties.

When my brother Edward, the 6th Lord Longford, died in 1961, there was a minute's silence in the Irish theatres. He and my sister-in-law, Christine, as brilliant a cultural figure as himself, had dedicated themselves for thirty-odd years to the theatre in Ireland. He had been made a Senator by Mr de Valera for his public work and was to the end a staunch and active member of the Synod of the Church of Ireland. His funeral service was conducted by the Archbishop of Dublin. Very many Catholics, including priests, attended, but only the boldest spirits, such as Brendan Behan and members of the family, like myself, entered the church. The rest stood outside in the icy February weather until we joined them at the grave. The restrictions seem fantastic today, and within a few years had disappeared.

My brother had undergone maltreatment at Eton as a Sinn Feiner when the 'troubles' were at their height. When he opposed a motion at the Oxford Union condemning as murder-

ers the men who assassinated Sir Henry Wilson (1922), a large
crowd of undergraduates waited for him and on his return to
Christ Church he was hurled into the pool called 'Mercury'.
His influence on my attitude to Irish Nationalism was profound, but slow-working. Paradoxically it was my meeting in
1932 with Mr de Valera, to whom my brother was at that time
opposed, which brought my intrinsic love of Ireland to a
political boiling point. Then came the studies which resulted in
my history of the Anglo-Irish Treaty, *Peace by Ordeal*.

By the time I had finished *Peace by Ordeal*, I was bitterly
critical of the methods by which Ireland had been partitioned
by the Coalition Government. I satisfied myself, and remain
satisfied, that without the Boundary clause, the Treaty of 1921,
to use Lord Birkenhead's phrase: 'Never would have been,
never could have been, signed.' The Irish leaders were led to
believe that the clause would apply the principle of self-
determination to the Northern counties, that two or more of
them would inevitably opt out of the Northern area and that
that area would then become non-viable, so that Irish unity
would come about after all. The story of how these expectations
were defeated need not be reproduced here. I suppose that my
first reaction was to press for a fresh attempt to redraw the
frontier, but then and subsequently I have never found much
support for this among Irish Nationalists. About this time,
Hugh Dalton suggested that I might make a suitable Labour
candidate for the U.K. Parliament in one of the Catholic areas
of the North. A non-Unionist was bound to win, if any anti-
Unionist front could be organised. But the complications of
my position would have soon been unbearable and I did not
pursue the idea.

The economic war between England and Ireland finished as
a sort of draw - in Ireland's favour - in 1938. Before leaving
London, Mr de Valera asked me to join him and his delegation
for coffee in the Piccadilly Hotel. Somehow the context led him
on to talk about America - 'A wonderful country,' he said,
'and so is Britain. But there are spiritual dangers in each case.
Perhaps we in Ireland, a small country in between, can do
something to rectify the balance . . . Perhaps the language can
help.' Alas! on that last topic, I am aware that I have always

disappointed him. When at various times he had told me how much I was missing through my ignorance of Irish, I have always prayed in aid the example of my brother and sister-in-law, who came to know it so well. But it has been a feeble rejoinder.

For the last eighteen months before the war, Mr de Valera was free to tackle the partition question. The I.R.A., as so often, were an unmitigated nuisance and a great impediment to a constitutional campaign. Yet it is possible that if the war had not come when it did, some real progress towards Irish unity would have been made between de Valera and Chamberlain. I had just begun to take a hand, though not effectively. In 1938 and 1939 I was beginning to raise my voice against Partition in the British Press. In the *Daily Telegraph* I called for the use of 'British good offices' in bringing about the unity of Ireland, employing a phrase which I derived from Mr de Valera, and which thirty-five years later has still much to recommend it. I came close to drama in January 1939 when I was due to lecture to the Queen's University Student Union on Partition, and was prevented from doing so by Unionist pressures of various kinds. I had promised already to speak the next night at the Town Hall in Newry. When the Press asked for my reaction to the banning of my lecture, I replied histrionically, 'Tomorrow I have been asked to speak at Newry, and providing that the invitation holds good, I shall be there.' I was, in fact, far from certain that I would be allowed to speak or, if permitted, would escape subsequent arrest. Newry, however, is mercifully close to the frontier. The Town Hall was packed and there was a large crowd outside. The police, armed as always in those days, were present in great numbers. I did not justify the use of force, but showed more sympathy for those who used it 'when every constitutional avenue is blocked' than I would approve of today. The moment my address ended, I was swept from the platform and whisked across the boundary into the safety of Southern Ireland. What Iris Murdoch might call 'a fairly honourable' exploit.

*

Then came the war. The Partition issue disappeared from

British politics. I was torn throughout the next six years between my regret that Southern Ireland could not play a part in resisting world tyranny, and my ever-deepening admiration for the incomparable nerve and dignity with which Mr de Valera sustained the only policy conceivable in the circumstances. I paid several holiday visits to Ireland during the period. On the golf links and elsewhere I came to know Sir John Maffey (later Lord Rugby). His services to Anglo-Irish understanding deserve a glowing tribute, which Tom O'Neill and I have sought to pay him in our life of Mr de Valera, published in 1970.

My earlier connection with Northern Ireland had been somewhat episodic, to use a word once applied by Harold Laski to my teaching at the London School of Economics. A branch of my family had lived at Langford Lodge, County Antrim, from the end of the eighteenth century until modern times. But our family home for three hundred years had been in County Westmeath and, once a border-line was accepted, we were indubitably Southern Irish.

In the early 1930s I used to stay regularly at Clandeboye, near Belfast, with Basil (Marquess of) Dufferin and Ava, to whom a great friend of his and mine, Eleanor Smith, the daughter of the first Lord Birkenhead, once directed an immortal reply, in the course of a dispute. He was always known to her as 'Ava', but on one occasion signed himself a shade pompously 'Dufferin and Ava'. 'Dear Ava,' she wrote back, 'you can go to Hell and take Dufferin with you.' Basil, 'the dark heavy-lidded companion' of John Betjeman's poem, 'Brackenbury Scholar of Balliol', the one Byronic figure of my youth, would have reached the very top in British politics if his temperament, his peerage and the holocaust of the war had all permitted it. Various notables from the small world of Ulster Unionism appeared at his table. As far as they were concerned, I was still a young Conservative, of a Protestant ascendancy family, though there may have been some whispering already about my brother's Sinn Fein propensities.

They seemed to talk freely enough in front of me. I asked one very high person whether they had much trouble with Socialism. None at all, he told me, the Protestant working class could be relied on to vote the Unionist ticket. The cause of loyalty to the British connection could always be employed to overcome class solidarity. I cannot recall that the words 'divide and rule' were actually used, but I had little doubt about the message which, I am afraid, in those days hardly shocked me. Bernadette Devlin has delighted and infuriated me in recent years. Her maiden speech enthralled not only myself, perched in the Gallery, but a large section of the House of Commons. 'I like her guts,' one Conservative member said afterwards. 'I like her sex appeal,' said another. My son-in-law, Hugh Fraser, as often, had the last word: 'I am not interested in her guts or her sex appeal. I admire her breathing.' Since then, she has said many brave things, and many unfair and exaggerated things. But I have never denied in my heart the truth of her contention that the sectarian animosities of Belfast in particular have owed much to the determination of the Unionist leaders to stay in power at all costs. Which is not to imply that they have deliberately embarked on violence, let alone the recent horrors, as an instrument of policy. It has simply followed as an ultimate consequence of their collective standpoint.

These wartime visits to Ireland had little visible outcome, although they gained me a rather peculiar reputation in high-level British circles.

Evan Durbin, whose great promise was to be so tragically abbreviated, was close to the top Labour politicians at the end of the war. He was anxious to find a Government opening for me even if I lost the Oxford seat I was fighting. He told me that there was much goodwill towards me in high quarters but my special relations with Mr de Valera puzzled them. I was in Dublin as the war ended when de Valera made his classic reply to Churchill's personal attack on him for denying Britain the Irish bases. His defence of Irish neutrality has now become widely accepted, but at that moment of intense national loneliness he spoke for the whole people of the twenty-six counties and won the admiration of most of those who heard the broadcast outside.

Soon after the war ended I assisted Randolph Churchill to meet Mr de Valera. Randolph, by his own account, which I have no reason to doubt, began: 'My father agrees that you had the best of the exchanges. He admits his mistake in taking credit for not invading Ireland.' I am under the impression that Mr de Valera replied, a little guardedly, that if he had been an Englishman he would have voted for Mr Churchill. He has certainly said that since to Tom O'Neill and myself.

Irish neutrality was, I repeat, inevitable, but inevitably it set back the rising hopes of reunification. Ulster Unionists had an easy task in pointing out the immense value to Britain of their own participation in the war. It could be demonstrated that recruiting from the South was at least as plentiful as their own. But there remained the indubitable fact that without the help of Ulster the Allies would have had no bases of any kind in Ireland. As the years have passed the value of these Northern bases seems insensibly to have disappeared. Since the Northern situation became critical one does not remember to have heard the need for them employed in the general argument. But for a few years after the war ended it was of much propagandist utility to the Unionist cause.

When Mr de Valera eventually disappeared from power in 1948 and a coalition took over, the whole issue of Partition seemed suddenly to come alive again. The new Irish Minister of External Affairs was the young Sean MacBride, leader of the Clann na Poblachta Party, a dedicated Republican whose father had been executed in 1916, a man full of culture and diplomatic initiative. It was one of those moments when someone like myself began to hope that something big might happen. Something did, but not at all what I had expected or wished for.

That summer Elizabeth and I were on holiday in Dublin. I was Minister of Civil Aviation at the time. Philip Noel-Baker, Minister for Commonwealth Relations, was staying with Lord Rugby in Dublin. On a certain evening in August, Elizabeth and I were having dinner with Sean MacBride in the Russell Hotel in Dublin. The only other guests were Dr Evatt, Australian Minister for External Affairs, and Fred Boland, at that time Head of the Department of External Affairs, later immensely distinguished as Ambassador to London, President of the United Nations Assembly, and Chancellor of Trinity College. At one point Fred Boland was called to the telephone.

He came back and whispered something to Sean MacBride, who left the room for a few minutes. Neither Elizabeth nor I thought anything about it at the time.

Next morning, however, as we read the papers in the Shelbourne Hotel, Dublin, we discovered that the Taoiseach, Mr Costello, had announced in Toronto that Ireland would be severing the last links which bound her to the Commonwealth. I shall always regret that this step was taken and, moreover, should have been taken in that particular way. It is no doubt true that it was pressure from Sean MacBride and other Republicans that caused the Fine Gael Party to break so sharply with their previous attitude to the Commonwealth. But at that dinner-party Sean MacBride had been discussing with me, quite genuinely, the desirability of Ireland attending the next Commonwealth Conference. Left to himself, he would no doubt have proceeded more circumspectly.

Philip Noel-Baker, a friend of peace if ever there was one, was placed in a painful position, and the British Government as a whole reacted strongly. It was not till the following year that a way was discovered of allowing India to declare herself a Republic and to remain in the Commonwealth. For the moment an Anglo-Irish showdown seemed unavoidable. Neither side emerged with special credit. The British Government put through the Government of Ireland Act, 1949. It may or may not have served its alleged purpose of reassuring the North. It did not fail to provoke immense hostility in Southern Ireland. It seemed to guarantee the frontier even more firmly than hitherto, not only a separate Northern Province but the existing frontier; it left the Unionist Party still more free to treat the minority as they chose.

Could I honourably stay in a Government responsible for such a measure? I took the unusual step of consulting John Dulanty, the Irish High Commissioner. He urged me on no account to resign, if I was concerned to be of help to Ireland. And so I stayed on, seeking and obtaining leave from the Prime Minister to appear before the Cabinet and make my protest. My older self respects my younger self for making that little demonstration in front of a chilly Cabinet. But today I am not sure that I would repeat the exercise, even if I retained my courage. A Minister who makes a protest in that fashion and is quite clearly not going to resign is greeted with contemptuous indifference. To adapt a phrase of Randolph Churchill's: 'He is like an explosion that goes off and leaves the house still standing.'

Ireland (II)

THE DORMANT YEARS

My next public appearance on the Irish scene, though as always I was paying regular visits, was in late 1954. At that time I became deputy chairman of the National Bank. I was chairman of it from early 1955 till early 1963, when I retired to leave myself free to serve in a Labour Government. The National Bank was by this time a unique institution. Founded by Daniel O'Connell in 1835, its headquarters were in London. Though it was one of the eleven British clearing banks, the great majority of its branches were in Ireland. It had more branches in the twenty-six counties than any other bank, and a handful of branches in the North where the customers were a mixture of Protestants and Catholics, as were the staff. I gained a limited but not insignificant insight into the Ulster mind by getting to know quite a few of them on a business footing. It would be absurd to say that religious differences don't enter into business connections in Northern Ireland, but our customers in their relationship with us were businessmen first and sectarians, if they were sectarians, afterwards. Banking on the whole transcended the partition line between North and South. In my eight years as chairman of the National Bank I never found our own work interfered with by religious issues.

I remember, however, asking some of the guests at a large cocktail party we gave for our customers and their wives in Belfast: 'Here half of you are Protestants, half Catholics; would you meet each other ordinarily in the way of business?' I was given the answer: 'Yes. We would but our wives wouldn't.' I realised that the fraternisation was precarious.

I have described in *Five Lives* two initiatives I took during these years in the Anglo-Irish field: one fruitful; one which came to nothing. Along with Professor Bodkin and Lord Moyne, who had been working at this cause for years, I helped to bring about a settlement of the long-standing dispute over the pictures left by the late Sir Hugh Lane. For half a century no one had been able to agree whether the pictures belonged to England or to Ireland, but since 1960 half the pictures have been exhibited in Dublin and half in the National Gallery, London, to general satisfaction. Professor Bodkin, Lord Moyne and I were given honorary degrees of the National University of Ireland from the hands of Mr de Valera, the Chancellor. It would have been agreeable if Professor, now Lord, Robbins could have joined us. As chairman of the National Gallery Trustees, he played an essential if painful role.

During the Lane Bequest negotiations I found myself calling on Harold Macmillan, then Prime Minister. The prospect of Ireland returning to the Commonwealth, even if she remained a Republic, stirred him notably. 'I suppose such a thing has never happened before,' he told me with some emotion. But perhaps for that very reason there was never in retrospect any chance of its happening then. Cardinal Dalton had suggested that Ireland might be reunited on the basis of the India solution - a Republic within the Commonwealth - and I espoused the proposition ardently in the *Observer* and elsewhere. Mr de Valera, left to himself, would never, I am sure, have snapped the last links with the Commonwealth. But he told me later that if the Dalton solution had been seriously taken up he would have returned to active politics and fought it to the death, which would have meant leaving the Presidency.

When I finished *Five Lives* early in 1964 the hopes of Britain and Ireland entering the Common Market had been dashed for the moment. I reiterated my conviction that the prospects of Irish unity would be much improved if entry into the Common Market came about after all. I drew attention to the improving worldwide relationship between the Protestant and Catholic Churches and to the reasonable likelihood that the whole psychological outlook should improve accordingly. None of these remarks look stupid today. There was no glimpse, however, in the minds of myself or of others who considered themselves well-informed of what was actually to occur.

There was never any doubt in my mind about Harold Wilson's friendly feeling towards Ireland or, as mentioned earlier, towards the Catholic Church. He said to Mr Jack Lynch, then Taoiseach, that he, Harold Wilson, had more Irish voters in his constituency (Huyton, Liverpool) than Jack Lynch had in his. Whether or not this is precisely true, it is very much a Catholic/Irish constituency. The cynics were quick to discover a voting calculation here, but to my knowledge they are wrong fundamentally. For many years before he formed his Government, Harold Wilson had a close first-hand contact with the Catholic population of Irish extraction, particularly with their priests. His natural benevolence and desire to understand people's problems gave him a thorough grasp of their case and set him working administratively on behalf of their schools.

Soon after coming to power, he returned the bones of Sir Roger Casement to Ireland. Churchill had seemed to sympathise with de Valera's request for the return when they got on well together at a Downing Street lunch in 1953. But he later produced the unconvincing reply that the legal objections could not be overcome. Harold Wilson overcame them in quick time. No gesture by a British Government has ever made so immediately favourable an impression in Ireland. The Wilson Government showed themselves well disposed to a Trade Agreement with the Lemass Government in Dublin. Wilson overcame a last minute hitch by personal intervention. It was the same in small matters. A Cabinet Minister has to obtain the leave of the Prime Minister before leaving the country, and formally that of the Palace. When I obtained leave in February 1965 to go over to Dublin for the England v. Ireland rugby match, Harold Wilson asked me at the Cabinet which side I was going to shout for. Ireland, of course, I replied. He seemed to find this perfectly proper. So did others, as far as I could judge.

About the same time I was approached by Harold Harris of Hutchinson's. Could I suggest a collaborator with Tom O'Neill of the National Library, Dublin, in a full-scale life of de Valera? It would not be official, but all his papers would be available. I gathered that he himself would give full assistance. Rather hesitantly I suggested myself. The suggestion was snapped up by Harold and found acceptable in Dublin. It was not by any means obvious that a British Cabinet Minister would be permitted to share in such a work, but Harold Wilson made no objection and was, I felt, sympathetic.

The book eventually appeared in November 1970. It was the bestseller of the time in Ireland. Sales were highly satisfactory in England and America. Predictably, the opponents of de Valera attacked him through the book, but few, if any, mistakes were detected and the English reviews were very pleasing. All this was far more due to Tom O'Neill than to myself. The great bulk of the work had to be done in Ireland, which meant that it was done by Tom. My lengthy experience of British politics probably strengthened it on that side. In my eyes the novel feature of a long personal assessment was an attempted account of de Valera as a man of religion. We received intimate help here from one of his spiritual advisers. The chapter on the family, to which his children contributed freely, brought to light important aspects of his character unknown outside his circle.

It is indeed as a family man that I came to think of him particularly, while the book was being written. I stayed with him quite a few times at the President's residence in Phoenix Park, arriving either in time for an early supper with him before he retired or, if I was speaking in Dublin, after he had gone to bed. In either case there would be Mass in the morning at 10 o'clock in his private chapel where the Blessed Sacrament is reserved and which he visits five times daily. Mrs de Valera and he are, as is well known, exemplary in their daily attendance. My visits are associated in my mind with a three-fold memory: the work on the book, the religious devotions, and the large family who were always dropping in and out.

Twice before I began work on the book I had been made aware of his exceptional concern for my family welfare. Once when my brother died. He has never ceased to take a great interest in my sister-in-law Christine. On the second occasion, at a time of great family distress, he rang me up at my home in Sussex and told me that he knew exactly how I was feeling, which demonstrably he did. When my daughter Catherine was killed in 1969 I was due to stay with him just afterwards. When I arrived he told me that Mrs de Valera specially wished to see me. Later in this book I repeat what she told me.

I have written much about Mr de Valera, beginning with *Peace by Ordeal*. I cannot hope to improve on the considered estimate of him provided by Tom O'Neill and myself in our full biography. But for forty years he has made so big an impact on me that a few more words must be offered. I have said more than once that he was the greatest statesman I have ever met. I repeat that opinion now, and indeed extend it to cover all statesmen of the twentieth century in so far as I can judge them. But everyone uses the word 'great' in their own fashion. What does it mean in my vocabulary? I need to find three elements in a statesman before I call him 'great', and his relative greatness depends on their magnitude and combination. Personal impressiveness; achievement; nobility of character. In a sense the three elements I have suggested are incommensurable. You cannot add them up on a common scale any more than you can add a loaf of bread and an Atlantic crossing.

Who, then, in the twentieth century are the competitors? The greatest villains, Hitler, Stalin, obviously fail at the third hurdle - the moral test. But the men we usually describe as 'great' from Napoleon's day to the present do not usually win many marks on a moral scale. Sir John Wheeler-Bennett and I recently published a volume on which twenty makers of the twentieth century were handled by experts. None of them - apart from Hitler, Stalin and, it may be thought, Mussolini - could be easily dismissed as 'bad' men, but hardly any would rank as outstandingly 'good' on any religious or ethical scale. Attlee would qualify here. Possibly Baldwin. But Attlee was in no sense an impressive personality. Nor was Baldwin, except in one of his best oratorical flights.

I would not for a moment dispute the religious dedication of de Gaulle or Adenauer, but there is an arrogant flavour in each case of which neither de Valera nor Attlee could ever have been guilty. Gandhi's claims to greatness are impressive, but he would hardly have described himself as a statesman. On the moral side we seem to be left with de Valera and Attlee as alone combining the skills and inflexibilities of a top politician with a true Christian humility. Both in a sense reached the top by accident, de Valera emerging from the executions after the

Easter Rising in 1916, Attlee from the Labour rout of 1931. Perhaps that is significant. Perhaps neither possessed the kind of egotism required if a man is to rise to the top on his own initiative.

In terms of achievement it is hardly possible to compare a leader of Southern Ireland with an American President like Roosevelt or a British War Prime Minister like Churchill. Unfortunately de Valera was almost always operating on a small scale. Relative to his opportunities, his Irish achievement was immense. When at the League of Nations before the war or in his struggles with Churchill and Roosevelt during it, he was thrown into direct confrontation with world figures, he more than held his own with vastly weaker forces behind him.

*

But what, the reader will ask, was I doing or saying about the Northern Ireland question during my three and a quarter years in the Cabinet, October 1964 to January 1968? I might as well put on a white sheet and stay in it. I have, of course, my excuses. One always has. There was certainly no special sympathy for the Unionist set-up in Stormont to be found in the Labour Cabinet. Every now and then one of us would raise the question of whether any steps were being taken to end the grosser forms of gerrymandering and anti-Catholic discrimination. The facts about these were not, of course, anything like as familiar as they became later. But I was by no means alone in being aware that much was wrong. Harold Wilson would reply that he was pressing O'Neill, the Prime Minister, hard; that O'Neill was very anxious to improve matters but was having great difficulties with his colleagues. Believing then, and knowing now, that all this was perfectly true, I can understand, but cannot condone, my own inaction.

It was not in fact till some months after I had left the Cabinet, in other words August 1968, that the Civil Rights movement brought matters to a dramatic head. The British Government forced the Unionist Government to announce a far-reaching programme of reform. The very announcement was an admission that things were in a shocking state. Terence O'Neill was at last able to move in the direction he desired, but the elements of reaction in the North, including the B Specials and many of the police, were violently opposed to altering the bad old *status quo*. Long before the I.R.A. appeared in any force, it became extremely doubtful whether a Unionist Government in Northern Ireland would be permitted by its right-wing elements to carry through a genuine reform programme.

At least, this is how I still see it. But many moderate Protestants will put much blame on extreme anti-Unionist bodies like People's Democracy who, they will always insist, reawoke the old antagonisms.

Ireland (III)

THE SLEEPER STIRS

It was at this point early in 1969 that Robin Denniston, at that
time managing director of Hodder and Stoughton and always
imaginative, asked me to write a full-length treatise on
Northern Ireland. I obtained by great good fortune a vital young
research assistant, Finnoula Deeney, a member of a leading
Catholic professional family from Lurgan, County Armagh.
I literally picked her up in the Shelbourne Hotel after yet another
England v. Ireland rugby match at Lansdowne Road. Finnoula
had many friends in both communities; since then she has
married the treasurer of the non-sectarian Alliance Party, a
young Protestant solicitor. Much assisted by her, I paid some
eight visits to Northern Ireland during the first half of 1969,
all of them brief but full of intensive interviewing. In the end
the book did not materialise. The scene was shifting too fast.
But the benefit to me was lasting.

I met representatives of nearly all the main groups, political,
religious, social and economic; also government officials,
lecturers and students. Terence O'Neill, still Prime Minister of
Northern Ireland, kindly found time to see me for an hour and
a quarter when under extreme pressure. He had recently held
an emergency general election, and while on paper he had done
quite well, he had failed in his main objective of crushing the
'hard line' opposition in his Party.

Since then I have come to appreciate Terence O'Neill in the
House of Lords and relish his companionship elsewhere, but at
this time I barely knew him. His family and mine had seen
much of one another when we were children. His father, like
mine, had been killed in World War I, which provided a bond
between his mother and mine, but Terence belonged to a
younger generation and I had never known him as a child.

Physically he seemed well and relaxed - no sign of nerves -

but he was most despondent throughout, both about the situation in Northern Ireland and his own prospects. On both subjects I kept trying - rather ineffectively - to cheer him up, expressing the hope that on no account would he resign. He agreed that he might possibly be taking too depressed a view of things, but he knew a good deal which I could not be aware of (most of it, I gathered, was gloomy). I began by suggesting that we should concentrate on community relations. I could get the economic picture from others. He agreed and said more than once that community relations had suffered a severe setback in the last few months and (he kept repeating this), 'Are now back to square one.' He felt that all his efforts had gone for nothing.

He dwelt sombrely on his own position, whose deterioration I gathered had gone hand in hand with the failure of his efforts to bring about better relations between Protestants and Catholics. I told him that I hoped to bring out my book towards the end of 1970. He said that it was extremely doubtful whether he would be 'holding his present job' by that time. All those I met in the next twenty-four hours seemed to agree that he would probably be out of office by the end of the summer. He had had a marvellous response to his broadcast to the people. But the election's result had been a sore disappointment. 'Yes,' he said, 'I know that the figures can be made to look all right, but everything depended on my defeating my twelve opponents in the Party and nine of them got back.'

I suggested that there was tremendous goodwill towards him in Northern Ireland. Was it not possible to broaden his support? I hesitated to point out that he had been criticised even by well-wishers for playing such a lonely hand which had possibly accentuated an impression of arrogance. He replied that the present Cabinet was probably the most liberal one available. He was glad to report that several of the Unionist M.P.s this time were not members of the Orange Order, but the more reactionary forces were strongly entrenched, working overtime to get him out. I gathered, however, that what was more painful was the personal hostility of large numbers of Protestant men in the street. Catholics he had found remarkably friendly in recent times.

I raised briefly the whole question of the Orange Order, which I ventured to describe as the curse of Northern Ireland, while not expecting him to agree or disagree. He certainly did not disagree. He touched on its history, in particular on Lord Randolph Churchill's statement (in 1886) that the Orange card was the one to play. This, he thought, was the turning point. He himself had never been anything like so active in the Orange Order as his predecessors in the Premiership.

On the subject of the working class in Northern Ireland, he commented that there had always been better relations between the professional classes than was usually supposed, but the hatreds between the Protestant and Catholic working classes had been undeniable. There was also a tradition of violence in Irish politics, including of course the North, which Englishmen found difficult to understand. At one point he seemed to imply that he and I were both English. I protested that I was Irish. He replied that so was he but we had both had an English upbringing. The very fact, however, that he felt apparently so much kinship with me made me realise how difficult it must be for him to feel completely at home as Prime Minister in Northern Ireland.

He had been accused of being very class-conscious and being most at home with Alec Home. Curiously enough I happened to ask how he got on with Lemass and Lynch, and he replied, 'Very well with both but I found it much easier to be intimate with Jack [Lynch]. It was just like talking to someone like Alec Home.' Later he mentioned Roy Jenkins as the Home Secretary he had come to know best. It seemed easier to think of him, therefore, as one who was most at home with men of refined manners than as any kind of snob. But I could well imagine, especially after meeting Craig the next day, that in the world of Ulster politics he would seem a 'superior person' to most of his colleagues.

Turning to long-term aims, the Prime Minister said that he and I probably differed. What he would be happy to see in the distant future would be a united Ireland but an Ireland united within a Federal system for the British Isles. In the immediate future he saw some very unpleasant possibilities. He realised that the Civil Rights marches were likely to continue but they would bring counter-protests of some kind, and the prospects of maintaining law and order were, to say the least, dubious. He himself had for some little time been the nut in the nut-crackers.

The British Government had been urging him to improve the civic rights and maintain freedom of speech. Every attempt he made to do so added to the difficulties in his own Party, but if he touched on the possibility of his resigning or being evicted, British Ministers begged him fervently to remain as the only hope. Certainly he was sure that if he went a much harsher regime would follow. He had begun to wonder whether the only answer was that Britain should assume responsibility for governing Northern Ireland directly (this I took to mean that the Northern Ireland Government would disappear). When he mentioned this in London, Labour and Conservative leaders shrieked with horror and told him (separately) that in effect they wouldn't touch the proposition with a barge pole. I left him feeling that I had spent an hour with a brave, honourable, civilised, Conservative gentleman.

I return to a direct quotation from my assessment at the time: 'Anything, I suppose, might happen this year but, short of civil war which I do not in my heart believe is possible, I feel sure that solid progress has been made which cannot be cancelled out by the eruptions of a few months. It may be that an emotional disturbance has to take place in the Protestant community before they accept the idea of equality after centuries of domination. If O'Neill passes from the Premiership shortly, as so many expect, he will not go down to history as a man who tried and failed, but as a man who did more than anyone else has ever done in Ulster history to build bridges.'

Obviously I did not then foresee the various horrors that started a few months later and have continued in one form or another. But I find nothing to retract in the final remarks about Terence O'Neill, which I am still confident will be justified by history.

*

The next morning I had a long interview in his office with

William Craig. I was struck by his quiet courtesy. He reminded me somehow of Molotov twenty years earlier, who was also very courteous, very quiet and rather frightening. Craig seemed to me as fanatical in the same kind of way, possibly more genuinely so. I never quite felt certain that Molotov believed all his own arguments. Craig seemed to believe his; to be indeed incapable of disbelieving whatever fitted in with his policy. He simply would not believe that discrimination against Catholics existed. It clearly did not exist for him. Keynes in his *Economic Consequences of the Peace* wrote that Clemenceau felt about France what Pericles felt about Athens - that all virtue resided in her. In spite of one or two references to Europe, Craig's whole world seemed to narrow down to the Protestants of Ulster, that is to say, the loyal Protestants who did not, at that moment, appear to include the O'Neillites.

Subsequently, as I read about his various activities and sometimes excited pronouncements, my opinion of him grew steadily more adverse. Yet four years later (February 1973) I interviewed him in London for the *Catholic Herald* and found myself writing thus:

In a personal sense, Mr Craig made a very favourable impression on me, far more than when he met me for an hour in his office in 1969. I found him courteous, friendly, gentle, disarming, no doubt still implacable, but that aspect did not obtrude itself.

His new proposal for an independent Northern Ireland seems likely to prove a non-starter. But his dream of 'shared loyalties' towards such a State being entertained by Protestants and Catholics alike seemed to indicate a genuine effort to remove sectarian hatreds. He is said to contain within himself a Jekyll and a Hyde. In February 1973 in his room in a London hotel, I certainly encountered a Jekyll.

In 1969 it was more encouraging to meet O'Neillites like Mr Bailey, the active young M.P., *not* an Orangeman, who had won a new seat at the election.

At dinner with Finnoula's parents, we met a number of their Unionist friends who all appeared to be O'Neillites, with varying degrees of enthusiasm; but a certain working-man we called on, the secretary of the local Unionist Party, appeared to me to be more representative of the rank and file. He obviously much preferred Paisley to O'Neill, still at that moment Prime Minister, whom he accused of having split the Party and lost the confidence of half of it.

Next morning I met the Reverend Eric Gallagher, Head of the Methodists in Ireland – a man of very convincing piety and obvious ecumenical spirit. He confirmed what O'Neill and Craig had both said from different points of view – that relations between the religious communities had suffered a great set-back recently. All three of them attributed this to the over-activity of the People's Democracy and other demonstrators. The Reverend Gallagher acknowledged sadly that many dormant fears had been aroused in his own community. This is not to suggest that either he or O'Neill put all the blame, or even the main blame, on the Catholic side. But all three felt that it was the marches which were the immediate occasion of the newly awakened animosities. The Reverend Gallagher told me, in strict confidence, that he, the Cardinal and the heads of the Church of Ireland and Presbyterian Church were in touch and had agreed to meet in the event of an emergency. Following this conversation, I was not surprised when the Peace Walk of the Church leaders took place in Derry soon afterwards.

Lunch followed with Paddy Devlin, chairman at that time of the Northern Ireland Labour Party, though now one of the leaders of the S.D.L.P. Naturally he much preferred O'Neill to Paisley as a man and as a politician, but he remarked that the supporters of Paisley – the working-class Protestants – were the people who must be won for a united front against Unionism. Before returning to England, Finnoula and I motored off to Cookstown where Bernadette Devlin had her bye-election headquarters. We left good wishes but cannot conceivably have promoted her remarkable victory. I was present, as mentioned earlier, in the Peers' Gallery when she made her maiden speech. Her rhetorical flair and capacity to think on her feet can seldom, if ever, have been exhibited to greater advantage by a maiden speaker. What struck me most forcibly, her performance apart, was the colossal enthusiasm of the Labour M.P.s. One felt that they had waited many years for someone to debunk the claim of the Unionist M.P.s to speak for Ulster, and to discredit a

Stormont regime that had too long been exempted from criticism at Westminster.

By this time I myself had little doubt about the right policy. The Labour Party of Northern Ireland had already suggested a Coalition Government. The morning after Bernadette's speech, I discussed the idea with Paddy Devlin, who had himself suggested it, and Gerry Fitt in the Irish Club, Eaton Square. They both agreed that it would be helpful if I floated the idea. This I duly did in a letter to *The Times*. In one form or another I have adhered unalteringly - not my invariable practice - to its main proposition. It was impossible, I wrote, to believe that as long as the Government was composed of 'Unionists only', it would be able to satisfy the minority, or bring about the required transformation of spirit. The chairman of the Northern Ireland Labour Party had suggested a coalition. 'This,' I was convinced, 'is the only policy that offers a clear possibility of a concerted movement towards peace and progress.'

My third visit to the North not long afterwards coincided with a Government crisis. Terence O'Neill had resigned, to my deep regret but not to my surprise. The choice of his successor lay between his cousin, James Chichester-Clark, and Brian Faulkner. The election was to be next day. My first task was to leave a letter of sympathy and immense respect at Terence O'Neill's office. I quoted Browning - 'leave him still loftier than the world suspects' - which still seems to me an appropriate comment.

The afternoon and evening I spent in the Parliament House at Stormont. One is accustomed by now to antagonistic feelings between rival groups immediately prior to elections. I was, however, surprised at the depth of the distrust between the Chichester-Clark and Faulkner factions, the one liberal or progressive by Northern Ireland Unionist standards, the other hard-line or 'not an inch'. More than one member of the retiring O'Neill Cabinet made it plain to me that he would never serve under Faulkner, but the reaction of even the most enlightened Unionists to the idea of coalition was disappointingly blank.

Phelim O'Neill, first cousin of Terence O'Neill, an old Etonian like so many of the Northern aristocracy, has shown himself throughout this period as unsectarian as anybody could be. He became a leader of the Alliance Party. A somewhat younger man than myself, he informed me that he was often mistaken for me. With his bald head and round glasses, this was admittedly a possibility. I expressed the fear that I might get him into serious trouble locally. Earnestly I pressed the urgent need for a coalition on him and a young O'Neillite M.P., Dick Ferguson, who has since given fine proof of integrity and has for the moment paid a heavy price. Both regarded the idea as utterly impracticable. Phelim admitted 'of course it is the only sensible thing. The only rational thing. But this isn't a rational place. This is Northern Ireland.' The conviction beyond rational discussion that Protestants and Catholics simply could not work together in a combined government had sunk all too deeply into even the most sensible minds.

I had a brief meeting with Brian Faulkner, but there was no opportunity for discussion. I had more conversation with two hard-liners, Messrs Burns and Mitchell. I knew Mr Burns to be a virulent opponent of O'Neill. He was rosy-cheeked and jocular, and felt sure that the parties would all get on well together now. The only real difficulty had come from Terence's personality. What, I asked him, about Paisleyism? Terence, he assured me, had created Paisley. Mr Mitchell seemed to share his view that there would now be no serious difficulty between the two sections of the Unionist Party. By this time the result of the election had been announced to a very considerable gathering of press from at home and abroad. Roy Bradford, the Unionist Chief Whip, had come down the stately staircase and announced that Chichester-Clark had won by one vote. The latter looked like a good-natured but very uneasy bull being teased and poked, growing ever warmer under the television lights. One wished him well. There was nothing else to wish him.

Looking through my notes for this and other visits, I was clearly much impressed by John Hume on a visit to Derry. I was attracted to Kevin Boyle, of People's Democracy, yet unable to discover a constructive approach on their part. I missed Ian Paisley at that time, though I have since met him on pleasant terms at Westminster. He is almost the only M.P. who

THE PAKENHAM FAMILY, 1948
Left to right, standing: Thomas, Rachel, Paddy
Left to right, seated: Catherine, Kevin, Lady Longford, the author,
Michael, Antonia, Judith

The two authors presenting Eamon de Valera with a copy
of his biography

THE WILSON CABINET, 1964

Left to right, standing: Fred Lee, Frank Cousins, Douglas Houghton, Anthony Crosland, Douglas Jay, Barbara Castle, Anthony Greenwood, The Author, Richard Crossman, Ray Gunter, Fred Peart, Tom Fraser, Burke Trend (Secretary to the Cabinet)

Left to right, seated: Willy Ross, Frank Soskice, Michael Stewart, Gerald Gardiner, George Brown, Harold Wilson, Herbert Bowden, Jim Callaghan, Denis Healey, Arthur Bottomley, James Griffiths

With friends at the Melting Pot, Brixton

has given me a cup of tea in the House of Commons tearoom. When I was trying to see him in Belfast in 1969, the conversation ended like this:

L. 'I wonder where I can get hold of your book. Your last book, I mean.'

P. 'You mean the one on Romans?'

L. 'Yes, that's the one. I have only read Luther on Romans and I would like to find out your views.'

P. 'I'll send you a copy to where you're staying.'

L. 'I am at the Grand Central, but you must let me pay for it.'

P. 'Oh, no! I'll give it to you, we don't eat Roman Catholics, you know, whatever you may hear about us.'

The book duly arrived and is full of interest, although Paisley's scholarship is disparaged by other Presbyterians. There are phrases which the outer world might expect from Mr Paisley. '. . . Today in Protestantism the priest has displaced the preacher . . . such Protestantism falls an easy prey to the wolf of Popery . . . the pulpit no longer dominates for the modern cleric cannot preach . . . the central position is occupied by what is called the altar . . .' But the book, as a whole, contains much more love of God and devotion to St Paul than hatred of his opponents.

I had about two hours with the Cardinal. At that time it was being freely said that the Protestant attitude towards the Catholics would improve if only the Cardinal would 'accept the border'. The Cardinal pointed to the *Belfast Telegraph*, to whose editor-in-chief he had just given a major interview. 'Cardinal Conway,' ran the headline, 'says the Catholic bishops have recognised the Constitution.' In other words, he had already done the very thing required of him. But it was obvious to me then that there was an ambiguity running through this discussion. What most Unionists wanted was not merely that the Cardinal should 'accept the border', i.e. recognise the Constitution in the sense of being ready to co-operate in a transitional arrangement. What they really demanded was an 'acceptance' of the border for any foreseeable future. And that there could never be any hope of his doing. In a negative sense he was extremely definite: 'I can't help feeling that what many

people want is a political declaration from the bishops or something that could be construed in the political sense like telling
their people that they should give up all hope of a United
Ireland. That, of course, would be quite improper for the
bishops to do. Just as it would be wrong for the Scottish bishops
to condemn Scottish Nationalism as a political standpoint.' In
other words, it was the business of the Catholic laity to make
up their own minds about the long-term future of Northern
Ireland without instruction or positive guidance from the
bishops. Certain methods, however, of achieving that end must
be condemned, e.g. the bishops' denunciation of the armed
campaign of the I.R.A. in the 1950s. Since then he has never
failed to perform both tasks of his delicate and unpleasant duty.
He has unwaveringly condemned violence, including, of course,
violence on the Republican side, but has been equally adamant
in standing up for his flock where they would appear to have
suffered oppression.

I suggested that Northern Catholics should refuse to abandon
the vision of a united Ireland and yet at the same time be
ready to take an active share in the responsibilities of the
present State. The Cardinal agreed. Indeed, he was the first
important figure in Northern Ireland outside the Northern
Ireland Labour Party who warmly approved of my suggestion
of a coalition: a government, that is, in which Catholics were
for the first time included. He called it 'rather a brilliant idea',
so that there was at least some firm ground under one's feet.

The border, we agreed, had not been an issue in the recent
election and was not likely to become one in the near future.
But as one born in a Catholic area of Belfast, the Cardinal
revolted at the discrimination against his people in every fibre
of his being. Until that was ended or began to be ended, no
reconciliation would make much headway.

Ireland (IV)

THE RECKONING

That was June 1969. I was back again in October; by that time
death and destruction had begun to operate. The origins of the
calamitous events of August 1969 have been explored in an
official inquiry. The ground need not be covered again. In the
event, the British Army were called in to save the Catholic
population from destruction in Belfast by the much more
numerous, better-armed Protestants, who had on their side the
'B' Specials and could count on the benevolence of the police
force. In the Falls Road area I was shown the marks where the
heavy machine-gun bullets had crashed through the outer
walls, killing in one case a small child. I was shown the
hundreds of burnt-out or wrecked houses, the vast majority
Catholic. I was told (and I have never doubted it) that the
Catholics at that time possessed hardly any arms in Belfast.
Those I spoke to had to send to Dundalk for a machine-gun to
defend themselves. The I.R.A. were a negligible force till
August 1969, but from then on many Catholics instinctively
looked to them as their only defence.

From autumn 1969 to summer 1970 a kind of race was in
progress. It was a race between the lagging reform programme
of the Northern Government and the strenuous efforts of the
I.R.A. to build up their own position by exploiting Catholic
fears and suspicions. The Labour Government in Britain,
following an outstanding report by Lord Hunt, had ended the
'B' Specials and disarmed the police. Protestant fears and suspicions kept pace with those of Catholics. But Jim Callaghan,
Home Secretary, had earned golden opinions in almost all
quarters. By summer 1970 one gathers that the Labour Government had its plans ready for introducing direct rule if necessary.

Soon after the election, again back in Belfast, I found an
extraordinary deterioration in the relationship between the

army and the Northern Catholics. A Stormont Minister told me with undisguised satisfaction that, now that the Tories had returned to power, his own Government felt once again that they were masters in their own home. It seemed more than a coincidence that immediately after a debate in the House of Commons, when stronger action was demanded by the Unionists, a curfew was imposed for a whole weekend in the Falls Road area. As always in Northern Ireland, violently conflicting accounts were available on all sides, but from that moment onwards a large section of the Catholic population regarded the army as hostile, and the army, doing their best to remain neutral, found themselves increasingly involved in guerrilla warfare with the I.R.A. In August 1971 the Faulkner Government persuaded the British Government to introduce widespread internment, a grave error committed against the opinion of the soldiers.

I was in Belfast before the end of the month, wrote a long article for the *Tablet* on my return, and spoke at length in the House of Lords on 22nd September. 'We are given to understand,' I wrote in the *Tablet*, 'that the British and Northern Ireland Governments are setting a high priority on restoring Catholic confidence and securing their increased participation in running the province. I cannot myself believe that while internment without trial continues, there is the least prospect of anything of the sort happening.' I had been shown by Cardinal Conway allegations of maltreatment by the British Army which had just gone to General Tuso. When I saw this highly civilised General, it is unlikely that my words added weight to those of the Cardinal. I may, however, have been useful in letting Simon Winchester of the *Guardian* know that General Tuso himself would positively welcome an inquiry into the allegation. Thence flowed the Compton Report, the majority and minority reports of the Parker Committee, the minority report a classic statement of a great liberal lawyer, Gerald Gardiner, and many other investigations, official and unofficial.

Old speeches are tedious to read, especially in paraphrase, yet I must pick out one or two points from what I said on 22nd September, 1971. I did not mince my words about the I.R.A.

'A lamentable development in the past two years, more particularly in the last year, has been the emergence of the I.R.A. and the fact that they have won so large a measure of sympathy from the Catholic working class, whose hostility to the occupying forces is now such a painful phenomenon.' I paid tribute yet again to the British troops. 'I am sure that no troops in the world would behave better than ours in the North of Ireland at the present time, perhaps none would behave as well'; but then I issued this warning: 'As long as they are regarded, as inevitably they are regarded today, as the instruments of an age-long Protestant domination, their task will become more and more impossible.' Which led me back to what I had been saying for the previous two years - the need for some kind of coalition.

Even when the reforms had been carried out and discrimination had been brought to an end on paper, there would still be two communities - one governing and one governed. There would still be the dominant majority, expecting what they called 'loyalty' from the dominated minority. There would be the gap between the governing and the governed which would be unbridgeable as long as one community remained in power everlastingly, and one community was everlastingly out in the cold. There could never, in other words, be peace or stability or loyalty or true identity for Northern Ireland unless the Catholic minority were granted some share of power, some part in the government. So I spoke in September 1971. I cannot put it more clearly.

My largest intervention in the Northern Irish question occurred on 1st February in the following year when I opened a major debate in the House of Lords. By this time the idea of some kind of coalition was being widely favoured in all kinds of responsible quarters. But for the moment the talk was of a community system of government, rather than a coalition in the ordinary sense. As I was to say in the debate, the kind of coalition government which I had recommended for two and a half years was now no longer an adequate formulation. The minority would no longer be satisfied with an arrangement under which the position of their Ministers in a Stormont Government was dependent on the grace and favour of Mr

Faulkner, or whoever the Unionist leader might be. 'It is now clearly essential,' I said, 'that the minority community should be accorded as of right a participation in the whole administration of the area, including their participation in the Cabinet.' In other words, they would be guaranteed a certain number of the crucial positions. I always left it open as to how exactly this should be provided for. Then and subsequently the difficulties were obvious, but the basic conception of including Catholics in any Northern Government left, in my eyes, no room for opposing argument.

But before I actually spoke in the House of Lords there had occurred the terrible event of 'Bloody Sunday'. Against that tragedy, it may seem tasteless to mention my minor debating embarrassment. I could not in my heart accept the account so quickly furnished by the army. Fortunately an inquiry under the Chief Justice had already been promised. No one, as I said, of Irish blood could fail to be horrified by the ghastly happenings in Derry, and the horror was not confined to Irishmen. But I was well aware that in the House of Lords there was profound, if suppressed, feeling on the side of the army, in view of all that they had been and were undergoing.

Just before I went into the Chamber, Lady Masham told me of a friend of hers whose son had sustained mortal injuries while serving in Northern Ireland and had just died after a heroic struggle. I was happy to pay tribute to him, and in doing so I convinced the House of my balanced, if conflicting, emotions.

In my August article in the *Tablet*, I had faced the stark question: 'Has Stormont a future?' 'I hover,' I had said at that time, 'on the brink of the conclusion that Stormont must go.' I still felt that one should pause at the brink, if it was humanly possible. I feared that direct rule would push the day of Irish unity still farther away, but I insisted that Stormont had by that time lost the capacity to put its own house in order, even if it wished to. The British Government alone had the power to force it to take the steps required.

I said the same, but more urgently, in the Lords' debate in February 1972 and finished with the sombre words that, unless action of a drastic kind were taken immediately, the last hour would have struck for Northern Ireland.

*

On 24th March, 1972, I sat in the Gallery of the House of Commons and heard the Prime Minister, Edward Heath, announce the suspension of Stormont. I found not only the content of his speech but his personal dignity in every way equal to the situation. The steps being taken were more statesmanlike and bolder than I had dared to hope for. All men of goodwill in Britain and in both parts of Ireland could at last get a breathing space to work out the right policy. As the year went on, I found opportunity again and again in the House of Lords and elsewhere to thank Heaven for the extraordinary chance that made William Whitelaw Secretary of State for Ireland. Whatever the future holds for him, during this year at least he has revealed an immense benevolence, fairness and courage. If I had been very prescient, I might have criticised at the time the proposal for the plebiscite, but in the circumstances it would have seemed ungenerous.

In the autumn appeared the Green Paper which contained a new and exhilarating, if still indefinite, concept. It was at last accepted that:

A settlement must recognise Northern Ireland's position within Ireland as a whole . . . It is clearly desirable that any new arrangement for Northern Ireland should, while meeting the wishes of Northern Ireland and Great Britain, be as far as possible acceptable to and accepted by the Republic of Ireland which, from 1st January, 1973, will share the rights and obligations of membership of the European Communities.

Here at last was an acknowledgment that the Northern Ireland problem was an all-Ireland problem and could not be solved in the context of the North alone. The passage quoted occurs in the section of the Green Paper called 'The Irish Dimension'. 'Whoever,' I commented, 'thought up that phrase must be a bit of a genius.' Certainly the problem was at last beginning to be discussed in the only rational context of the whole island and, therefore, for the first time there were underlying grounds for hopefulness. The Green Paper did not actually suggest the creation of an all-Ireland Council, but it pointed clearly in that direction. Such a Council, although an advisory and not an executive body, could, in my eyes, play an even larger part within the new E.E.C. framework, concentrating always on practical co-operation without political commitment.

The Irish scene waits for no man, least of all for authors and publishers. While the manuscript of this book had still to reach the printers, Mr Whitelaw produced his eagerly awaited White Paper with its far-reaching plans for legislation. Vital options were still left open, but one supreme task was explicitly assigned to the Secretary of State. If Ulster were to have any kind of government of her own in future he must ensure that, for the first time, the Catholic minority had a fair share in it. The White Paper was greeted very favourably in Britain, and approved overwhelmingly in both Houses of Parliament. I gave it my full support in the House of Lords. In Northern Ireland the non-sectarian parties were highly favourable, the Catholic groupings rather favourable, the Unionists' attitude very mixed. Long before this book is published, elections will have been held and we shall know whether a government, or rather an executive, will have been set up in Northern Ireland in which, for the first time, the Catholics are allowed an adequate representation.

Everything turns on this last point as the British Government themselves at last appear to recognise. After the White Paper came out, and before speaking in the Lords, I paid yet another flying visit to Northern Ireland and Dublin. In the North I met with few surprises. A talk with Cardinal Conway was, as always, invaluable. I acquired a better understanding than ever before of high-minded Protestant attitudes after a full discussion with leaders of the main Protestant Churches. I came away asking myself how many of their fears could be said to be rational and how many irrational?

When I raised this point at an impressive conference on the Northern Irish question which was held soon afterwards at Cambridge, much clarification followed, though some obscurities remained.

Meanwhile, in the South, Jack Lynch, so sensitive and acute a politician, so brave and patient, 'a holy man', as I once heard Mr de Valera describe him, had given way to Mr Cosgrave. On my Dublin visit he very kindly allowed Mr Garret Fitzgerald, the brilliant young Minister for Foreign Affairs, son of my old friend Desmond Fitzgerald - Minister for External Affairs in his time - to bring me to see him. I was already aware from past meetings of his patent integrity, which was underlined on this occasion. Mr Lynch had already made it plain that if and when Irish unity comes it will not be a takeover of the North by the South. It must be a true partnership on equal terms. I have no doubt that this will be the attitude of Mr Cosgrave and his colleagues.

*

What are one's outstanding reflections after retailing baldly this troubled history and mentioning one's own persistent, if not very significant, efforts to affect its course? Looking back, it seems extraordinary that Catholics were treated as if second-class citizens for nearly fifty years under the rule of Stormont, while constitutionally members of the United Kingdom. It is astonishing to reflect that it needed the events of 1968 to destroy the all-too-effective British convention that the internal affairs of Northern Ireland could not be discussed at Westminster. The minority were less protected under the prevailing system than under any other conceivable. If Northern Ireland had been a separate country, they could have obtained help from the South, or more effectively from the United Nations. If they had been treated like other members of the United Kingdom they would have enjoyed the democratic rights of the English, the Scots and the Welsh, rights, incidentally, enjoyed by the minority in Southern Ireland. As it was, the British Governments, including Labour Governments, without any particularly ill-intention, underwrote the oppression.

If one is asked, however, why the lamentable discrimination in the North was not brought home to people in England many years earlier, the answer must be found in the inability of Irish Nationalists, North and South, to agree in any way as to how the goal of unity should be pursued. Mr de Valera had said from 1920 onwards that force must be ruled out. 'Ulster must not be coerced,' but that still left open the question how far the six-county government should be recognised and in what sense, therefore, co-operation was possible. And in the North there was endless dissension among Catholics as to whether Republicans should stand for Parliament and, if elected, whether they should take their seats. Meanwhile, the men of physical force were always a disturbing factor whether or not at any particular moment they were statistically numerous.

The British public can be excused for considerable ignorance, but those who counted themselves well informed, among whom I must include myself, are devoid of this alibi.

Where do we find ourselves now? In regard to the ultimate unity of Ireland, I can fairly say that I have never wavered since the light first dawned on me in the early 1930s. Perhaps too often in the past, however, Irish Nationalists like myself have talked in terms of an abstract vision and been over-anxious to persuade the English that England was responsible for the crime of partition. Today, in the age of the E.E.C., there seems a growing recognition in England that nothing except a united Ireland makes any sense at all. For over thirty years people such as I have tried to persuade the English that a united Ireland was in their own interests. For a long while the war experience and the preservation of Ulster as an allied base seemed to point in an opposite direction, but as mentioned earlier the British defence interest in maintaining partition seems to have disappeared without trace. Economically the heavy burden of subsidising Northern Ireland and maintaining an army there to keep order have probably disposed the average Briton to 'get shot' of the whole thing, if he is consulting selfish interests only. The loss of British lives in the army strengthens the tendency. If Britain maintains the connection today it is for reasons of obligation, alike to the Protestants and Catholics. How long that sense of obligation will predominate, who can say?

But when the time comes something much more positive will be required from the South. It will not be a question of a few adjustments to the constitution of the Irish Republic.

There are features of life in Southern Ireland which cannot be expected to appeal to non-Catholics, although some of these have passed or are passing. There can be no dictation by one part of the country or denomination to another. There must be a fundamental starting afresh, with the twenty-six counties and the six counties sitting down together to originate a constitution and life-plan for a united Ireland.

What are the prospects of the Northern Protestants agreeing to reunification? No one who has watched the Irish rugby XV drawn from North and South alike and raised to great heights of endeavour on behalf of Ireland can doubt that in crucial ways the Northerners are, in fact, Irish. I doubted it least of all after an international match at Lansdowne Road, when I found myself late in the evening with two of Ireland's most famous players, Noel Murphy of Cork, with his arm round one of my shoulders, and William John McBride of Bally-mena, with his arm round the other.

Mr Paisley would be generally regarded as an Irishman wherever he found himself, and whatever he called himself. When a group of his clergy made a protest in Westminster Abbey against Father Corbishley speaking there, I was told by the police afterwards that a lot of 'Irish clergy' had been causing trouble. They judged only by the accent, the denomination escaped them. Historically, of course, the sectarian division dates from the time of the religious wars. Since then, as mentioned earlier, it has served the interests of the ruling class and too often been kept alive for that purpose. But since the Second Vatican Council and many Protestant initiatives, such as the visit of Archbishop Fisher to Rome, the religious basis for the mutual animosities has disappeared. In the last few years the Ecumenical spirit has late in time impinged on the Northern religious leaders and on all genuine Christians in Northern Ireland. The sectarianism has therefore been severed at the roots, though it may take a long time to die.

The British defence interest gone, the sectarian basis mean-ingless, what fundamental reason can a rational Ulsterman point to for wishing to preserve partition? Up till now there has been an economic case for it. Ulstermen could seriously argue that while there was an economic customs barrier between Southern Ireland and England, it was altogether to their advantage to stay on the British side of it. This meant keeping a customs barrier between North and South. But with the coming of the E.E.C., this objection also has vanished. The overwhelming natural arguments for unity in a single small island should at last prevail.

PART THREE

Prisoners (I)

PUNISHMENT AND AFTER

'Those whom we call criminals are only tiles blown off the
roof by the wind.'   SIMONE WEIL

'I believe that we are all, whether we are criminals or, as we
think, respectable members of society, a part of the same
human race. I believe that all of us, whether we be criminals
or respectable, are equally dear to God, and unless one does
start from that point of view, it seems to me that one cannot
possibly call one's approach a Christian approach. On the other
hand, we are all aware that law and order must be preserved
and that everything possible must be done to that end, and
certainly violence - violence in particular - must be discouraged in every way open to us. The problem of penal reform
is to reconcile these two starting-points.'

I was speaking in a major television debate, in January 1973,
and leading the opposition to the proposal that we should take
sterner measures to curb the increase in crimes of violence. It
had been moved the previous Sunday by Mr Peter Brodie, till
recently Deputy Commissioner at Scotland Yard. I was supported by Mr Anthony Storr, the psychiatrist, and Mr Brodie
by David Napley, the solicitor. There were three sessions altogether. Robin Day was in the chair. The 'assessors' were
Reginald Maudling, former Home Secretary, and the Reverend
Don Cupitt. Four members of the general public were introduced into the third programme. We were allowed two and a
half minutes or so for our initial statements. Naturally we all
took much trouble to summarise our best thinking and deepest
convictions.

'I don't just hold the opinion,' I went on, 'that we ought to
treat everyone as members of the human race. I also hold, as a
Christian, that the supreme force in the universe is love, and

that all human beings are capable of redemption.' I said that I had known many criminals well and been friends with a number of them who had been convicted of terrible crimes. 'I know,' I said, 'from my personal experience that redemption is possible and refuse to believe that it cannot occur in every case.

'I assert, as a Christian, that kindness can bring about kindness, and cruelty can only produce cruelty. Therefore I say that any policy that is based on enlightened kindness has some chance of succeeding; a policy based on inhumanity is bound to fail.'

This is my autobiography, not that of the other participants, so I will report on the discussion from my personal point of view. The actual proposals of Mr Brodie and Mr Napley were not so very extreme. Neither of them was proposing, in the immediate future at any rate, the restoration of hanging or the arming of the police. They made it plain in a general sense, however, that they wanted tougher measures. I did not feel myself that anyone, except Mr Brodie, challenged my statement of principles. When Mr Maudling was asked to sum up, he did so along what might be called classical lines. 'I think, myself,' he said, 'there are three purposes of punishment. There's deterrence, there's retribution, and there is redemption. I agree,' he went on, 'with Mr Napley that retribution is part of it, because I believe the old-fashioned point of view that, just as a good deed deserves its reward, a bad deed deserves its punishment.'

If he had cast an eye over my book *The Idea of Punishment*, published in 1961, favourably noticed by Mary Warnock and other philosophers, he would have known that I myself found a major place for retribution. And I have, in fact, not changed my opinion in that regard. The word has acquired, as I said at the time, vengeful undertones and maybe should be superseded. Justice might be a possible alternative but, strictly speaking, it should cover a wider area. At any rate, since I became involved in these arguments, I have never deviated from Mr Maudling's proposition about the connection between a good deed and the reward, and a bad deed and punishment.

I had stressed, as had Dr Storr in different language, our conviction that no one is irredeemable. Reggie Maudling went almost as far. 'I have seen some cases,' I said, 'which I believe are almost beyond redemption, but they were very few indeed, and I don't think anyone should abandon hope of any individual human being.' He also stressed what the rest of us should have mentioned, but had rather taken for granted, that a high detection rate is the best deterrent of all.

When he finished, I was able to say that I agreed with every word, or almost every word, of his approach, but pointed out that he still left it obscure whether Mr Brodie's side was right, or ours was. We had just been informed that the public appeared to be on his side rather than ours, but I exclaimed with unusual passion, 'To me, it is not an open question at all. Mr Brodie is totally wrong. If a million people hauled me to the stake, I hope I would still go on saying, "Mr Brodie is wrong." It's not a question of public opinion. It's a question of basic morals.' I selected something that Mr Brodie had said on the previous Sunday as epitomising his approach. 'He tells us,' I said, 'that a lot of people are thugs and will go to Hell,' and although that is rather a crude summary it is not an unfair quotation.

I think Reggie Maudling was perhaps rather embarrassed by my identifying his point of view and mine. In his main statement, he had talked of the necessity for tough sentences, which we all agreed with. In my view they are already very tough indeed in many cases, but in the end he was found saying that he wanted to see *tougher* (my italics), longer sentences for violent crimes, which seemed to concede a large part of the Brodie case. He stoutly maintained, however, that once they are in prison, we should seek to return the criminals to society better than when they went in. In that sense he finished up somewhere in the middle. So it appeared did the other assessor, the Reverend Don Cupitt, although I gathered afterwards that he basically sympathised with us.

At the end of the debate, where did I feel the issue stood? Obviously to some extent the difference was one of emphasis. No one was advocating extreme brutality and no one was saying that violent criminals should not go to prison, at any rate until much better alternatives had been worked out. The debate was specifically concerned with violent crime. If the subject had been crime generally, I and others would no doubt have had a lot to say about the necessity of keeping out of prison all sorts of people who ought not to be there at all.

Inevitably the public were left with a distinction between those who wanted *more* severe measures - Brodie and Napley - and their opponents - Storr and myself - who presumably wanted *less* severe measures. But this was not my explicit position, although matters might sometimes work out that way.

What I have been concerned with for many years is *a more constructive* approach to prisoners. This clearly means that I would welcome every conceivable plan for employing prisoners constructively outside prison. But then one is left with the old problem of the deterrent consideration - this arises whether we are talking of hardened professional criminals or violent young hooligans - what Mr Brodie and many others would call thugs. It is not enough to ask ourselves, what is best for *them*? What is most likely to turn *them* into civilised and law-abiding members of society? We have got to think of deterring or, if you like, frightening others who might be inclined to commit similar crimes. In other words, punishment must include an element of pain. Years ago, I took the chair for Gilbert Hair, that outstanding prison governor. 'Yes,' he said, 'I know you don't think much of prisons as a way of treating human beings. No more do I. Perhaps you prefer execution or mutilation, pillory or stocks; or flogging; or you may have your own ideas. If so, I'd like to hear them. But if you can't suggest anything better, and if you want any sort of law and order, then prison it's got to be.'

While I was preparing for our television debate, I visited a number of hostels where very constructive work was taking place. But I face the fact that institutional treatment, whether in approved schools, borstals or prisons of one kind or another, is going to play a large and inevitable part for as far ahead as we can see in our struggle with delinquency. I pass over here the whole question of how far prisons or institutions should be medically or psychiatrically orientated. Every time I go to

Grendon Underwood psychiatric prison, I am more than ever encouraged. A regime not dissimilar to it has now been started in 'C' wing, Parkhurst, and Broadmoor holds out a better prospect for the long-term prisoner than any prison known to me. Let us assume that in an enlightened penal policy all such psychiatric facilities would be duplicated and reduplicated. There remains the crucial residual fact that large numbers of young, and not so young, persons will be dispatched to prisons in the years ahead, and that on our present showing very little will be done for them.

Again in preparing for our debate, I inquired how our young people from New Horizon were faring in prisons, and quite a few of them go there. I was told of one of our young men, aged 22, who had been for three months in one prison and spending twenty-three hours out of twenty-four in his cell. The fact that he was awaiting allocation seems to me a pretty feeble excuse. I was told of several young men who had been in another house up to a year and never met a welfare officer.

Following up that clue, one discovers that at the present time the average welfare officer has to cope with a hundred and twenty prisoners, so that they have little chance of making a serious impact on any individual.

In *Five Lives* I gave one chapter the heading 'Quantity and Quality'. Was it not Karl Marx who said that at a certain point quantitative turns into qualitative change? The only man I ever met who admitted to enjoying prison was one of six prisoners in Cork jail, before it was closed down for want of custom. There were six prison officers, one per head of prisoners. The whole prospect of psychological improvement and moral redemption in our prisons would be transformed if we provided vastly more uniformed staff, welfare staff, psychiatric staff, and far better material facilities. That means setting aside a very much larger share of our national resources than ever hitherto. The magnitudes involved remain, however, very small. We spend about fifty million on prisons at present, compared with somewhere near three thousand million each on defence, education and health every year. The calculation of what we spend on after-care is bound to be imperfect, depending on our national allocation of probation officers' time. A figure of, say, three and a half million is probably about right. One could double all these quantities without difficulty, after an inevitable transition, if the will were there.

But there comes the rub. The prison service remains the Cinderella or, to use another veracious cliché, the last in the queue, for at least two obvious reasons. In the first place, prisoners will never represent an organised lobby, or seriously speaking any body of votes. More obstructively, the cry goes up, 'Why should we spend it on them, when so many deserving people are short of houses, or health services, or adequate social security?' Even the humane Mr Maudling in the debate referred to seemed a little startled that my main proposal for dealing with violent criminals was to give them *help*, to confer a benefit on them. It is, however, of the essence of the standpoint I tried to ventilate that this more enlightened caring for the prisoners is at once a Christian duty and a policy of social self-preservation. Certainly it is a Christian duty to leave the ninety and nine sheep until we have recovered the one lost in the wilderness. But it is just as fundamentally true that there is no other way than this which holds out any hope of bringing about their redemption and turning them into social assets, instead of grave liabilities. This is the policy (I even venture to call it a philosophy) which all penal reformers, religious or secular, are dedicated to in practice, whatever words they use.

We heard from the BBC that the great majority of letters and postcards favoured a hard-line approach rather than that unfolded by Anthony Storr and myself. There were few signs of that in my correspondence. In the past when I have be-friended notorious delinquents, I have had a pretty abusive postbag, along with gratitude and appreciation. This time I admittedly drew some hostile fire, but most of those who wrote said that we had expressed their feelings, and a number of the letters were deeply moving. Not a few came from prisoners or their families.

*

Edward Richardson, serving a long sentence in Hull, brother of Charles Richardson doing twenty-five years, wrote with special warmth. 'I agreed a hundred per cent with everything you said and, although I know you would have put up a strong case entirely on religious grounds, I don't think it would have got through half so well with the general public, or been anywhere near so effective as the very constructive argument you did put forward.' He was speaking for almost, though not quite all, prisoners known to me. Then he went on: 'At present, apart from Grendon, prisoners get almost no assistance to forge a new life. The longer a person stays in prison, the less able he becomes to fend for himself and his family on release. At present, prisons make far more criminals than they deter.'

Among those who seemed to be much encouraged by our efforts was Mrs Violet Kray, mother of the Kray twins, who had called on me more than once. 'I was so pleased to hear,' she wrote, 'that you do think there are some prisoners who learn from their mistakes. I know my sons, Reg and Ron, very much regret being where they are, and I know from the bottom of my heart they will never mix with bad people again. They have certainly learnt their lesson. I still do not believe all the bad things that have been said about them.'

I took an early opportunity of visiting Reg and Ron Kray in the top security wing at Parkhurst, or rather in the Acting Governor's office. I had met them in prison once or twice before. It may even be that they gave me some little credit, perhaps undeserved, for persuading the authorities to bring them together in the same prison. Strange to say, they and I have various friends in common in the outer world. This was the first occasion on which I had talked to them for any length of time. They have always, I am sure, had plenty of charm. I have never, of course, had experience of the other side of their character which produced such appalling crimes. Ronnie Kray receives, I believe, a good deal of medication, which means that Reggie Kray undertakes most of the talking. If anyone, however, tends to leave Ronnie out of the discussion, they find out their mistake. He broke in at one point with very strong conviction: 'We've done wrong, and we've got to be punished.' Which is some support at least for his mother's account of their attitude.

Naturally they were hoping against hope that I would be

able to say something promising about a release in the distant future, but I don't think that they really expected it. In their own eyes, the best that they could hope for, in any foreseeable future, was a transfer to Maidstone, where their brother Charles was serving, and even that, they understood, must be a long way off. They had no substantial complaints, though Reggie Kray understandably was annoyed that a letter of his to me had been stopped by the Home Office. This was presumably because it enclosed some poems that he had written. They were not, it is true, great poetry, but full of decent wistful feeling, and could not conceivably have injured anybody.

At an earlier date, Ian Brady had been prevented from sending hand-painted Christmas cards to his mother, Myra Hindley and myself until after a lot of tedious controversy. In each case the obstacle appears to have been some rule that prisoners could not send out works of art, at any rate without special permission. I mention this now to indicate the kind of petty restriction for which prison staffs lay the blame, rightly it would seem, on the inflexibility of the Home Office.

Looking at the twins now, one would not connect them instinctively with atrocities and gang horrors. They still, however, retain the look of very tough customers - good friends but, one would imagine, bad enemies. They had, after all, begun life as boxers, and when I talked about Eton Manor Club in Hackney Wick, recalled that they had boxed there in their amateur days. The wide topic of physical fitness gave us plenty to talk about. It seemed incredible that they could have ever controlled a small empire.

I reminded Reggie that on the last occasion I had asked what started them off on the wrong track, and that he had replied: 'The drink.' He agreed that that had come into it, but they both seemed to feel that the explanation must be sought in 'the environment'. They had grown up in a society where you had to fight to survive, where family loyalties were dominant, and a violent way of life was part of your inheritance. Talking to me that afternoon, I am sure that they had made a resolution 'never again'. They were aware, of course, that by the time they came out they would be past the age when violence was likely to help them. But even apart from that, they seemed to listen tolerantly, even eagerly, when I talked about turning over a new leaf and seeing the error of their ways. They were ready to consider my suggestion that in building a new image in prison and, for that matter, a new character, they should avail themselves more than hitherto of the help available from prison visitors, welfare staff and chaplains. But Reggie warned me that people of that kind, however well-meaning, knew little of the life from which the Kray twins came. I was left uncertain whether they would, or would not, overcome their palpable suspicions. They expressed the hope that I would visit them again. I gladly assented.

It is tempting to pick out prisoners with a record of sensational violence, but the vast majority of them are totally different. Many, like Roy James of the train robbers, have notable talent and energy: many are very helpless.

From time to time, at my home, my office, or at the House of Lords, a call was passed to me and a husky voice announced, 'It's Reg' - Reg D., for many years my most constant protégé. Reg's evil genius, as he said, was the drink. He couldn't take it; even one was fatal and led to trouble - had led, in fact, to twenty-nine convictions in all. He got in touch with me in 1952, following a spell of eighteen months in Wandsworth and Winchester, the culmination of six years of minor convictions after his discharge from the army, when still only 18 years old, as medically unfit. He had joined up as a driver in the R.A.S.C. when his mother remarried and he found himself rejected. Since then, he said, he had always felt alone.

Years of sleeping rough, walking the streets, dossing down with felonious room-mates in sleazy lodgings, had left their mark. Wan-faced, diminutive, undernourished and generally deprived-looking, Reg nevertheless had a keen native intelligence and was highly articulate, with a histrionic streak which he was sometimes tempted to make use of to his own undoing. Yet he was always presentable, even when in the direst straits, always affectionate towards myself and Elizabeth, never devoid of an underlying charm.

He used to pop up after a period of silence, for a loan, or with a request to be visited in prison, or for me to act as referee. He was often on the brink of sudden good fortune - at last a job with prospects, once even the pools. One drink to celebrate and the mirage collapsed. Reg was back to the start. During his prison spells he had acquired some skills - cooking, decorating, oil painting; and when he did work was known to do a good job. But never, not even in the mental home where a thoughtful magistrate endeavoured to ensure some constructive treatment, had he ever been really helped to overcome his basic problem.

Last year he spent five months under remand in Brixton Prison on a charge of uttering a forged cheque. He was convicted, but the conviction was subsequently quashed on appeal. Lord Justice Edmund Davies appears to have perceived that Reg, in spite of his record, had some good qualities in him, gave him encouragement and ordered his release.

Last Christmas, as so often, homeless and facing a bleak and miserable few days, he found his way to a centre run by the Young Quakers' Action Group, which made an instant and, it was hoped, a lasting impact. He was befriended and made to feel wanted, his services being enlisted as cook. Not least, they helped him to come to an understanding with himself, to face up to his problem and to resolve to overcome it. They maintained contact with him, sustained him over an attempt at suicide, visited him in hospital, and generally encouraged him. He was looking forward to spending Easter with them, as at Christmas. His daemon, if not altogether vanquished, was at least receding.

But in a mundane sense it was not to be. One day an urgent call came from him in hospital - two police officers had arrived to interrogate him and were insisting that he accompany them to the police station for questioning in connection with a recent theft. He was well enough to be moved, so that the hospital could not refuse to let him go. He returned much shaken by the experience, though no charge was made against him. Left to himself, he would have stayed in the hospital indefinitely, but his place was wanted urgently. He was once again befriended by the Quakers, who took him under their care in the true spirit of the gospels. Yet one more call came from him, which reached me in the middle of a meeting. I asked him to come and see me the next day, but by that time we heard that he had taken an overdose. Like the apostle Nathaniel, he was a man without guile.

At this point I must explain briefly the main facts of my connection with crime, prisons and prisoners. For those specially interested, *Five Lives* gives a full account of my activities up to 1963. It all began with my period as a prison visitor in Oxford just before the war, which was resumed immediately afterwards, but suspended whilst I was in the Attlee Government. Then came two years (1953-4) carrying out research with psychiatric and other expert help into the causes of crime. My book on this subject was published in 1958 and was followed by my monograph *The Idea of Punishment* (1961). In the middle fifties, I and others started the New Bridge, a society for befriending ex-prisoners, of which I was chairman for quite a while, and am president at the moment. The name was supplied by Edward Montagu, who has made such a great success of his family and business life since those days. Bill Hewitt, well known as C. H. Rolph in a number of altruistic connections, and other dedicated persons, brought great experience of helping prisoners.

I was chairman of the Pakenham-Thompson committee on the whole problem of after-care, which reported in 1960. Here the initiative was not mine, but that of Peter Thompson, a young public relations consultant of deep Christian convictions, though with psychological problems, which he has since described. The committee was the means of bringing Jack Donaldson into the penal field. I take personal pride in all he has done since - most recently as an electrifying chairman of the National Association for the Care and Resettlement of Offenders. Our committee, I think, can fairly be said to have had an influence on governmental action. Perhaps we can take some credit for the existence today of the Probation and After-Care Service. With all its limitations it represents a great advance on what existed when I first became involved. But while Peter was desperately striving to help others, he was himself collapsing under a variety of stresses. A spell in Broadmoor was an inevitable consequence. Four years later he emerged with a book, *Bound for Broadmoor*. I was honoured to write the Introduction to a work that was extremely well received. As I said in the Introduction, Peter is a man who has never failed to use his own sufferings for the benefit of others. Since his Broadmoor days, he has made good, not only as an author, but in his profession of public relations and as a spokesman and planner for the Festival of Light. He will never rest until there is a genuine national system of mental after-care.

I should add that from 1961-2 I was chairman of a committee set up by Justice to draw up a plan for compensating victims of violence. The government measure that followed must have owed a good deal to its findings. I am never surprised if those who know of my activities on behalf of criminals, but don't know me personally, expect to disconcert me by asking, 'Why don't you do something for the victims?' In the television debates already quoted, it was the first question put to me in both the second and the third programme. In a sense, I have a water-tight answer. I can reply, with absolute truth, that I have twice gone quite a long way in trying to start a society for victims. On the second occasion, two or three years ago, David Astor, Jill Tweedie and others less famous worked hard with me on a plan to bring victims together with the criminals who had damaged them. But nothing came of it at the time. While, however, this book is being published, a start is being made in Bristol. For reasons all too understandable, it is not the criminals but the victims who are reluctant to come forward.

*

I have touched on social research and inquiries, and on starting the New Bridge for ex-prisoners. I cannot here begin to retail all sorts of speeches made by me in the House of Lords and elsewhere, and the friendships with individual prisoners during these earlier years. I notice that in *Five Lives* I opined that I was better known as a 'prison person' than under any other label. I added that if I were allowed only one form of impact in the years ahead, I would rather make it in penal reform than in any other sphere. Nine years have passed since I wrote those words, and it is salutary and a little mortifying to ask how far

I have lived up to them. The answer must be 'not very far'. Yet there are one or two things to point to.

While *Five Lives* was going through the press, I was asked by Harold Wilson, Leader of the Opposition, to preside over a committee on the prevention and treatment of crime. Joan Bourne was our invaluable secretary. We worked fast, faster perhaps than was really desired of us. Our report was, in fact, published before the election of October 1964. Though not official policy, the distinction of our membership made it certain that it would have a large effect if Labour won the election. In fact, when the Labour Government was formed, eight of our members were included, for example, Gerald Gardiner, who went to the Woolsack, and Alice Bacon, who became Minister of State at the Home Office. Later on, Bee (now Lady) Serota was included. Probably no individual had a more constructive influence on our work than she did. As chairman of the Children's Committee of the L.C.C., deeply versed in all the social services, she helped myself and the other members to take a much more fundamental view of the factors early in life which lead to crime later on. From outside the committee, Barbara Wootton, with her vast experience as a magistrate and her stylistic cogency, pressed the case for a radical transformation of the juvenile courts, so that we ceased to treat children as little criminals. Peggy Jay, so highly qualified in everything connected with children, brought home to us the possibilities and urgency of a far-reaching family service. *The Children and Young Persons Act (1969)* was the culmination of a long argumentative development. The influence of our report was a crucial link in the chain.

The list of our proposals cannot be recited here. The abolition of hanging was, of course, among them. It did not need our committee to convert the Cabinet to that conviction, but there was a moment when it was at least unclear what priority it would be given. At that time, and not in that connection only, the presence in the Government of half a dozen Ministers committed to a particular report was patently significant. Frank Soskice, Home Secretary, whom I describe in my book *Humility* as 'morally the best of us', was not a member of our committee but, as T. E. Lawrence would have said, 'he was of the creed'. Nor was Victor Stonham a member, though he gave us impressive evidence. No Minister ever went to the Home Office (where he became Minister of State) with as much knowledge of all concerned for prisoners, no one ever kept faith more thoroughly.

Of all the measures, apart from hanging, which we recommended and which the Labour Government carried into law, the introduction of the Parole System was to me the most satisfying. It represents in my eyes by far the most valuable advance in the prison system in recent years. With parole operating, one can preserve the deterrent effect of announcing a heavy sentence. Yet one can hold out hope, even to men serving thirty years, for example, that they can emerge from their incarceration after a tolerable period, if they can earn their remission. No one could have been a more trusted chairman of the Parole Board than Lord Hunt, a man of iron nerve as the whole world knows, but also of a sensitive heart. Not so long ago I sent him a letter from a prisoner's wife:

My husband is in prison serving a sentence of three years for dishonestly handling. It was his second offence of this nature, the first being a £50 fine. He was convicted of receiving 47 cases of whisky, valued at around £1500 – and personally I think three years was a vicious sentence and appealed against it. After waiting eleven months for his appeal to be heard, it was dismissed, so all I had to look forward to was his parole, which everyone said he would get.

He went before the local review board and was recommended for parole, but the Home Office turned him down, giving him a review in March . . . I think I will go mad, as I couldn't *go through it all again*. It's only for our children's sake that I carry on.

My husband worked so hard for this parole, and has never been in any trouble since he has been inside; also he has been a trusty for about six months, which shows you what kind of person he is. We have been married for ten years and both come from very respectable families, so it was a great shock to all of them, but they have all stuck by him. He is a very good husband and father, and they are very hard to come by these days, and I will do all I can to help him, as I love him very much.

I added the comment: 'I am sure that you receive many poignant letters but none surely more poignant than this.' He wrote at the bottom of his reply: 'Yes, we receive many stressful and distressing letters. It is one of the heart-rending aspects of the job.' He means that, and a bit more.

I know from plenty of experience how much encouragement and incentive are provided to prisoners even when they are doing relatively short sentences. If anything, I would feel that the Parole Board have played too cautious a game, but I doubt whether they had any other option. Certainly there have been times when the Home Secretary has intervened, as he is fully entitled to do, and refused parole which the Board themselves would appear to have recommended. Strictly speaking, news of this kind is not released in individual cases, but sometimes it gets out. Walter Probyn at the time of writing has been in prison for about fifteen years. His last offence was shooting 'with intent to cause grievous bodily harm' while some years ago on the run from prison. When I was first in contact with him he was immensely articulate and extremely bitter, though always grateful to me personally and to others, like Lady Wootton and the saintly Merfyn Turner, who took up the cudgels on his behalf. He deluged me and everyone else with communications and was determined to drag the authorities before the European Rights Commission at Strasbourg. Every now and then he brought forward a grievance that appeared to be justified. But what I was desperately anxious to persuade him of throughout was that there was no truth whatsoever in the notion that the authorities wished to retard rather than accelerate his progress.

At the end of 1971, he was writing: 'I have been more than convinced that I will not be allowed to live any existence other than that of a criminal.' But as time passed, a great change came over his outlook and for a most interesting reason. For the first time in all those years of imprisonment, Walter Probyn began to get full opportunities of study and, still more important, to find an assistant governor with a deep interest in him. He became for a time a member of some kind of joint committee between the staff and the prisoners, which discussed prisoners' complaints. His own studies in sociology seemed to have helped him to appreciate the old adage, not, I think, to be found in sociological textbooks in precisely these terms: 'To understand all is to forgive all.' He wrote to me: 'I have been so busy taking up other people's complaints that I have not been able to think about my own.' In discussion when I visited him, he confirmed that this was so. For anyone who had known him previously and been overwhelmed by his volume of complaints, this was an astonishing development. I wrote to the Home Office to say that I had never seen so beneficent a change in a long-term prisoner and yet, a few months farther on, he was writing a sorry story. He was convinced, and I cannot believe him wrong, that the Parole Board recommended him for parole and that the Home Secretary turned him down, for reasons unknown. Transferred to an open prison, he might in theory have seemed to be still moving forward, but the shock of the refusal of parole was for the time being traumatic, and in the open prison he found that the Wormwood Scrubs facilities for study were no longer available. This bitter cry was wrung from his heart: 'The blatant betrayal of my trust in the authorities has made it impossible for me to ever believe in the integrity of any official again . . . The pledges and assurances I gave to you about my future are no longer valid. I would urge you to withdraw any guarantees you have given about me.' I wrote back, begging him to reconsider his extreme language about the authorities. Of course his words are not justified, but can anyone with any human feeling fail to sympathise?

Who knows what his position will be by the time this book appears? A visit to Leyhill, the open prison, in April, left me with a vivid memory. The Governor, accompanied by Walter Probyn, met me some way from the prison and picked up my bag. Walter tried to relieve him of it, but the Governor told him firmly: 'No, Walter. I'm not as old as all that.' Our little procession moved forward, the Governor carrying the bag, the prisoner and the visitor walking beside him. I was left alone with Walter for an hour - a facility not accorded me in enclosed prisons. At once I urged on Walter that the alleged ill will of those in charge of him was demonstrably non-existent. He took my point with a smile, but continued to reserve his position. After fifteen years in prison, I expect that I would have done likewise.

To put my point succinctly. Parole offers unprecedented encouragement and incentive to prisoners, but the system with its inevitable uncertainties can impose a severe strain on a prisoner whose public reputation makes him a dangerous prospect in the eyes of the Home Secretary. A new responsibility is placed on the prison authorities to make sure that a despairing reaction is averted and that the last state is not worse than the first.

I had hoped that my experience as a prison worker would be of use to a Labour Government, but it did not turn out that way. Whether through my own weakness or otherwise, I found myself less able to help individual prisoners while I was a Minister than hitherto. I have told in *Five Lives* of my friendship with Niven and Christopher Craig, and my efforts to assist them, to which they had unmistakably responded.

Soon after the Labour Government was formed, Niven Craig was allowed to work out of prison on the Hostel Scheme - a remarkable opportunity in the circumstances. He had been in prison for many years, but he had many more years still to serve, and the step taken was admittedly exceptional. In fact, he justified it abundantly and on one occasion later on, himself took me down to Broadmoor to help a prisoner who had been removed there. At the time, however, a fellow-prisoner became so envious of Niven that he wrote to two Conservative M.P.s to complain. He attributed Niven's opportunity to undue influence by Ministers, especially myself. Indeed, he went further and asserted that there was a homosexual connection between us. The two Conservative M.P.s descended hot-foot on Pentonville Prison. I have no right to say that they were exhilarated by the prospect of a scandal, but they were nothing loth to perform this part of their duty. The prison official who was present when they interviewed the mendacious prisoner assured me that, as soon as they saw that the sexual allegation was totally false, they dropped it promptly. One of them, nevertheless, persisted in raising the issue of undue influence in an adjournment debate in the House of Commons, and not in relation to myself only. It was easily demonstrated that there was nothing whatever in the charge, but the results were unfortunate. Harold Wilson imposed a rule that Ministers would not be allowed to visit prisoners without the Home Secretary and himself being informed. One gained the impression that such visits were not desirable. I am afraid that I restricted my own thereafter partly out of deference to the Prime Minister, partly out of a desire not to embarrass Frank Soskice, the Home Secretary, probably the most gentle man who ever held that office.

Soon afterwards I received a letter from Niven's brother, Christopher, informing me that he was soon to be married and inviting me to the ceremony. I was touched and honoured, when I thought of all that he had been through, and the rather feeble efforts that I had made to assist him. But here was a small dilemma. There was little doubt that if I attended the wedding, after the recent publicity attaching to myself and Niven, there would be all too much newspaper interest at a time when the Labour Government, with its tiny majority, was in the toils. Three courses were open to me - to decline the invitation, to go to the wedding without telling anyone in advance, or to inform the Prime Minister that I intended to go. The last course I adopted, but it was not a wise one. It produced a long, earnest letter from the Prime Minister, begging me to avoid inflicting this particular burden on the Government at that particular time. After considerable hesitation, I fell in with his view and tried to salve my conscience by giving dinner to Christopher and his charming fiancée on the eve of the wedding. This piece of action, or inaction, I regret more than anything I did or failed to do during my time in the Cabinet. Even if I had been cast in a heroic mould, I would not have found it an easy decision.

Finally, back to the New Bridge. It has struggled along for fifteen years or so and at times has seemed close to foundering. Having some means of comparison, including our establishment of the New Horizon Youth Centre, I am aware that help for prisoners comes low down or last in the queue, alike for public and private beneficence.

For a long time we were suspected, it seems, by the Home Office of undue interest in homosexual prisoners. Our origins gave a plausible, if flimsy, excuse, and we were also for rather more understandable reasons disliked by the voluntary bodies already undertaking after-care. Our very existence was an implied criticism of their performance.

While I was chairman there was a certain amount of controversy within our ranks as to how official we wanted to become. Were the benefits of State assistance a justifiable reason for losing our freedom to help anybody in any way we chose? We have been very lucky in our chairmen, Lord Croft and now Lord Hertford. Also in our staff, at once so human and so practical in the office tucked away at the side of St Botolph's Church in Aldersgate. Finance remains a problem, but we are now receiving a £2,000 a year grant from the Home Office, generous support from some of the City livery companies, from our 250 members and many others who respond to our appeals. Princess Alexandra is our Patron, and showed herself fully equal to her responsibilities when invited to meet some ex-prisoners.

Today our active voluntary associates are in touch with a considerable number of men both in prison and outside. This voluntary associate scheme has been the mainstay of the New Bridge's work, with individual associates befriending one and often more men, preferably getting to know them while still in prison. The associates in London, who form the majority, are divided into five groups, each meeting once a month with a group leader and a probation officer sitting in to advise. There are more cases at present than the associates can take on, and a publicity campaign is starting to try to recruit more volunteers.

When we began, we accepted with open arms the help of anyone who would work with us, but as time went on, we gradually became more selective - rightly, I am forced to agree, though I was one of the last to admit the necessity. The frigidity of the official world has evaporated. Liaison is now very close with the probation services and with a prison, such as Pentonville, for example.

Today, all prospective associates attend N.A.C.R.O. (National Association for the Care and Resettlement of Offenders) courses, after going through the New Bridge's own selection panel, and become accredited Inner London Volunteer Associates. There are also volunteers working in the areas of

Chelmsford, Littlehampton, Birmingham, Dartmoor and Bristol. Much help is given by wellwishers of all kinds.

Until last year we operated primarily as a befriending organisation. Friendship all along involved the strengthening and encouragement of many battered and disconsolate human beings, handicapped by temperament, or the experience of prison, or the consequent stigma, or all three. Help in finding accommodation or work has often been its concrete expression. Since last year, however, there has been added an organised Employment and Advisory Service. In the first year about four hundred men were referred to New Bridge for jobs - 70 per cent of these from the Probation Service. Of these, 265 were interviewed in prison or kept appointments in the office; 250 interviews were arranged with employers - 152 of which were kept. Eventually 77 men obtained jobs found for them by the New Bridge, while 66 found their own employment. All very promising, yet still very small.

Who shall say that any one man has made a measurable difference to our penal system in the last ten years? I would certainly not claim it for myself. Least of all if the price for doing so was to accept responsibility for things as we find them. Martin Wright, director of the Howard League for Penal Reform, set out some essential facts in *The Times* on 8th February, 1973, two hundred years to the day since John Howard was appointed Sheriff of Bedfordshire and required to inspect the local jail. Despite all the improvements since the time of John Howard, there is no cause for complacency today. More than a third of all prisoners sleep two or three in a cell built a century ago for one, and which has no sanitary plumbing. In 1971, over 50,000 people awaiting trial were held in prison; 22,000 of those convicted were not given prison sentences, and 2,500 were found not guilty. Ten thousand men are discharged homeless from prison every year.

All whose hearts and heads are in the right place aim to reduce the numbers in prisons, to improve conditions inside prisons, and to provide much better after-care. Those who will the ends must will the means, and this is where success has hitherto been so limited. For all our laudable efforts. We have failed up till now to convince the British public that the human and material resources which would make the job possible should be forthwith provided. In the world of penal reform, those who know the subject best are least likely to award any medal and, for that matter, least anxious to receive one. But the yearning to improve the system burns indomitably and painfully inches are gained.

*

For years in all my penal exercises I drew much strength from the formula that one must hate the sin but love the sinner. It has recently ceased to appeal to me as much as previously. St Francis de Sales wrote long ago: 'The judgments of men are rash, because the malice of sin depends primarily on the intention which is kept secret in men's hearts and, as far as we are concerned, is hidden in darkness. They are rash because we have enough to do to judge ourselves without trying to judge others.' And modern psychiatry underlines the lesson. But even apart from that, and even if accompanied by a recognition of our own sinfulness, 'to hate the sin but love the sinner' somehow suggests an attitude struck from a moral pedestal, and the older I get the less happy I am in that posture. Let us say, therefore, that one should condemn the offence and care for the offender. It is less arresting, but it seems more Christian.

Prisoners (II)

A LIFE SENTENCE

Ian Brady and Myra Hindley came into my life at the end of 1968, more than three years after they were sentenced to life imprisonment for hideous offences. The Moors murders probably horrified the general public more than any other crime in this century. Once it became known that I was visiting Ian Brady and Myra Hindley, I was naturally asked, even more than usual, whether I had no concern for the relatives of the victims. It goes without saying that their agony is never far from my mind. They are regularly in my prayers. I have let it be known that I would do anything in my power to render them service. Not surprisingly, this offer has not yet been taken up.

At the end of 1968 Myra Hindley wrote to me from Holloway prison in my known capacity of someone interested in prisoners. She wanted me to help her get permission to visit, or have meetings with, Ian Brady. A regular correspondence was taking place between them, but neither then nor later were visits allowed. She argued, as did Ian Brady, that normally visits were allowed between common law husbands and wives, and that that in effect was their relationship until they were arrested. I felt that I could not pursue the matter further without meeting her, so I obtained Home Office permission for a visit. Psychiatrists and others must assess my motives as they wish.

Before I set off, I had formed the opinion that the meetings would not be desirable, either in her interests or in those of the community. Here had been a girl, aged 18, and of blameless record when she met Ian Brady, aged 22, working under him as her immediate boss. Ian Brady had been at Borstal and had been involved in trouble of various kinds over the years. After five years of the association, she herself was convicted of complicity in the terrible crimes. Anyone who wished to do the best for her would surely give her the chance to break away from his influence, whatever her immediate inclinations.

When I met her, she was totally different from the ferocious Medusa-like blonde so familiar from the police photographs. To start with, her hair had reverted to its natural dark colour. She was quiet, unassertive, good-mannered. I would never have recognised her. She pressed hard, though respectfully (as always, there was a governor present), for the meetings with Ian Brady, to whom at that time she was totally dedicated.

I did not make up my mind immediately. But I found that a lady who had been visiting her every week since she had come to Holloway was convinced that her whole mental equilibrium depended on her being given some hope. And this was the only hope conceivable. So I agreed to work for the visits, and proceeded to do so sincerely, exhaustively, but quite ineffectively. Three years later it had become clear to me that Myra no longer wished for them, so I ended my unsuccessful exertion. For many months she hesitated to send word to Ian Brady that the old relationship was over, although she would never cease to wish him well. She was aware that her new attitude could easily be misunderstood by him and by others. It was all too obviously in her own interest in a worldly sense to break the connection. She was encouraged to think that she would be released eventually - not soon, but one day. It was not difficult to calculate that the severance with Ian would expedite her freedom. She took a long time to clarify her own motives before she acted. Above all, she was fully conscious of the terrible blow to him. By now she had developed quite a few friendships in prison, or among those visiting the prison. Apart from his mother, he had no one in the world but her. To someone like myself in touch with both of them regularly by correspondence and otherwise, it was clear that they were drawing apart. Each was working out his or her own salvation and finding an utterly different solution. Myra was reaching a deep fulfilment in Catholic belief and practice. She had been baptised a Catholic, but not brought up as one, and knew very little of the Catholic Church until she came to prison.

There came a moment, 'I wish that I could put complete

trust in God, but I am frightened to do so, for my faith is full of doubt and despair that I'll ever be good enough to merit complete forgiveness.'

But it was not so very much later that she was able to tell me, 'I don't think that I could adequately express just how much it means to me to have been to Confession and received Holy Communion. It is a terrifyingly beautiful thing; terrifying because I have taken a step which has taken me on to the threshold of a completely new way of life, which demands much more from me than my previous one, and beautiful because I feel spiritually reborn. I made such a mess of my old life, and I thank God for this second chance, and in my own "small way", to quote St Teresa, I hope to prove that I am worthy of His blessing. It doesn't matter whether I live in prison or outside, there is a small way wherever one is.'

I am occasionally asked whether it is true that I converted her to Roman Catholicism. It would be quite untrue to say any such thing. Those who helped her most were priests and others inside the prison, including the Governor, Mrs Wing. My assistance, if any, was minimal. Ian Brady, on the other hand, continued to reject all churches with disdain, reserving his special scorn for the Catholic Church which had come to represent the deepest things in life to Myra. No real intimacy of thought or feeling was possible any more.

The correspondence between myself and Ian Brady for 1969, 1970 and 1971 lies before me as I write. It runs to over fifty letters from each of us. His letters until near the end keep coming back to the possibility of visits, by which he means meetings with Myra. In the last few months he appeared to accept the inevitable. If she did not wish to see him, it would have been too absurd to demand that the Home Office should bring them together. His various hunger-strikes, until the end of 1972, were nominally justified in his mind as a form of protest about the denial of visits. But even after the prospect of visits had disappeared, he still hunger-struck on occasion, offering the following reply to my perplexed inquiry: '. . . in regard to the present demonstration, you say you cannot understand my intellectual reasons. It is essentially a spiritual choice. It is between two futilities. That of doing nothing. That of doing something. To do something naturally infers a degree of hope, no matter how infinitely small or subconscious. To do nothing acknowledges complete hopelessness. It is like either being dead or alive . . .' So his struggle with the authorities in prison was not solely motivated by the argument over visits. Yet that argument was a recurrent theme.

But it was by no means the only one. In a letter of 22nd January, 1973, he writes:

Our correspondence has been pretty stilted and foreign these past few months. I think back to our letters at Durham. The early years of our correspondence were both the best and the most constructive. I suppose you recall the Dietrich Bonhoeffer books which acted as a spring-board for our lengthy dialectics on religion.

I have all your letters, of course, and draft copies of my early replies. I recently re-read our early correspondence and was struck by the closely reasoned objectivity and balance of my replies, and was left with the impression that a better person wrote them, not I . . .

Reading that letter, which is not quite fair to him, I feel no little sense of guilt. As I will explain in a moment, Ian Brady is at his best as a student and lover of great literature: Tolstoy, Dostoevsky, Dickens, Wordsworth, Blake and not a few others. He has never failed to read carefully and comment on books I have sent him, such as my wife's *Wellington* or my daughter's *Mary Queen of Scots*.

A poignant conclusion could be drawn from his impression that a better person than his present self wrote the earlier letters. Inevitably one may be told a long-term imprisonment produces a deterioration of this kind. In his case there has been the additional factor that in the early years he took, and passed, examinations, and later abandoned organised study, though continuing to read intensively. But he has just told me that he intends to work intensively for a Koestler Award, and that the intellectual stimulus is coming back to him. For a long time he made no complaints of his conditions of imprisonment, apart from the denial of visits; occasionally there was a wry comment. I had told him that Mr McClatchey, the Bishop of

Durham's chaplain, had commented favourably on his sense of humour which I myself have frequently noted.

He was probably referring, wrote Ian, to my strong sense of the ludicrous, both in myself and in others. Only last night, while talking with Mr Clarke, I had a particularly trying paroxysm of uncontrollable laughter, while trying to relate to him some very flattering comments about myself and the other prisoners on this landing, made in an article in the *Sun* this week, in which the words 'high level of intelligence' figured. Viewing such comments through a montage of swinging fists and flying tea-jugs, how can one help but laugh? . . .

But broadly he was favourably impressed with conditions at the top security wing at Durham and, in retrospect, came to look back on it as a 'golden age'.

The general question of top security wings cannot be embarked on here. Penal reformers like myself have denounced them as living tombs and, on the face of it, there is something utterly inhuman in confining prisoners for years in such a small space, unless they are moved to a space just as small elsewhere. But Ian Brady valued the peace and quiet. When I first visited him he had emerged from his isolation and was engaged in cooking, along with other prisoners whose crimes bore some similarity to his. As in Myra's case, there was no resemblance to the police photographs. The lines round his mouth suggested an almost exaggerated sense of humour. When I visited him next in Durham he was alone with a prisoner named Straffen, in a wing that could have housed a good many others. The wing itself was being brought to an end as a top security unit. Ian Brady and Straffen were the last to move. At one time he sent me a book on the philosophy of solitude. If I suggest that he would be more capable than most prisoners of enjoying solitude, I might seem to imply that he should be content with it indefinitely. But that would be altogether unfair to him; the solitude which he would value would be solitude alone with nature. The fact of confinement, much of it solitary confinement, bears on him at least as heavily as on other prisoners, more perhaps than on most.

Those who recollect the crimes for which he was sentenced have asked me, understandably and heatedly, whether he does not feel remorse. I hesitate to answer that question as clearly as I would wish to, but the following passage makes possible a charitable assessment:

I want to prove myself, not by doing useless jobs such as mailbags year in, year out, but by giving something tangible and worthwhile. I mean, not so long ago, after the previous hunger-strike, at the risk of making a fool of myself, I seriously considered the possibility of inquiring about donating a kidney to some hospital, for the satisfaction of knowing I'd done something *real* to balance the past. But I eventually decided that such a gesture would be perhaps too ostentatious and that my motives would be misinterpreted or construed as the passing fad of a mental defective.

'Surely,' I wrote to the Home Office, in forwarding his letter, 'it is very encouraging, if we believe in the possibilities of human reform in prison, that he should now be seriously offering to *donate a kidney*. It is noteworthy that he looks upon this as a way of beginning to "balance the past", which is not far, surely, from a down and out expression of remorse? May I respectfully beg you to investigate the possibility of his rendering the service in question? People sometimes ask me whether I think he is sincere in what he writes to me. I reply that I am sure that he is, but I cannot prove it. To surrender one of one's kidneys is a pretty definite indication of sincerity.'

I am sorry to report that nothing happened.

Since leaving Durham in 1971, he has alternated between Albany Prison and the hospital at Parkhurst, both close together in the Isle of Wight. The year 1972 had been an unhappy one for him with the gradual recognition that the old relationship with Myra Hindley was finished, and he had had various difficulties with another prisoner in Albany. These developments have led to his making many complaints and adding to them when the complaining letters were, he claimed, interfered with. But as I write he has begun - which is new in our relationship - to welcome visits from me so that a fresh and more hopeful phase may be opening. By and large he has shown unreserved gratitude to me over the four years of our friendship and, coming from him, this means more than it would from most other people.

Quite early in the day I offered to visit him, but he kept postponing the event. On one occasion, admittedly with good reason as he was under punishment, he cancelled the visit at the last moment. When I gently reproached him about his reluctance to accept obligations, he replied: 'I'm afraid that your estimate of my attitude to obligation is not quite correct. I'm not afraid of all obligation. But I can't accept obligations I know that I cannot remain constant to under certain circumstances, circumstances which I think in all likelihood will occur. And, moving from a general to a personal level, it is not a question of distrusting you, but of distrusting myself . . .' But his attitude to obligation is quite unusually cautious. A Dostoevsky character admits that he finds himself shrinking away as soon as anybody becomes too intimate. Ian Brady drew my special attention to the passage.

From the beginning, he felt an element of embarrassment in the very cordiality with which I approached him:

I have a confession of sorts to make. You would be right to speculate that I am not a person who easily feels guilty about many things. Yet I feel so whenever I receive your letters. I look forward to receiving them, more than I can say, but this feeling always accompanies them. I have tried to make clear, in past letters, in the course of discussion on morals, etc. that my ability to discuss and apprehend moral arguments cannot be equated with my ability to practise my findings. Recognition of Right or Good is, by itself, worthless . . .

Shortly before the cancelled visit I had referred to him, though not by name, in a speech in the House of Lords, and explicitly in reply to questions in *The Times* Diary. Immediately afterwards he was involved in hostile encounters with other prisoners and felt that he had let me down after what he called my generous reference to him in *The Times*. 'I have already,' he said, 'betrayed your trust even before it was finalised by a visit.' When, later on, I paid him two visits at Durham, it was very much on my initiative.

During 1972 I feared that our relationship was endangered by the breach with Myra. He never said so in so many words, but certainly it was not unnatural for him to attribute her moving away to her new-found religious life and to cast the responsibility for that, rightly or wrongly, on me. There were moments when it seemed all too possible that our correspondence would be suspended. Possibly my defence of Myra when Mrs Wing took her for a walk, and there was a good deal of Press outcry, may have tided us over a difficult patch. At any rate, quite unexpectedly a most welcome letter arrived from him for the first time taking an initiative in asking me to visit him. Then came another SOS involving a further visit, and now we seem to have settled down to a new pattern of friendship.

What kind of man emerges from this prolonged and, in spite of prison censorship, revealing correspondence? Certainly no one basing himself on the written words would associate him with anything remotely approaching the terrible actions for which he was convicted. But he seems to be conscious of a deep conflict yet unresolved in his own nature. He is embarrassed, as already explained, when I seem to ignore his darker side in things I have said publicly or written to him. That he is capable of delicate feeling, I know at first hand, from my own occasions of bereavement and family illness.

On pornography, he adopts a position that would normally shock me, except that it is close to that apparently held by many literary journalists. His arguments are the usual ones for not interfering with it, but there is a special interest in a passage like this:

I have no time for the Mrs Whitehouse types, who studiously ignore real obscenities such as war, poverty and exploitation of the lower classes, but have an ever-sharp eye for anything to do with sex. People are more intelligent and selective and have outgrown the need for such anachronisms as censors. I hope you find nothing personal in my remarks; I have strong views on the subject exacerbated by the way these 'prohibitionists' have used me personally as an example for censorship.

He is often supposed to have been much influenced by the writings of the Marquis de Sade. His interest in him, but not necessarily his support, can be deduced from the following passage:

147

If you accept that real evil must be based on a deep philosophy, you must accept that such philosophy must hold some intelligence, some appeal to reason, some pragmatism? If so, then it is better to educate rather than withhold by censorship reason, intelligence, pragmatism of this sort? If you wish to have a textbook example of such a philosophy, there is a biography you may find of interest: *The Life and Ideas of the Marquis de Sade*, by Geoffrey Gorer.

On politics, he is vehemently anti-Tory. In his view, a Labour Government in power should take steps to make it impossible for the Tories to return to office! As might be expected, he does not love politicians as a class, but has some kind words to say, rather surprisingly for Trade Union leaders. On religion, he is crudely disparaging about all churches, particularly the Roman Catholic Church, but he never says a word against Jesus Christ or his teaching.

'As stated to you in the past,' he wrote on one occasion, 'I am agnostic. But as also repeatedly stated, the difference between wanting to believe and actually believing is too great a void for any serious pretensions. Who doesn't want to believe at some time in this life? Even atheists must succumb to such hopes, albeit momentarily.'

More than once I have urged him to face the challenge of Christian historical evidence, to which he has replied: 'I admit that the man Christ existed, and that he voiced many eternal truths which, in aggregate, comprised a philosophy of ideal standards, but I doubt any suggestion of there being a divine factor involved.' He is a heart and soul follower of Tolstoy in an undogmatic version of Christian ethics. Among certain great writers he is completely and unselfconsciously at home and knows his way about them at a moment's notice. In 1970-1, I was writing a book on 'Suffering' and benefited not a little from his comments.

You ask my opinion, he wrote, regarding the Tolstoyan doctrine on Suffering. I would say that Tolstoy regarded it as essentially a force for spiritual good. He continually has his characters spiritually cleansed by it. In *War and Peace* (Part 10, Chapter 37) there is a very moving example of this (especially the final paragraph), when

Prince Andrey finally meets his enemy, Anatole Kuragin, in the tent for the wounded at Borodino. Prince Andrey himself is suffering, but it is his seeing the suffering of his enemy, Kuragin, that makes him feel 'a passionate pity and love for that suffering man'. Then there's Princess Marya, *War and Peace*, an almost saintly person, whose father causes her much suffering, though he loves her. She is able to discern that his cruel attitude towards her is only his way of hiding his affection for her and accepts the suffering. And when the Old Count, her father, is eventually suffering his death agonies, his only concern is to beg his daughter's forgiveness for the suffering he has caused her. And, lastly, again *War and Peace*, Pierre Bezukhov, who is purified both morally and spiritually while in a prisoner-of-war camp by his own suffering and that of a fellow-prisoner, Karataev.

You may say that these are only Tolstoy's characters, but the interesting thing about Prince Andrey and Pierre Bezukhov is that they are actually the two parts of Tolstoy himself.

I took up with him the whole question of the views of Tolstoy and Dostoevsky on suffering. I agreed that the redemptive effect of suffering was strongly held by Dostoevsky, but not obviously so by Tolstoy. And he replied:

Your question juxtaposing Tolstoy with Dostoevsky and the re-demptive effect of suffering, I would not agree completely that it is not to be found in Tolstoy. What about Nehlyudov in *Resurrection* (again, Nehlyudov is Tolstoy himself)? Didn't the suffering of Mazlova *lead* to his redemption? (You may say his complete redemption takes place at the end of the book, when he reads the passage in the New Testament, but it was Mazlova's suffering which tilled his mind for the seed.) Secondly, didn't the suffering caused by Nehlyudov's conscience produce spiritual good in him?

If I had completed my book on 'Suffering', I would have made no apology for quoting his conclusion:

Incidentally, when I use the word 'redemption', I mean purity of conscience not the, to my mind, narrower theological sense. There are so many paradoxes in the subject of Suffering, and the mind gets caught up in a chicken and egg situation. Suffering is, I think, a catalyst of higher Awareness, of self and others, and Awareness is Life. But there are so many different combinations of the nature and degree of awareness, that it is impossible, in my opinion, to decide whether suffering produces more good than evil; but at least we're sure (at least, I am) it certainly produces both good and evil, so is therefore neither completely one nor completely the other.

Ian Brady is often referred to as having exhibited early in his life a streak of cruelty to animals. He implies in one of his letters that some such charge might have been justified, but was long out of date.

When young, I myself was cruel to several animals, yet for the past sixteen years or so my opposition to mistreatment of animals has been, and still is, dangerously extreme, producing a blind and immediate reaction of intense hatred.

On another occasion, he told me that he had now reached the point where he literally could not hurt a fly or any kind of insect.

And what of his attitude to the authorities? He has plenty of good words for individual gaolers, the prison staffs in general and, by implication, for particular officers, notably the former Governor of Durham, Mr Chambers, on his departure. But for the Home Office collectively nothing but denigration. Yet the much-abused censorship must be given some credit surely for allowing his comments to reach the outer world.

Again and again I tried to convince him that one day, a very long way off, no doubt, it would be possible for him to achieve his release if he could demonstrate its justification. He has always treated the very idea as a total fantasy. He has argued, moreover, that release on the only terms conceivable would focus on him an intolerable amount of public attention; that he would even prefer continued and unlimited confinement. I was told at one time in Durham that in a sense his acceptance of lifelong incarceration had enabled him to effect a psychological adjustment superior to that of prisoners who were perpetually wondering when release might come. But I cannot think that this is a final or, in any way, a satisfactory answer.

As I complete this book, I appreciate his dissatisfaction with the conditions under which he is serving. I am in discussion with the Home Office concerning them, and the means of their improvement. I do not under-estimate their problem in trying to provide him with companionship. I do not accuse them of ill-will towards him, but imagination and initiative in dealing with an admittedly difficult situation have hitherto not been in evidence. Let us hope that by the time this book appears, or soon afterwards, I shall have occasion to eat my words.

For a long time he was disappointingly reluctant to engage in any serious discussion of penal reform. So many intelligent prisoners lay themselves open to the same comment that I must suppose that if I myself were in prison I would find it almost unnatural to put myself in the place of the Home Office and seek to formulate a satisfying penal policy. But lately Ian Brady has been able to bring his mind to bear on fundamental penal issues. His interest was much stimulated by *Psychological Survival*, a book written by two sociologists about the top security prisoners in Durham, including himself. He appears under the name of Frank, which happens also to be my Christian name. He did not let the coincidence pass.

I sent him my small book on *The Idea of Punishment*, and was pleased that he liked it as a theoretical exercise, although he reserved his position about its applicability to the real world. If I quote an extract from his last letter before this book goes to press, it will be realised that it is taken from a continuing dialogue. 'I intended,' he wrote, 'to tackle you on the question of retribution (which the book seems to postulate), but as you wrote it over ten years ago I was wondering if you had reached any new and clearer definition of the word. My argument was that the law cannot possibly function on the Christian ethic of forgiveness.' He went on to argue that if certain well-known delinquents had been given suspended sentences instead of being sent to prison for many years, they themselves would be unlikely to repeat their crimes. 'But others would be encouraged to emulate them. So leaving aside all academic arguments and ethical convolutions, it seems quite obvious that prisoners are here to stay.'

Putting this into my own words, I take him to mean that the deterrent argument requires a policy of long-term imprisonment for certain criminals, which is in conflict with Christian ideas of forgiveness. No one who has ever visited long-term criminals for more than a few minutes, or claimed any kind of friendship with them, can ignore the urgency of this question. In Holy Week this year I gave a quarter of an hour's talk on the radio on 'Christian Forgiveness of the Criminal'. With Ian Brady, but not only him in mind, I concentrated on the question: 'How can we say to a prisoner serving a long sentence, we as Christians forgive you? We embrace you in Christian fellowship, but you will quite understand that we find it our Christian duty to keep you locked up for very many years.'

In theoretical terms, the answer should be provided by drawing a distinction between our *emotional* and our *administrative* attitude to the prisoner. We should continue to love him, even while we give effect to the social duty of keeping him in prison. But can that mean anything, or sound like anything except pure humbug to the prisoner? Can we persuade ourselves that long-term imprisonment can actually benefit a prisoner in terms of his moral improvement, and can we, what is bound to be still more difficult, persuade him that this indeed is so? Something of a conflict of duties between what we owe to society, and what we owe to each individual member, be he delinquent or otherwise, is, I suppose, ineluctable. But once the issue is formulated in all its starkness, it surely becomes impossible for Christians and other ethical persons not to give an altogether new meaning to the task enjoined on us in Matthew 25 of seeing Christ in each convicted prisoner. The longer the sentence, the more glaring the duty becomes.

At the Side of Youth

My connection with youth work goes back a long way. It began when I was an adolescent, no older than the so-called 'old boys' of the Eton Manor boys' club in Hackney Wick, East London. The presiding genius of the club was my mother's brother, Arthur Villiers, D.S.O., merchant banker, athlete, soldier, philanthropist, freeman of Leyton, freeman of Hackney Wick, who lived at or near the club for over half a century. I myself loved all vigorous games, the vigour declining as the years increased. I ran races, played netball or basketball, tennis, squash and rugger. I played for the Eton Manor rugby fifteen in their inaugural match, getting my eye cut open. I was never much good at billiards, but there was a time when at table tennis I could compete with all except the London champions. I played quite a bit of squash with Douglas Jardine who showed me scant mercy. Incidentally, at a leaving dinner at the Manor given for some of the M.C.C. team for Australia in 1932 he demonstrated body-line tactics with Larwood.

After I married, I contributed little to the club, though continuing to visit it from time to time till my uncle's death at the end of the sixties. It was quite in character, therefore, in 1959, to act on a hint from Edward Boyle, M.P., then at the Ministry of Education, and suggest a fundamental inquiry into the working of the Youth Services, whose gross neglect had recently been exposed by a select committee. While the subsequent Albemarle Inquiry was still sitting, I initiated the first debate ever held on the Youth Services in the House of Lords. Nor did I abandon the topic there or elsewhere. After a couple of years in Harold Wilson's Cabinet, I began to realise that I was not going to be what Lord Reith would call 'stretched' or, indeed, used at all seriously in the Social Services. I took the bit between my teeth and asked permission from the Prime Minister to conduct an overall inquiry. This would not only investigate the Youth Service, which came under the

Ministry of Education, but the other main provisions for youth, including the treatment of young delinquents - a Home Office responsibility.

The Prime Minister was nothing loth. An old 'Beveridge' boy himself, he was always ready to concede my credentials as a social inquirer; but the Ministers concerned, presumably on official advice, dug their toes in. I had to threaten and clearly intend resignation before I was allowed to undertake a rather emasculated inquiry. Anthony Crosland, Minister of Education, and Roy Jenkins, Home Secretary, wished me - I do not doubt - well, but Tony felt that he would be letting down his junior Minister, Denis Howell, responsible for the Youth Service, from which Tony had somewhat detached himself.

Roy reminded me the other day that at the end of the argument I said to him and Tony: 'I shall be kind about both of you in my next volume of autobiography, but not quite so kind as I meant to be.' I had forgotten that I used such impertinent words, but I am glad that someone with such an ear for language as Roy should treasure them.

With Joan Bourne once again my colleague, I ranged far and wide up and down the country. In a short space of time we collected an immense amount of information before my resignation from the Cabinet more or less nullified the project.

Soon after my resignation, that is, in the spring of 1968, Ray Gunter, Minister of Labour, asked me to take over from Lady Albemarle the chairmanship of the National Youth Employment Council. This was an advisory council with members representing different employment interests and some special knowledge of vocational guidance. Given my preoccupation at that time, I welcomed the opportunity to learn about this aspect of social policy. The more I saw of young people in difficulties, the more it seemed to me that their troubles and tragedies were rooted deeper than we could reach. We needed to look farther back for a moment of truth where a productive impact might be made, and in this context vocational guidance was obviously of the utmost importance.

At this point I myself underwent the tests of the excellent Vocational Guidance Association answering, if I remember rightly, about two thousand questions. My higher marks were for what was called 'Writing' and 'Church and Welfare'. My marks for 'Selling' were abysmal. The conclusion was, I seem to remember, that I would do well to concentrate on social work, with writing as a side line, but that I would be well advised to avoid any career that involved *persuasion*. As I had just come from over twenty years on one front bench or the other in the House of Lords, I wondered if I had chosen the wrong calling. But whatever advice they might have given me earlier, the guidance which they gave me at that moment seemed, and still seems, to be remarkably apposite.

I wish that I could say that the experience of being chairman of the National Youth Employment Council was uplifting. It saddened me that such a vital service was - and still is - expected to operate on an annual budget that would scarcely finance five minutes of Concorde development. The Youth Employment Service was generally controlled and partly run by the Department of Employment, but most local services were operated by education authorities. It was a time of traumatic uncertainty about the future. Rumours of impending structural changes circulated wildly and created deep division between those who supported local authority control and those who preferred the Service to be amalgamated with the national manpower service.

The issues are clear enough, but it was clearer still that the tug-of-war was destroying the Service, and more energy was spent on who should run it than on how it could be improved. The struggle for power became almost obsessional. It went on for longer than I was chairman, and by the time I left, it was evident that any solution would have been preferable to the absence of one.

However, I can record one small achievement, which was to concentrate attention on the particular problems of disadvantaged young people; and our report, *At Odds*, prompted some useful work on their behalf, notably the community industries scheme in areas of high unemployment.

I was especially concerned, not surprisingly, with the employment position of black young people. But I had little success to point to. Not long ago the Department of Employment reported that unemployment among black youths was double the percentage for the population as a whole. The situation during my period of office was worst of all in Brixton. I have been honoured recently to become a patron - I hope an active one - of the Melting Pot Foundation, set up by a Barbadian, Ashton Gibson, in that very area, to bring self-respect and fresh opportunities to the black community, and reconciliation generally.

I was not sorry to end my term of office, partly because the internecine battle saddened me, when so much constructive work needed doing, but also because I began to doubt the value of the Council system itself. So many opposing interests were represented that we rarely reached agreement; and when we did, I wondered if our views would divert Ministers one centimetre from a course which had already been charted. It is difficult to see how policies can be divulged at the confidential planning stage to members representing such diverse outside interests. I could not escape the suspicion that the Council was a mere figurehead, a corporate rubber stamp assembled at discreet intervals to place the seal of public approval on settled policies, which we had no effective power to change.

There were, however, many compensating joys - mainly people. I travelled about meeting many careers officers and civil servants, as well as local authority specialists working incredibly long hours with deep devotion, in spite of the pitiful resources allocated to them and their work.

For whatever reason, I have come nearer to official recognition in the field of youth policy than in any other sphere. In autumn 1970 I was approached by Alec Grant, chairman of the Further & Higher Education sub-committee of the Inner London Education Authority. The idea may have come to him from his friend and colleague on the G.L.C., my son-in-law Alec Kazantzis. At Alec Grant's request, I undertook the chairmanship of the major inquiry into the whole future of the Youth Service in the I.L.E.A. area, and its relationship to adult education. I was well aware of the significance of the opportunity; what I.L.E.A. does today is likely to be widely followed tomorrow. The committee contained a score of expert representatives from all the main areas of youth work, statutory and voluntary. It was too large, but that was the only thing wrong with it. Much else was right, notably the quality of the personnel, from Miss Adams who frequently deputised for me in the chair, to Miss Compton, our secretary, who drafted our report after eighteen months of strenuous argument. We were assisted at every turn by outstanding officials.

In February 1973 I received a letter from Alec Grant informing me that our report, *A Chance to Choose*, had been approved by I.L.E.A. as a policy document: 'The substance of the recommendations,' he wrote, 'has been accepted for implementation as soon as sufficient financial resources may be made available,' subject to one or two points mentioned. So it seems that we did not labour in vain.

Youth policy documents are almost unintelligible to the uninitiated. I will confine myself to our broad emphasis. In our own words, 'We concentrated mainly on the needs of young people and concluded that, in order to protect their interests, the separate identity of the Youth Service should be preserved.' To this conception I had clung inflexibly throughout. In this, of course, I was not in any way alone, but the idea of a *community* service to cover all age groups was exercising in my eyes a dangerous fascination. I myself was convinced that if the Youth Service did *not* retain its separate identity, the share of national resources would be fatally diminished. Its political pull, always pathetically weak, would more or less disappear. On the other hand, amid many conflicts of opinion, there was complete agreement that there should be less rigidity, far more flexibility between the various services provided for young people and adults, and internally within those services. We all agreed that there should be no longer any imposed age limits, though in my passion for the separate service, I was less keen on this than the others. Still, they were giving their lives to youth work; in spite of my powerful concern, it was a relatively small part of mine. So in a general way, I hope, we got the best of all worlds.

We had very lively discussions about the respective meanings of education and of leisure as guides to the future of the service. Myself, I am still old-fashioned enough to talk of character-training. Those who are now bearing the main brunt are as morally earnest as I have ever been, but they seem to feel that the old aspiration must be presented in semi-disguise. Through the Youth Employment Council and the I.L.E.A. inquiry, I was enabled to cover not a little of the ground I tried to investigate as a Minister. And I did not stop there, as will be seen in a moment.

*

I am occasionally asked why I have taken this persistent interest in youth, which has shown no diminution with the passing years. Is it some craving to maintain an illusion of personal youthfulness? A Peter Pan complex, or what? Who can answer that question precisely? To describe a social service as a Cinderella is to use a very tired metaphor as mentioned in connection with prisoners. But it is equally appropriate to the youth and delinquency services, and most of all to the treatment of juvenile or adolescent delinquency, where the two neglected services come together. In the fifties and the sixties I was coming to the fore in these overlapping fields.

I was fully conscious by 1964 that the New Bridge for understandable reasons had so far done little for the young. While it was still uncertain whether Labour would win the election or, if they did, whether I would be a Cabinet Minister, I was deep in discussions with a charitable trust for a kind of junior New Bridge. I had in mind an advisory centre where I myself would work full-time. Four years later, by the time I was out of the Government, my friend in the charity concerned was dead. So I had to cast about elsewhere.

For several months in that year (1968) I was preoccupied with student issues. I spent much time in the summer preparing for a Lords debate on higher education, visiting half a dozen universities and other colleges. It was a bad year for university staffs and particularly for vice-chancellors. I was conscious that they knew the precise distance between their desk and the windows, if the worst came to the worst and they had to escape the mob. At one point I descended on the Hornsey College of Art during the revolutionary take-over by the students. This led later to my becoming chairman of the Hornsey Commission set up jointly by staff and students (more enthusiastically by the latter than the former), to lay plans for a happier future.

For four months we met at least once a week, with many informal contacts. Finally at a great meeting in a North London cinema, our report was adopted. On paper it contained much democratisation. The highlight of the meeting was the address of the chairman of the governors, an alderman, prominent in the laundry business, who addressed the students with jovial disrespect. 'I know you fellows,' cried the alderman. 'You think I don't know about academic life. You are quite right, I don't, but I know what it is like having to wash your shirts, and I can tell you it is a very nasty job.' Martin Walker, a small, dark, brilliantly good-looking revolutionary student, a leading member of the commission, wound up with a peroration from Kafka. What struck me was the moral courage he showed in braving the scepticism of his fellow-students and convincing most of them that these were the best terms that could be got. From the prolonged and often exciting discussion, I carried away one clear recollection. What the students demanded beyond all else was a 'real tutorial system'. No one could doubt the justice of their demand for a much closer relationship between themselves and the staff, but if they had known what a real tutorial system was in the Oxford University sense, they would have rejected it as grossly paternalistic. I came away from the commission feeling that I had learnt more than they had.

Now I began to give effect to my dream of helping youth. By the end of the year, the essential steps had been taken on my initiative to establish what became the New Horizon Youth Centre. The first friend I spoke to about it was the Reverend Meredith Davies, unrivalled as a chaplain in prisons and borstals, and invaluable supporter of the New Bridge. He became our first chairman, with myself as director, theoretically a full-time appointment, except that there was no money available. Notable members of our Council were collected by Meredith Davies from the City, and by myself from elsewhere. Some brought an intimate knowledge of social work and a special concern for young people. Our first treasurer was Mr Leslie Prince, and now for some time we have been nursed and nourished by Sir Matthew Slattery. Our debt to both of them is immeasurable. Sally Trench, author of the best-selling *Bury Me in my Boots*, a first-hand authority on junkies, and Jack Profumo, already a name to conjure with among all who knew his work at Toynbee Hall, have inspired us from the beginning.

In *Five Lives* I paid tribute to Jack Profumo and his splendid wife, Valerie. I said that at that time (1964) he was nearer to the Kingdom of God than I was or, for that matter, than the general run of politicians. The words look rather patronising now, though I am not sorry I used them. Today he certainly requires no certificates from me. By the time we started New Horizon (1969) I was already aware of the great impression he had made in social work. I mentioned him to Stella Reading, unrivalled in the situation, and she at once found him a post at Toynbee Hall. At Harold Wilson's request I had become chairman of the Attlee Memorial Fund, for whose success Jack was more responsible than anyone. I had seen him in the rather sombre surroundings of Toynbee, improving morale and adding gaiety all round. A foundation member of New Horizon, he has won the special devotion of our young workers and never attends a meeting without contributing something live and novel. When the Queen greeted him at the opening of the new Attlee Building, it was like the last scene in *The Four Feathers*. The underlying worth of the man had overcome every obstacle.

After our first Press conference, our purpose was described by *The Times* as 'unclear', and that was a euphemism. But we decided from the beginning that we were going to help all young people with problems, not only delinquents. In practice a high proportion of all our clients, as we have come to call them, have been in trouble with the courts.

Angela Lambert, unfailingly helpful, produced a young secretary for us - Nikki Hunt, petite, dark-eyed, vastly attractive alike to council members, staff and clients, always spreading warmth in the coldest moments, of which there were plenty, physically and psychologically, at the beginning. Our office at the back of St Botolph's Church was so small that if Nikki wanted to work in it, I had to move out, and vice versa.

For many weeks no one came near us. One client did indeed show up, was eagerly fastened on by all, but quickly disappeared in embarrassment. We had nothing but faith to feed on. Not a few were heard to say that we would fail and would deserve to. Through the intervention, however, of Joan Abbott, an experienced children's officer and New Bridge friend, and the kindness of the clergy at St Anne's Church, Soho, we were able to rent a large room there, which had once been a café.

When we first arrived at Dean Street, Nikki Hunt and I occupied the main area, but a kind of cubicle was constructed out of it, where Joan Abbott could interview people. In the event, Joan was not able to stay with us very long, embarking on social work out of London, so that the original plans were completely altered. I had not lost touch with Martin Walker of Hornsey, and he now joined us as a full-time worker. Like Nikki and myself, he had no professional training. Once Martin arrived, I retired to the cubicle, which was indeed for the whole of 1969 the only office I possessed and my base for multiform activities. It was, however, of immense value to have run the place actively day by day with Nikki's help for a short time, and to have answered telephone inquiries of all kinds, including requests for abortions to which I was chilly. Even after Martin took over, I lived the life at close quarters, sharing a lavatory with the drug addicts.

Martin Walker has written, and my firm have published, the story of the New Horizon Youth Centre during the year and a half he was in executive control under my supervision. No one interested in youth work, certainly no one interested in New Horizon, should neglect his book. He has quoted me at some length, with my full permission. His readers will notice, however, that I differ sharply from him in his account of the attitude of the officers of the St Anne's Church towards our activities. The truth is that the church authorities found us very uncomfortable tenants and I cannot conceal the fact that they found Martin our most uncomfortable member. Martin insisted at the time, and in his book, 'that there were conflicting interests between the work New Horizon were attempting to carry out and the ethics of a Christian approach, which was inevitably bound up with Establishment tradition'. Then and later I strongly resisted this notion. As I wrote in a footnote to Martin's book: 'The issues were in no way ideological. Nor can I accept for a moment the idea that there has been a clash between Christian ideals and those of New Horizon, which was started by the Reverend Meredith Davies and myself, both Christians.' It was built up (with much help, of course, from the Council and Nikki Hunt) by myself, completely dedicated to Christian ethics, and Martin, who repudiated them utterly in so far as he understood them. 'Handing out soup and sacraments,' he wrote in his book, 'was one thing, but an attempt to change the nature of the established order was another.' Whatever may be meant by that last phrase, I am quite sure that New Horizon would never have been a suitable instrument for achieving it.

But some of Martin's other comments are irrefutable. He gives a vivid account of my inviting him to breakfast at the Royal Court Hotel in Sloane Square and asking him to join New Horizon. He quotes me, no doubt correctly, as saying: 'I felt a strong urge to do some real social work, as opposed to talking about it, or making speeches about it in the House of Lords, or referring to my own past, whether in social work or in politics. I wanted to do something real, and have first-hand contact with young people.' In those rather flat sentences my motivation, as far as I can judge, is set out accurately. Lurking in my subconscious also was probably a sense of responsibility, a sense of failure perhaps in relation to all the young people for whom the raising of the school-leaving age had been postponed. Martin exposes, fairly enough, my complete uncertainty at that stage as to what form our organisation would take. As I told him when he was writing his book, in many ways the project was like the South Sea Bubble: I had to ask people for their support for an organisation the purpose of which would become clear at some later date. The difficulty of raising money on such a prospectus makes one tremble, looking back. But today I have no regrets for the folly of rushing in where angels were so hesitant to tread.

We settled down with a new pattern. Martin and Nikki dealt directly with the young people, while I, from my adjacent cubicle, played the part of an avuncular figure to staff and clients, and helped them whenever called upon with any prestige I possessed outside the centre, with government departments and others. The rest of the Council between regular meetings rendered assistance in all sorts of different ways.

*

Whatever theories were developed by Martin or myself (Nikki was too wise to promulgate theories), the centre had soon come to differ in two vital respects from my original conception, though to be fair to myself I had always (in a phrase made fashionable since by Harold Wilson) 'kept the options open'. In the first place, it was an advice centre and a community centre rolled into one. It possessed a little community life of its own, in which the young people, or many of them, participated. They could feel that they belonged to it and it belonged to them. It would have had nothing like the same appeal if they had come in one by one, been given advice and departed. In so far as there was therapy, the sense of community was a considerable part of it. But all this was subject to the underlying fact that we were dealing with young people adrift in the West End, who could never therefore form a stable population for very long. Yet somehow or other we preserved a sense of community. The second point, clear to anyone who reads the above, was that my glorious idea of myself advising young people had not proved the answer. In one sense those who said I was too old for such a task were abundantly justified. On the other hand I was, by the end of 1969, somewhat like Liddell Hart, shall we say, whose relatively brief active service in the First World War had enabled him to become a great strategical thinker!

Long before this, I had gone round propounding the slogan: 'It is the young who must help the young.' Several years earlier, I had urged that much fuller use should be made of adolescents in helping adolescents who had gone wrong. It was disappointing for me personally, but it confirmed my theories to find that young people like Martin and Nikki, and subsequently many others, were able to win the confidence of these rather shattered young clients, in a way impossible to me. Large questions here suggest themselves. Martin and Nikki were very definitely not trained in social work. They were not only forty years younger than me; they were quite a few years younger than the average probation officer. Am I saying that training and experience are of no first-hand value in such situations? Obviously not. In my considered opinion, every kind of age group, with every kind of background, can make its contribution. It was the special originality of New Horizon to make use of workers whose talents would otherwise have been neglected. But let me say at once that we were exceptionally lucky in finding Nikki and Martin.

I have in front of me as I write the last report of New Horizon, dated January 1973. In the early days I was obsessed with the difficulty of attracting those whose problems were greatest. 'Those,' I used to say, 'who need help most are the last to come for it.' Gradually that position changed and, on the whole today, we find it hard to cope with all who come to us. We must be careful to avoid becoming, in Lenin's phrase, 'giddy with success'. Every now and then something terrible happens.

Jon Snow, who succeeded Martin in autumn 1970, told me that of the 300 drug addicts that used the centre at the beginning of 1972, 20 were dead by the end. For various reasons outside our control, of which the move from Dean Street to Macklin Street, Drury Lane, was the least important, the drug addicts have come to figure much less prominently. Drug addicts can make one feel overwhelmingly sad, but they are not violent. Recently, violence has flared more than once. On one occasion a knife was used, with almost fatal results, on a voluntary worker, by a young man under the influence of drink and barbiturates. What won my undying admiration was the fact that our young workers called a meeting next day at which the whole matter was fully discussed by the clients. The assailant had by that time been arrested, but his companions attended the meeting until the act of violence was condemned by the general feeling. At that point they took their departure, but gradually they have been readmitted to the centre.

At the moment at which Martin Walker left New Horizon, a

kind of watershed had been reached. The centre had begun to come to grips with the various problems associated with the West End. There was less difficulty in making contact with those most in need of help, which had been experienced at first. Although there was a fairly wide spread of problems - drugs, loneliness, homosexual prostitution, and petty crime - drugs predominated. The centre was open during office hours only, but within that time solid relationships and some useful case-work were achieved. Certainly for some, enough support was being given to prevent their getting worse. And for a few, their lives were actually improving as a result. But particularly among the young drug users, we seemed in most cases unable to halt a continued deterioration. Indeed for some it was only possible to help make the process of dying slightly less painful. How was it possible to expect them to reduce the drug taking if no improvement was effected in their overall social situation? For most of us, the initial response to the problems being encountered was one of horror and pity. But as time went on, the underlying causes became clearer. So that by the time Martin left, the centre had moved from the point of responding to the individual's immediate needs to looking farther. In-evitably, accommodation, support, lasting relationships, and some sort of occupation became more important than dressing abscesses or allowing someone to sleep for an hour on the floor of the office.

The question was whether making contact with a problem during office hours was all that New Horizon was concerned with. Having established that there was a *problem*, was there not a duty to go further and start providing more facilities? There were three possible solutions: to continue as we were, to stop altogether, or to expand. This last choice was made. Whereas the decision to start New Horizon had been mine, this second step was based on a decision arrived at jointly by the workers, our Council, and myself. This represented the role that I have since continued to play, viz. that of keeping closely in touch with events, and sharing and supporting the ideas developed by those actually working on the projects. By the end of 1972, New Horizon had moved from employing three workers and providing day centre facilities during office hours, to providing a walk-in centre open seven days a week until late at night. A separate hostel had been established to house those young people whom it was felt could survive on their own if given intensive support for three or four months. The total staff of New Horizon was now thirteen. The budget had increased from £5,000 a year in 1969 to more than £20,000 a year in 1972.

Perhaps more than at any other time, the centre is now concerned with precisely those young people in mind when we started up in 1968, and is moreover in fundamental contact with some of the main aspects of the 'youth problem' so-called. We are dealing with the outcome of the conditions under which so many young people today are growing up. There are too many common factors in their backgrounds for it all to be mere coincidence. Of 2,000 young people who used the centre during 1972, 80 per cent came from the provinces, of whom some 700 were from Greater Glasgow alone, the rest mainly from industrial cities, within which similar conditions show up again and again - poor housing (old and new), limited recreational, educational and social facilities. Unemployment is usually heavy in such areas, and these factors, combined with unsatisfactory domestic circumstances, leave young teenagers in a vulnerable position, liable to become delinquent or at least anti-social. They are frequently taken into, and out of, the care of local authorities, or else remain with very unstable families. When eventually lack of opportunity or the pressure of events, such as, for example, continued arrest, gets too strong, they uproot themselves and make for an alternative situation. London supposedly provides this; in reality, of course, it does not. Accommodation is desperately scarce, even for the most adequate; employment is not easily come by, and these factors, with the acute loneliness which young people experience when on their own in London, render them quite helpless.

Despite the changes in New Horizon since its inception, the overall picture has remained constant: that of young people helping other young people less fortunate than themselves. The objectives, too, have remained the same - to enable young people to make a free, fruitful decision about what they really want to do with their lives. This in itself may sound very straightforward. But it is far from so, particularly when a young person has a background of institutional care, tending to deprive him of the opportunity to make a choice.

Those who work at the centre are themselves young. The average age is 24. Of a dozen workers, in 1972 two were specifically trained in social work. The rest had varying backgrounds; in purely 'establishment' terms they would be regarded as 'unqualified' as, I explained, were Martin and Nikki. But qualifications in this particular field are in any case debatable, not least because it is one in which so little certainty has been achieved. New Horizon represents an experiment. Our workers have seemed to find it an advantage in some cases to function without the pre-conditioning of a training course and formal instruction. But some who have worked at New Horizon have gone on to related courses with much benefit. I cannot repeat too often that on no account do I disparage training in general - I simply offer our particular experience over this limited period as a contribution to the general pool of understanding.

Right from the start I never felt that New Horizon would remain static. I see the need for us to develop and to keep on developing, particularly in the field of providing homes. But of course, for this we shall need money . . . money, and still more money!

*

I record below interviews with three young people typical of those who come to the centre - although no three examples could do justice to the human variety.

TED: a likeable Cockney, heavily built for his age (28), very fit; dark, round-faced, clear complexion, but with no particular pride in himself when he first came to the centre. Has learnt to give of himself - very popular all round - a sort of father figure to the rest. Has been convicted several times for violence and handling stolen goods.

I began by asking him, 'What help does New Horizon give you?'

TED: Gives me quite a lot – because you're able to sit down and talk to the workers about your problems, y'know, get yourself sorted out at the same time.

L: Do you think a lot depends on there being many other people in the Centre?

TED: Yes. You can only get out what you put in. Some chaps say to me, y'know, you don't get anything out. I think when I first came here, it was something to keep me out of the streets and out of the arms of the men in blue. Since then, I have got myself pulled together. I think I have done myself some good by being here.

I turned to his past and asked him about the sort of troubles he had been in before he came to New Horizon.

TED: I have had offences – violence, – all the usual sort of thing, and gang fighting in the East End.

L: Were you a member of a gang?

TED: I was on the outskirts of the gangs in the East End – no special one, but I did know most of the people in the East End. I did not belong to any particular gang.

L: I am on the side of law and order, you know that, and if people begin stabbing people, they have got to be punished quite heavily. When you think it over calmly, you will agree.

Jon Snow intervened. 'Ted, do you think things would have been any different if you had not come to New Horizon?'

TED: Yes, I think they would. I think I would have been in prison serving a pretty heavy sentence as well.

JON: What is going to happen to you now? Are you living where you have been helped to find a place by New Horizon?

TED: Yes. I am now living in Chiswick and hoping to start some work with Community Service Volunteers in two weeks' time, in a Children's Orphanage, and then I will see how the future goes, y'know.

L: That's wonderful. At any rate it reflects great credit on you and great credit on New Horizon.

DAWN: a most attractive, well built, neatly dressed, dark 16-year-old, very mature for her age, with graceful gestures. Looks about twenty. Has been on the run since she was 13, and living at New Horizon hostel since 15. Her difficulties would seem to be largely temperamental. Until the age of 10, she had an unsettled, rather than unstable existence - father in the army, moved from Cyprus to Singapore to West Germany, taking his family with him. Mother very dominant. Dawn at loggerheads with mother and sister, proved a disrupting element in the family and was placed in care of Cheshire County Council. Has now been accepted at Kingsway College to study for five G.C.E.s, and with encouragement is likely to do well for herself.

I asked Dawn how it was she came to New Horizon.

DAWN: I came to London again last May from Cheshire and met a few old friends and we spent the night in Odhams Press (derelict building in Covent Garden). And in the morning we split up and went down Trafalgar Square and met another friend I knew and we went into one of the cafes, and there was a guy I knew and they brought me up here.

L: What did they tell you about New Horizon?

DAWN: (laconically) Nothing. Just brought me up here.

L: Do you like it?

DAWN: It's all right sometimes. (hesitantly) Well . . . it's all right if I'm not coming here all the time, because if you're coming here all the time . . . I don't like the same place all the time.

Jon Snow asked the same question he had put to Ted. Can you say if things would have been any different if New Horizon had not been around?

DAWN: Well . . . I would not be living in London. I would still be running away from Cheshire. They would keep taking me back to the Approved School and in the end to Borstal.

(Note: When in care to Cheshire C.C. she was continually running away from the Approved School.)

JON: Do you think things on balance are slightly better now than they might have been, or not?

DAWN: They are, yes.

I turned to her own background.

L: What about your home? Did you quarrel with your family? Or did they quarrel with you, or what?

DAWN: Not really. I still go and see them and visit them and I ring them up.

L: But you didn't like living at home? It is not a question of a broken home? They are quite happy together, your parents?

DAWN: No ... No.

JON: But you have been running away from home since you were about twelve?

DAWN: I didn't like my sister – she used to argue with me. She was bigger than me.

I came back to the present and New Horizon.

L: Here you get a feeling of security, do you? You are among friends. People are ready to help you?

DAWN: Yes, they do help me. They do things for me and I do things for them as well.

L: What sort of things? Cooking?

DAWN: No. This month I am going to do the magazine for them. I do all the shopping for the hostel.

RAB: a typical, wiry little lad from Glasgow, sharp-featured, with a heavy accent, very likeable and honest. His chief problem is loneliness. Comes from a broken home, father alcoholic, mother ran away leaving five children. Rab has always sought work in vain, until the psychiatric hospital provided the opportunity. Work now considered a privilege (packer in warehouse). Has consistently attempted suicide, but responded rapidly to the psychiatric treatment and stimulus of a job.

I began by asking him how old he was and how he came to New Horizon.

RAB: Nineteen. When I first came here, I was violent – always carrying knives. I have just come out of a psychiatric hospital last Monday ...

ON: Did we know you before you went in?

RAB: I used to come to Dean Street.

L: How long were you coming to New Horizon?

RAB: I was in the hospital for nine months. I had a lot of psychiatric trouble and was on drugs. I just cracked up with drugs, barbiturates and everything . . .

L: While you were coming to New Horizon? So you have seen plenty of life.

I asked him what it was like in the psychiatric hospital.

RAB: I was out working. But sensibly I went out to work from there. I think the treatment – where you have to go out to work, you learn something about independence. They have helped me well and got me off drugs. I am no longer violent: I don't carry knives any more.

L: When we started New Horizon, of course, most of the people we were seeing were on heroin and there was very little violence, because most of them were just helpless. How did you take to barbiturates? Did somebody persuade you to take them? They make one violent?

RAB: No. I just started to take them for fun.

L: How did they help you – did they train you at the psychiatric hospital?

RAB: I did not go in because of drugs, but for suicide – several times – in a state of great depression.

L: But they helped you that way? What did they give you?

RAB: A different kind of drugs; they put us on sedatives.

I turned the discussion to the future.

L: Will you be able to work now that you are better? Do you feel that the Centre can now help you?

RAB: They have helped me in the past . . . if it were not for Jon I would be dead by now . . .

L: Would you say that the other people here are helping you? I mean on the whole . . . I understand the workers do, but apart from the workers?

RAB: You make new friends and you learn other people's problems. They help you with yours and you can help them.

L: People sometimes say that at places like Borstal people do corrupt each other – but you don't find that happening here? So the only trouble is this depression?

RAB: I think I'm cleared of that now. I am getting married next month to a girl . . .

Ted was sitting with us and came in helpfully.

TED : I have known Rab for quite some time. I have seen him in his ups and downs. I can see a change in him now to when I first met him. I do feel, that as Rab knows, he has got back on his feet because he decided to put something into it. Otherwise he would be at the end. I am glad he decided to make a go of things.

L : If you were one of the workers here, you would persuade people to put something into it, otherwise they wouldn't get anything out of it?

RAB : I have helped Jon about the office and went to court a few times. It's good to help a chap. I helped to get . . . off. I done as much as I could for him and to get probation instead of going to prison. He is all right now – working – first time he had ever been given a chance. He has got a girl-friend . . .

I said there was one other question I wanted to ask.

L : I suppose all three of you have had experience of other forms of social work. How do you think New Horizon compares with others? One of the features is that the staff are young people.

JON : Average age of the workers is 23 – average age of clients about 18.

TED : The thing is that here you can sit down and discuss with people here and you know whatever you say won't go beyond the four walls. The thing is there is a much easier atmosphere to discuss your problems here than going to a Probation Officer to discuss your problems – a much easier atmosphere. The workers here are much more approachable. The ones that work in local offices – the social workers look down on you. The people here are just as qualified, but no airs or graces. What they say is right . . .

L : They treat you more like an equal here?

DAWN : If they want like to do something for you, they discuss it with you first – everything – they wanted to get me into a hospital which I didn't want. If it had not been for New Horizon I would have had to go there.

L : I get the idea. Rab, do you feel you are treated more like an equal?

RAB : Yes, quite different from the authorities. They put your wick up . . . as if they were God or something . . .

TED : This is it – I wanted to go into voluntary work with handicapped children, but I didn't have any qualifications, I didn't think I would have to go to college for three years . . .

DAWN: Most of the workers have done the Social Work Course, but most have said it is no use at all.

L: The thing about doing courses is that you learn a lot in a short time.

So there we left it for the moment. No doubt the so-called authorities have much to offer which is not comprehended or appreciated by those they are trying to help, but the conversations above give some idea of how many young people seem to prefer our sort of establishment.

PART FOUR

The Permissive Society

There is not, as far as I am aware, any authoritative definition of a permissive society or trend towards a permissive society. In some sense or other, for good or for ill, we all seem to agree that our society is more permissive than it was some years ago. That is far from true universally. Some years ago Elizabeth and I asked permission to build a modest house for a hard-working member of the Foreign Office on our small estate. The plans were, of course, approved by a first-class architect, but permission was refused. It is hardly conceivable that this could have happened a generation earlier. When we talk of our society today being more permissive, we are referring to only one part of human activity, mostly concerned with culture and personal morals.

In the book already referred to about British politics in the sixties, Mr McKie picks on the liberalisation of the laws on divorce, homosexuality and abortion, and the freeing of authors and playwrights from what he calls the censor's hampering hand as evidence of a powerful movement towards the freedom of the individual. The Obscene Publications Act passed in 1959 had been an early and, in his eyes, laudable fore-taste. He argues that the abolition of hanging was seen by its supporters as an integral part of the campaign to civilise Britain, by its detractors as an equally integral part of the nation's steady descent into permissiveness. Mr McKie refers to the character of the new Labour M.P.s in 1964 and 1966 as young, middle class, well educated and sceptical. Faced with a moral prohibition, their response was likely to be 'Prove it!' Above all, to use a word which, in the sixties, was one of the highest tributes a man could pay to himself, they were 'rational'.

That word 'rational' bids one beware. When we discuss pornography, we shall notice the famous conclusion of the Arts Council working party report, a typical specimen of the high-water mark of 1969 permissiveness. It is argued there, plausibly and entertainingly, that there is *no evidence* that pornography corrupts or degrades anyone, and that therefore there should be no interference with the natural rights which attach to freedom of speech. That sounds rational, until you look into it closely. The real truth is, of course, that evidence of the kind demanded here has never been available for social policies. In other words, it was one thing for John Stuart Mill, a hundred years earlier, to insist that there should be no interference with freedom unless damage would result to others. It is quite another, with the coming of the social sciences, to insist that there must be *scientific proof* that this damage would ensue. Throughout the sixties, a rational policy could seem to mean a policy based on scientific evidence. By the end of the decade, it was beginning to be realised that, in the world of social reform, there was here a misleading analogy.

In an article in *Socialist Commentary* in February 1973, a writer under the nom-de-plume of 'Catalpa' put the McKie standpoint more crudely. He started with an attack on Mr Ross McWhirter for trying to secure the banning of a television film about Andy Warhol. He went on to argue at some length that the Left and more particularly the Labour Party had promoted all the significant reforms in the direction of cultural freedom and that the Right had done their best to stop them. He avoided, incidentally, mentioning our Pornography Report and dismissed me as a lone eccentric. Among the cultural reforms which have either been carried out already under the left-wing pressure (or soon would be), he mentioned the Race Relations Act, equal treatment for men and women, the abolition of hanging, and the reform of the laws relating to homosexuality. (Personally I was active in the latter two reforms and I was, and am, strongly in favour of anti-racial measures and complete equality for women.) 'Catalpa' then proceeds to place on the same footing of liberal merit, the Obscene Publications Act of 1959, the Abortion and Divorce Law Reforms, and all attempts to make contraceptives available to everyone.

Most of us would agree that not a few of these measures have been part of a movement towards the so-called permissive society. I have said several times, before and after I got caught up in the pornography debate, that I am neither for nor against a permissive society. I have often said that I am *in favour* of the permissive society if it involves a more humane attitude to prisoners, drug addicts, unmarried mothers, and other outcasts. I insist that I am utterly *against it* if it involves a lowering of moral standards, whether in sexual or other fields. But this second proposition can be resolved into several others. One may have in mind a relaxation of the criminal law in its relation to moral conduct. One may have in mind a relaxation of social pressures on those who relax their moral standards, or one may have in mind a falling away of moral standards, by which I mean here a departure from Christian principles.

The difference between the second and third points is surely palpable. A parent today may be no more in favour of pre-marital fornication than in past years and yet be less ready than of old to condemn a child who indulges in it. But it is one thing to say that this is a *non-judgmental* age, which I believe to be relatively true. It is another thing, which is also relatively true, to say that there is a good deal more pre-marital fornication than there used to be and a good deal more sexual promiscuity. The two points are separate. Yet they are surely in some way connected with each other and with a third one - the much greater freedom of discussion of sexual matters now prevalent. I would not like it to be thought that I altogether regret this last phenomenon.

Any one of us is at liberty to place the start of the modern trend of permissiveness where he chooses. Personally, I find a turning-point in the publication of the Wolfenden Report in 1957, more particularly in its conclusion that homosexual conduct between consenting adults should no longer be a criminal offence. A decade later that reform, as we are all aware, passed on to the statute book through the initiative of Lord Arran, Mr Leo Abse, and many others. When the Wolfenden Report first appeared, the House of Commons didn't dare debate it. I initiated a debate in the Lords in which I indicated my clear support for the proposal in question. I believe that I was called by Lord Boothby, 'the non-playing captain of the homosexual team', but at that time I certainly did not venture to test the issue by a vote. I call the Wolfenden Report a turning-point, not so much because of the particular recommendations on homosexuality, but because of the principle which it laid down, and on which it based its individual conclusions. I will quote the key passage from the Wolfenden Report of 1957:

The function of the criminal law, in so far as it concerns the subject of this Inquiry, is to preserve public order and decency, to protect the citizen from what is offensive and injurious, and to provide sufficient safeguards against exploitation and corruption of others, particularly those who are specially vulnerable because they are young, weak in body or in mind, inexperienced, or in a state of special physical, official or economic dependence. It is not, in our view, the function of the law to intervene in the private lives of citizens, or to seek to enforce any particular pattern of behaviour further than is necessary to carry out the purposes we have outlined.

I simplified the point of view of the committee in these words of my own: 'If someone is doing wrong, the law must not intervene to stop him or her, unless they are harming someone else.'

In 1957 I went on to ask: 'Can we accept this doctrine, that is to say, the doctrine that the law must not intervene to stop someone who is doing wrong, unless he or she is harming someone else? By and large,' I said, 'though it is for each Member of the House to decide for himself, I think we can.' I gave a reason in words, which as far as they go, I would not try to improve on today. I said that I was not arguing that it would be morally wrong for the State to intervene in all cases to protect people from themselves, or their friendly associates. I was arguing that, from long experience, it had been found as a general rule that that could not be done without interfering with private life and human liberty so drastically as to undermine the whole growth of moral responsibility.

What has been the agreed contention behind the ten years of successful agitation for the removal of the criminal sanction on homosexual conduct between consenting adults? Basically, it has been the argument that I have just set out. It has not been, at any rate on the face of it, a new argument about the morality or immorality of homosexuality as such. That is still condemned by society as a whole as sinful, or immoral, or anti-social, or whatever words one likes to use. It is probably not quite so much condemned as it was, in view of our greater understanding of its causes and, at this point, it is rather difficult to keep away from my third heading, a greater leniency towards offenders. (I am glad that I ended my 1957 speech with an adaptation of some words from Ruskin: 'Let us be merciful while we still have mercy.') Basically, however, I would submit that the major change in the last ten or twelve years in this field has not been due to acceptance of homosexuality. It has been due far more to increasing acceptance of the Wolfenden principle that the law must not step in merely to prevent grown-up people from hurting themselves.

Then came abortion. I am not concerned here with the merits or demerits of abortion which, in fact, I detest: I am simply using it to illustrate the concept of permissiveness. On the face of it, one might argue that it stood on the same footing as the Wolfenden amendment. But I would point out two distinctions between the Abortion and the Homosexual Bills.

An act of abortion does, after all, involve someone else in addition to the woman who secures it. There is the unborn child or, as it can technically be called, the foetus. I realise that those who support abortion wholeheartedly do not pay a great deal of attention to this consideration. However, the logical distinction between abortion reform and homosexual reform is unmistakable. Again, the movement to legalise many kinds of abortions was a movement that was aimed, by a high proportion of its champions, not just at altering the criminal law, but at altering our whole attitude to abortion, at persuading us to recognise that abortion was far more often the right thing to do than society had previously admitted.

When the nation altered the law about homosexuality, they were not being asked to say that homosexuality between consenting adults was morally right after all. But that is exactly what they were asked to say about abortion under a wide variety of conditions, and they gave an affirmative answer. In this case, very much more clearly than in the homosexual one, the change in the criminal law was intended to indicate our carrying further a change in moral conduct.

Look for a moment, and for purposes of symmetry, at the

Divorce Law Reform which became law in 1969. Divorce Law Reform is not, of course, something new in the last fifteen years. I was election agent for A. P. Herbert in 1935 in the Oxford University election. Divorce Law Reform was perhaps the most striking feature of his programme, and certainly the Act that followed his election facilitated divorce immensely. Some years after 1935 I became a Roman Catholic. I look forward with some apprehension to extra years in purgatory on account of my 1935 activities. What perhaps was most striking in the Act of 1969 was the provision that enabled a guilty party to obtain a divorce after a separation of five years in the shortest case. Strictly speaking, the Wolfenden principle would not be sufficient here to prevail on its own. Suppose X leaves his wife Y and lives for five years with Z and then wishes to divorce Y. It is clear that X and Z are not just like two consenting adults who, in theory at any rate, have no one else to consider. They are, in fact, likely to be damaging Y, the first wife, very seriously.

I said to the House of Lords: 'I acknowledge that in a few cases these provisions for getting rid of an unwanted wife after a few years may, on balance, increase rather than diminish the total happiness. But I would say, with absolute conviction, that in the vast majority of cases these provisions will have a very cruel impact and for that reason I am totally against this Bill.'

In general, the supporters of the Bill took their stand on an argument from liberty and an argument from suffering. They certainly would claim to be moved by both ideas or emotions. They also had, of course, the additional advantage of being able to point out what nonsense the existing law had become. Whatever may be said about Divorce Reform as a whole, I cannot believe that the provision I have just referred to, that is, the right of the guilty partner to 'get shot of' the innocent one after five years, would have been accepted by the nation if the argument had been confined to the balance of suffering. I feel sure that it was the product of a more libertarian age in which we are much less inclined than hitherto to stop people doing what they want to do in the moral sphere. So here again, the change in the criminal law and the change in moral attitudes, both as cause and effect of the legal change, are fairly well mixed up.

*

Most of my ideas on the permissive society were worked out by October 1970 when I gave an address on that subject, one of a series of religious essays which were published afterwards. The date has significance for me because pornography was no more than a peripheral interest, although I had already been disgusted by *Oh! Calcutta!*. I had certainly no plans for a debate, let alone a major inquiry. But what I said at that time still seems to be true when so much dubious water has flowed under the bridges. One aspect, I agree, of the permissive society, or if you prefer the civilised society, is a greater toleration. But I added that the argument for toleration is reinforced by a widespread view that artistic values have a standing of their own which puts them so to speak on an equal footing with moral values. When there is a clash or appearance of a clash between them, there is no reason, we are told, why artistic values should give way. I had forgotten that I had written those prescient words until some time after our pornography report appeared. I have certainly learnt to appreciate their wisdom even though the artistic lobby, in the widest sense, are seldom ready to admit to a dichotomy in quite those terms. What I think I was less aware of was the powerful undercurrent in favour of a looser code of sexual morals which might shelter under the general cry of freedom, but was at least as closely connected with ordinary human frailty. For young people today the temptations to pre-marital sex are far greater than they have ever been in this and other countries, now that contraception has reduced so considerably the risk of untoward consequences. The fact of women's emancipation, of which I remain a fervent supporter, has brought boys and girls together in an intimate relationship a good deal earlier, and this too must be regarded as adding not a little to temptation.

The fundamental propositions of the Wolfenden Report have already been quoted. The insistence that if someone is doing wrong the law must not intervene to stop him unless he is harming someone else is neither Christian nor non-Christian.

Sir John Wolfenden always strikes me as religious in the best practical sense, but his report gave the humanist a chance to break through a good many established positions which Christians had traditionally supported. The movement towards a permissive society gathered momentum until checked, for the time being at least, when James Callaghan, Home Secretary in 1969, turned down bluntly, discourteously it may be thought, the Wootton Report which would have reduced the penalties for possessing cannabis. What he, a Labour Home Secretary, said about the permissive society, amidst the general approval of the House of Commons, seemed to mark the end of an epoch.

He was glad, he said, that his decision against the report had enabled the House to call a halt to the advancing tide of so-called permissiveness. 'I regard it as one of the most un-likeable words that has been invented in recent years. If only we would regard ourselves as a compassionate society, an unselfish society, I would feel prouder of 1969.' The phrase 'permissive society' seemed from about that time to become discredited. It would be premature, however, to assume that the intellectual pressures it represented had spent themselves. Roy Jenkins suggested that what we were looking for was a civilised society, but this phrase in its turn is full of its own ambiguities, if we study it in the words of a disciple like 'Catalpa'. Jim Callaghan's phrase about the compassionate society also used at that time by Harold Wilson seemed to be more widely acceptable. I hope that that proves to be so, but the end is not yet.

From the days of the Wolfenden Report onwards, I was, of course, fully conscious of the difference between crime and sin. Homosexual conduct, though not homosexual feeling, remains wrongful - even though here again to understand all is to forgive all - but the criminal law was not in that case the appropriate means for enforcing morals. To summarise my attitude to the changes carried through, always by private Members' legislation, during the period of the Wilson Government, I was in favour of the Homosexual Law reforms; I passionately supported the abolition of hanging; I was against the Abortion Law reform, touched on earlier, and the reform of the Divorce Laws, with the new and execrable provision that a guilty party can expel an innocent one from the marriage after a lapse of five years. Sitting there in the Cabinet till early 1968 (Divorce Law reform came later), one seemed to be somehow remote from these powerful tides that were carrying the nation forward, here as I think for good, there as I think for ill. Looking back, as one who has written so often about the Christian in politics, I am disappointed that the Christians of all denominations in politics did not come together to discuss these issues from a Christian standpoint.

On the whole, leaving out hanging where the Christian conscience came out firmly and potently, one would say of Christians, very much including Catholics, that they were on the defensive in relation to these problems. Collectively they cannot be said to have been enthusiastic about what was happening. Intellectually they knew that the case for the old-fashioned conventions was not as strong as they used to suppose, but there was an absence of positive alternatives. The clergy looked to the laity and the laity looked to the clergy, and meanwhile bodies like the Abortion Law Reform Society got on with the job and took advantage of an unrivalled opportunity. When Lord Silkin's Abortion Law Reform Bill obtained a second reading in the House of Lords in 1966, the voting was 72 to 8, but the 8 consisted of 7 Roman Catholics and one peer married to a Roman Catholic. After the division, Lord Barrington, whom I barely knew at that time, came across to me and asked me: 'Is it permitted for a heretic to join in?' So far had the idea of resisting abortion become identified with the Catholic minority. Lord Barrington joined in to some purpose. He inspired a movement which produced 500,000 signatures quickly.

Uncertainly and disjointedly the Christians had begun to move.

Pornography (I)

A MORAL IMPERATIVE

'Say not the struggle nought availeth.'
ARTHUR CLOUGH

'Excuse me,' said the taxi-driver, as he dropped me at our flat in Chelsea, 'I can never remember your second name. I know you are Lord Porn, of course, but your other name slips my memory.' A personal sketch in *The Times* three days before our report came out referred to me as having eighteen months before been 'a well-liked, but comparatively obscure, Labour politician', and now a contemporary folk-hero. It is no doubt true that like all but a few politicians I was not well known to the millions. Then I became involved in pornography and my notoriety went forward apace. The time was to come when *Life* magazine could say of me: 'To every Englishman, Francis Aungier Pakenham, the Seventh Earl of Longford, K.G., P.C., is better known as "Lord Porn".' On the day our report came out, I appeared on nine radio and television programmes. By the time these words are read, I may or may not have relapsed into my 'comparative obscurity'. If so, I shall have had a crowded hour, if not of glorious life, at least of unremitting limelight.

I am asked repeatedly how I became so interested in pornography. It is often assumed that it has been a life-long obsession. I am not readily believed if I say that the word never crossed my lips in public until I announced my House of Lords motion for 21st April, 1971. By the time the debate occurred, the interest was building up fast. I had received a thousand letters, nearly all of support, and I felt justified in announcing that I and some of my friends proposed to set up an inquiry. But when I put down the motion originally, I had no idea that it would arouse any more interest than others I had initiated, on prisons, youth, homosexuality, universities, for example.

Oh! Calcutta! (summer 1970) was, I suppose, my decisive moment. I had hitherto given the obscenity debates rather a wide berth. At the time of the *Lady Chatterley* trial, I was approached by the solicitor for the defence, presumably as the kind of liberal who would be only too happy to come forward on the right side. I told him that I would be glad to be lent the book, not then on open sale, if only to refute Elizabeth's criticism that I was too much inclined to condemn controversial works without reading them. I warned him, however, that I would be likely to give evidence for the prosecution rather than for the defence. 'Why so?' he asked. 'Because I'm a Puritan.' He knew the answer to that one. 'But D. H. Lawrence was a Puritan.' 'Ah!' I replied with confidence, 'but not my kind of Puritan.'

Time moved on. The Obscenity Act of 1959 came into being. The theatre censorship was abolished, but I remained on the sidelines, absorbed in many other controversies. I walked out of a play called *America, hurrah!* when a huge four-letter word revealed itself before my petrified gaze, with worse to come, so my companion assured me. But it remained for *Oh! Calcutta!* to leave me with no excuse for continuing to close my eyes. The nationwide controversy, in *The Times* and elsewhere, brought out of his retirement Sir Alan Herbert, President of the Authors' Society, doughtiest of all the champions for literary freedom. In an article in *The Times*, he left me in no doubt that we had entered a new phase and that the old restraints on indecency were in danger of total extinction.

I went to *Oh! Calcutta!* with my son-in-law Hugh Fraser in a spirit of inquiry, but admittedly with my mind more than half made up against it. I left halfway through, having seen more than enough. The organisation of a major debate in the Lords is not as easy or as rapid as it sounds. There has to be considerable support and negotiation before a full day can be obtained, but by 21st April, 1971, the way was clear, and the debate was opened by myself before a crowded Chamber. I rose to call attention to the problem and impending menace of pornography.

I had a good speech ready, though my delivery on these set occasions never satisfies me and tends to become more rigid as I proceed. Today, in spite of all the unforeseen happenings which followed, I could not much improve on the text as a preliminary statement. I had had lots of help. The Home Office enabled me to set out the highly complicated legal position with considerable confidence. Professor Anderson then and in time to come was an indispensable ally. Professor of Oriental Law and Director of Legal Studies at London University, chairman of the House of Laity in the Church of England, father of Hugh Anderson who had been cut off at the outset of his career but left behind him a unique memory, Norman Anderson was not known to me personally before this business began. But Mary Whitehouse and the Reverend Eddie Stride introduced me to him; between us we had evolved the idea of an inquiry. In the event he was to become our vice-chairman and to contribute what many regarded as the most effective chapter of our report.

Every now and then, not as often as I could wish, one hits on a phrase or sentence coming from one knows not where which exactly sums up one's attitude. So it was, mercifully, on this occasion. I was dogmatic, I said, in my conviction that pornography has increased, was increasing and ought to be diminished. I used the same words a hundred times afterwards without apology, but I also said what our critics afterwards found hard to swallow. I was absolutely open-minded as to *how* the diminution of pornography should be effected. I also threw in something which came to my mind after a talk with my daughter Antonia, herself a member of the Arts Council, styling herself a neutral in our controversy. 'Most people,' I said, 'dislike pornography; but they also dislike censorship.' The problem was how to curtail the first without extending the second. With those words I can fairly claim to have grasped and stated the essential problem from the opening moments.

I have been told interminably since that I 'made up my mind' before our inquiry began. Let me deal with this once and for all. After sixty-five years on the planet, I was sure that pornography was harmful before I spoke in the Lords. Incidentally, I had already studied by that time the work of the American Commission. But I was anything but sure what ought to be done about it. When Lord Beveridge undertook his most famous inquiry, he was sure that 'Want' ought to be abolished. When our committee at Harold Wilson's request inquired into crime in 1963/4, we were sure that crime was anti-social beyond question. No social investigation has ever borne fruit in action without some pre-suppositions. Some of our committee turned out to be more hawk-like than I was, some more dove-like. A ready-made opposition existed, basing themselves on the report of the Arts Council Working Party of 1969. This had concluded in effect that there was no reason to think that obscene publications did any harm and that all restrictions on them should therefore be eliminated. Already by the time of the debate, Ben Levy, the gifted playwright who was credited with the authorship of that report, had sharply criticised me on the 'World at One' programme. He had belittled me in friendly fashion as a representative of a minority (R.C.) of a minority (Christian). At the end of the debate in the Lords, which side had more cause for satisfaction? Probably, but not certainly, ours, and that mainly because we had got our blow in first, rather than by reason of any superiority in debate. The actual exchanges produced hard and level slogging.

The first Government spokesman, Lord Eccles, welcomed our inquiry, and Lord Beswick, the Chief Labour Whip and official Party spokesman for the day, showed plenty of sympathy. Numerically the majority of the speakers favoured our side, but the sponsors of a broad motion can usually rely on that happening. Arnold Goodman, Jennie Lee, Dora Gaitskell and Ted Willis spoke vehemently against us. It was clear that large numbers of 'communicators' would be bitterly hostile. As night fell on my final words, a sharper criticism of sexual promiscuity than anything I had said earlier, it was very much 'all to play for'.

At almost the precise moment that I had emerged as an anti-pornographer, Dr Martin Cole swam into the news as my antithesis. Whether this was pure coincidence can be disputed. Perhaps our joint notoriety represented the inevitable collision about this time of two irreconcilable tendencies. His film *Growing Up*, in which a young woman teacher performs an act of masturbation, and sex relations for children are treated favourably, was being shown to various audiences and offered to Education Committees. I had walked out of it myself a few days earlier. I said some unpleasant things about the film during my opening speech in the Lords. All this belonged to the atmosphere of that over-charged moment.

I announced in my speech that I and a few friends proposed to set up an inquiry into pornography, unless the Government intended to institute one of their own. I could not, and did not, expect the latter occurrence. I was highly satisfied with the welcome that Lord Eccles extended to our project. At that moment, as I wrote later in the preface to our report, I did not know where sixpence was coming from. I had a hunch from the multitude of friendly letters that enough could probably be scraped together to make some small investigation feasible. But in the event, the six thousand pounds so generously provided by the Dulverton Trust dropped on us out of the sky. The idea of an inquiry had everything to recommend it. Without it no sensible programme could be drawn up by ourselves or, for that matter, by the Government. In Britain, the subject had never been explored on any governmental or systematic academic level. (The Arts Council Working Party document was a slender, brilliantly written *jeu d'esprit.*) Assuming that the Government were not going to do the job themselves, it was our imperative duty to go ahead as best we might. In the situation of 1972, steps to deal with pornography could not wait indefinitely. A time limit of a year or so seemed, and still seems, about right for an inquiry. Academic research in the strict sense would, of course, take very much longer. It could indeed continue for years without positive conclusions. I have never called ours a scientific inquiry any more than Government inquiries, those of Beveridge, Wolfenden and Robbins, for example, deserve the name of scientific. I would claim with confidence that we were well equipped as a group to collect and evaluate the existing evidence and point the practical moral.

When the committee was formed we could easily demonstrate that it included respected and eminent members of the relevant disciplines: the churches, the law, medicine, psychology (a psychiatrist and a psychoanalyst), the arts, communications, education, business, youth - nine members under 30 - surely a record! Norman Anderson, our vice-chairman, brought in a number of outstanding members, including Sir Frederick Catherwood our experienced and incisive treasurer, and Lord Justice Edmund Davies, who played a decisive part in our legal sub-committee.

Our staff was small, but very efficient. From beginning to end, my own private secretary, Gwen Keeble, was closer to me than anyone else. Fred Catherwood discovered an organising secretary in Patricia Winter, an extraordinary find as it proved. Though still under 30, she had already worked in Africa and done Christian counselling in universities at home for several years. Somewhat later, Antonia put me in touch with Marigold Johnson, whom we came to refer to as 'our Scribe'. Except where there was clear evidence to the contrary, as with the signed articles and reports, the actual drafting can be attributed to her skilful and sophisticated pen.

Our terms of reference when eventually drawn up were these: To see how the problem of pornography could be tackled in a manner acceptable to public opinion. The only explicit assumption in the committee's mandate was that pornography was a problem which ought to be tackled. It was a deliberate act that we did not invite anyone who did not believe that pornography was a problem at all, whether a pornographer or an extreme radical. I have no reason, however, to suppose that such people would have agreed to serve under my chairmanship if asked. Any evidence was the other way. In some ways we had advantages denied to a Government inquiry. We certainly investigated some matters at first hand from which they would have drawn back, but I am ready to believe that a Government inquiry would have obtained a stronger representation of the arts than was achieved by us. Writers, however, including critics and publishers, showed an edifying readiness to give us evidence. So did the president, secretary and former secretary of the Film Censorship Board, and the directors-general of the BBC and ITA.

The immediate reaction to my announcement of an inquiry somewhat staggered me. Lord Goodman, a man of intuitive sympathies and a delicate touch, ponderously advised me against it, in our own interest it seemed. I could not refrain from asking sarcastically whether the right of carrying out inquiries was now confined to the Government and the Arts Council, of which he was then chairman. (*The Times* was later to treat their inquiry as private, in the same sense as ours.) Two days later, Arnold Goodman sent me a most generous letter on my being given a notable honour. Others were not quite so broad-minded. Certain journalists let out what can only be called a snarl of baffled rage, as though I had in some mysterious way broken unwritten rules of controversy.

When the committee was announced but not even set up, the *New Statesman* devoted a leading article to us entitled 'Full Frontal Hypocrisy'. A talented writer in the *Guardian* was still more offensive. Some liberal opinion became rather shame-faced at this illiberalism in its cruder form, but the antagonism to the inquiry in many intellectual quarters was based on deep-rooted emotion. The members were at first treated as stooges of mine. When I demonstrated that I did not know more than half of them previously, the contention persisted that they thought the same as I did on essentials and would inevitably reach the same kind of conclusion as myself.

And so we plunged forward into the unknown. No one had ever done anything quite like this before, but I had had an experience of inquiries which no one in politics could equal. Three years as Lord Beveridge's personal assistant; two years looking into the causes of crime for the Nuffield Foundation; presiding over a committee on the prevention and treatment of crime set up by Harold Wilson in 1963, and the committee set up by Justice on compensation for victims of violence. Nor was that all. Incidentally, these rather striking qualifications of mine were never mentioned as far as I am aware in the Press. From beginning to end, the scale of the publicity out-distanced all expectations of myself and others. Early in the day I was interviewed in major broadcasting programmes by William Hardcastle ('World at One' three times in all before and after the debate), by Robin Day on the radio in reply to an hour's questions from the general public, and by Robert Kee, assisted by Jill Tweedie, Michael Parkinson and the Reverend Trevor Beetson. 'Why does Robert Kee dislike you so?' I was asked afterwards. But in fact we have been very good friends for years.

At the end of the programme he said to me with relish, 'A discussion with you is like a very fast game of tennis.' Either Jill Tweedie or Michael Parkinson pressed me as to whether I was always against oral sex. I can't remember exactly what I said, but the legend started at that time that I did not know what it was. I should doubt whether I suffered damage. A radio programme under Robert McKenzie was built up round me, as was a Jimmy Savile programme for a large audience which included stalwart supporters from the Festival of Light but also representatives of lurid publications. I was delighted that Jimmy Savile joined our committee. I only wish that we could have included his comment when he signed the report: 'The ways of man get more and more complicated. Jimmy Savile finds it simpler to follow the ways of God.' He lives up to his words, an idol of the public, who works most of the time as a porter in a Leeds Hospital or in Broadmoor.

I was featured in the *Evening Standard* as 'British worthy No. 4', my predecessors being the Duke of Norfolk, the Archbishop of Canterbury, and Mick Jagger. I was interviewed times without number and was chosen by the *Sunday Times* as the most caricatured figure of 1972. The impetus was never altogether lost during the following year. Some weeks after the report came out, I was one of two speakers at a huge Savoy luncheon on behalf of the selected 'Men of the Year'. The theme was courage and achievement. Naturally I disclaimed anything of either except the achievement of notoriety. But the episode rounded off a period (spring 1971-autumn 1972) in which for the first and last time I became indubitably well known to the general public. My citation as a 'Man of the Year' referred to me as Crusader Extraordinary. I have to accept the fact that my notoriety, favourable or otherwise, is based on the conviction widespread among friends and foes alike that I was leading a campaign against pornography. One should be, and in a sense I am, profoundly honoured by such a label, but I seek to turn it aside or play it down. If I *had* been leading a campaign I hope that I would have been a far more active and ingenious champion. As it was, we had no campaign staff whatever. Certainly no public relations officer or agent. I never took an initiative in seeking to arrange articles or interviews with the media. On one occasion I did protest to the *Sunday Times* about their flippant coverage of our exertions. An article for them resulted – almost the only article I wrote during this time. I addressed plenty of meetings but never at my own suggestion. If I had described myself as leading a campaign, I could rightly have been denounced as an impostor.

But apart from much local protest, there *were* two campaigns of national significance, whose primary assault during this period was levelled at pornography, although their aims are wider and deeper. Both as I write continue and flourish strongly – the Festival of Light aspires to bring Jesus Christ into all our activities, public and private, its members mostly young, its leadership wise and self-effacing, its spirit inspirationalist and ardent. Mary Whitehouse, founder and general secretary of The National Viewers' & Listeners' Association, is passionately concerned with the whole quality of broadcasting. She is by now, after much ridicule and contemptuous treatment, well established in the national life as a moral force. An extract from her diary, quoted in her book, is more revealing than anything she has said in public.

One of the hardest things for me just now is to accept how the strain of the battle is showing in my face and telling on my health. I suppose I've aged ten years in the last three and particularly during the last weeks.

This is the Cross – to realise there is no glamour, no appreciation to be asked or expected, nothing but ridicule, pain and loss. Friendship there is, and love, but even this does not touch the central core of loneliness in a battle of this kind. It is in this loneliness, and in this alone, that one finds Christ. In Him, and in Him alone, not in family or friends, must I seek comfort and sustenance.

The Festival of Light and Mary Whitehouse, on behalf of VALA, acted in complete independence of our committee, though they gave us valuable evidence from outside. More than once I took the opportunity of showing my goodwill towards both movements. In September 1972 I found myself in one of the boats in the armada organised by the Festival of Light on the Thames. The young people were fervently calling the name of Jesus from one boat to another. A senior clergy-

man next to me in our boat commented: 'I am sure that this
appeals to Jesus more than it does to you and me.' Maybe so,
but it *did* appeal to me, and moved me, though it was hardly
'my scene'.

Two days after the debate in the Lords it was announced
that I had been made a Knight of the Garter along with R. A.
Butler and Lord Waldegrave. The cognoscenti were well aware
that there could be no connection between the controversial
debate and the signal honour. Many members of the public
obviously felt that there was and that I had been given this
accolade by my Sovereign for my projected service to national
purity. Certainly apart from the intrinsic glory, the timing was
providential for me. I was about to be subjected to critics who,
to say the least, were going to accuse me of ineptitude and un-
worldliness. The Garter was a clear reminder that I was not
without recognition. And of course a strong boost to my
morale in a stressful period. After the election of 1935, David
(later Lord) Margesson told me that he was overwhelmed with
requests for honours, including peerages. None of the applicants admitted that they were personally interested. 'My dear
David,' they would say, 'I couldn't care less. But it's my wife
who keeps on about it; you know what women are?' At last
David Margesson checked the latest arrival. 'I suppose your
wife insists on it,' he said wearily. 'Good Lord! I don't give a
damn what she wants; I want it for my business.' In the story
at least he was the only one that got an honour. In our case, it
would be hard to say whether Elizabeth or I were more pleased,
and the children were very happy for us. BBC 'Panorama'
wished to film me dressing for the Garter ceremony. I hesitated,
not feeling that dressing was quite my thing. Elizabeth recalled
that when Wellington heard that he was receiving the Garter,
he asked immediately, 'Which way does it go on? Does it go
over the right shoulder or left?'

For myself as for other Garter Knights, the fact is all important that it lies in the personal gift of the Queen. I am a
staunch monarchist but hardly a rabid one. Yet I have cherished
a particular devotion to the present Queen since I wrote an
article for the *Guardian* after the Coronation, called 'Thoughts
in the Abbey'. I forecast that her special contribution would

be her influence on the side of religion, family life and morals in general. And I have surely been right.

People sometimes ask me, 'Do you know the Queen well?' To that there is only one answer, 'No, I wish I did.' But when I was Colonial Secretary I once had lunch alone with her. I am asked at this point in the recollection, 'Do you mean that there were only one or two secretaries present?' I reply, truly, 'No, quite alone, just the two of us.' But I am not always believed. She had just returned from a visit to the West Indies and was eager to talk over the details with someone equally absorbed. We had, in fact, read the same briefs, supplied by the Colonial Office; we were, if I may say so respectfully, in a situation of fellow students. But she was well ahead after fieldwork on the ground.

The conversation never flagged for a moment. I came away conscious not only of her distinctive charm at close quarters, but of her grasp, her earnestness, her intimate interest in the personalities involved, and her deep concern for the peoples.

Pornography (II)

'STRAIGHT AHEAD, OF COURSE'

It was obvious from the first that some of us would have to visit Denmark. The Arts Council Working Party and other libertarians had made much play with the alleged decline of sex offences in Denmark since the Obscenity Law was liberalised. Mr Gummer, M.P., had already replied effectively in his book on the permissive society. But for us there was only one way to counter the propaganda - to go and see for ourselves. Through the good offices of the Danish Embassy in London, a series of discussions was arranged with, among others, government officials, leaders of the police, and the sociologist Professor Kutchinsky, whose researches were being widely quoted by the libertarian school. Visits were also arranged to pornographic films and (with some difficulty - the Danish Government did not want to be involved) to so-called live shows. Also for good measure to a real-life pornographer: a young man who was supposed to have made a large fortune out of the trade and to be able to lay on the hardest of hard porn, including bestiality if wanted.

Our party of six were not in retrospect an ideal selection - my fault and no one else's. I, as chairman, was clearly a 'must'. Dr Christine Saville was a perfect choice, with her years of medical work in the prison service and more recently among drug addicts, as we knew to our great benefit in New Horizon. So was Perry Worsthorne, deputy editor of the *Sunday Telegraph*, attractive in person, challenging in mind with ready access to discussion on the media. But two out of our six were employed on our staff and not therefore members of our committee. Joan Bourne, an old and dear colleague of mine in social investigations, acted for a while as secretary to our committee till with much relief she handed over to Patricia Winter. Sue Pegden, 21 years old, altogether delightful, selected as a research

assistant out of 200 applicants, came to us on obtaining her
M.A. in social psychology. Later she moved to social work of a
more congenial character. I blame myself for letting her be
exposed to the Press on the Danish visit. One paper took the
opportunity to invent a split between myself and the other
members of the party. Sue was said to be in tears over my
alleged obscurantism. This, I am assured, was pure fiction.
But if anything went wrong there the responsibility was mine
only.

And then there was Gyles Brandreth. Again my responsibility
was unquestionable. I had met Gyles a little earlier when he
was a highly versatile president of the Oxford Union. He had
impressed me considerably, and also Elizabeth, who had joined
him in a television programme. Mary Whitehouse called my
attention to an excellent article of his in the *Manchester Evening
News*, on our kind of topic. We were admittedly anxious that
for reasons of the public attitude, but not for those only, we
should include our share of bright young people. The 40-year-
old phrase seemed to have been coined for Gyles's benefit. On
the face of it his appointment to our committee, and still more
to our little Denmark party, was to prove disastrous. In due
course he wrote an article about the visit in *Nova*, basing himself on his confidential knowledge in defiance of all known
conventions and guying us pretty thoroughly. This led to his
membership of the committee being terminated. The committee who, by implication in his article, were referred to as
old bores could hardly be expected to retain him in their midst.

But there is another side of the story. We were initially
pilloried as a monolithic junta, everyone supposedly sub-
servient to me, or at least thinking exactly as I did. By the time
we had returned from Denmark our opponents were peddling
the alternative line that we were at loggerheads with one
another and in a state of disintegration. This description was
rather easier to disprove than the monolithic fable, and in
that sense the air of public independence assumed by Gyles
may have helped rather than otherwise. He continued to the
end to treat me as a holy fool but one who curiously enough
possessed sufficient devilish cunning to get his own way all too
often on the committee. I never fail to enjoy his company. I

realise that at this stage of his life his desired image could hardly be reconciled with my kind of purpose or with that of the rest of the committee, but I shall always follow his career with unusual interest.

When we reached the aeroplane to take us to Copenhagen, we found that representatives of nearly all the national Press were coming too. I had said beforehand that it was not for me to stop anyone coming. This was treated as a warm invitation. If I had known just how much excitement our trip would arouse, I might have been less cordial. But it might not have made much difference. The BBC were already awaiting us in force in Copenhagen without any suggestion from me. (Incidentally, they were invaluable in unearthing the 'hot spots' to be visited.) The ITA and the *Daily Express* discovered rather late that news was being made in Copenhagen and hastily dispatched their representatives to the scene of the action.

What did the visit amount to on a sober view, if such a phrase can be applied in the circumstances? The official talks were thoroughly worthwhile. A full interpretation of the facts could not be arrived at by letter. In our report we concluded that the Danish experience could not honestly be used in the present state of knowledge either on behalf of those who wished to strengthen the controls on pornography or of those who wished to remove them. In England one would not take the movement of sex crimes as much of an indication of the moral effect of pornography. But in Denmark alleged developments of this kind had been clutched at eagerly by the libertarians. In fact, the official figures showed that on paper sex crimes have been dropping throughout the sixties and the largest drop occurred in the year before the first of the new laws came into force. The deputy chief of police cast grave doubts on the reality of the figures, in view of the growing disinclination to report sexual offences. He much doubted whether there had been, in fact, any decline in sex crimes at all. In a negative sense, therefore, we had exposed the flimsiness of an argument on which much reliance had been placed in the preceding two or three years by those who wished to sweep away the existing controls on pornography.

But it was none of these discussions, conducted in any case

in private, which aroused the intense publicity and associated my name it seems for all time with Copenhagen. 'Aren't you the chap who went to the Continent?' a taxi-driver asked me a year later, as though, for a good Britisher, 'the Continent' was still unspeakably dangerous. About the same time I was asked as I waited in the London Airport lounge, 'Off to Copenhagen, I suppose?' as though it was the freshest joke in the world. A stranger in a train, learning from me that I had just paid a visit to Manchester, asked me knowingly, 'Not quite so exciting as your last visit, I imagine!' This again was a good year after Copenhagen.

On the first evening after dinner we split up into three parties. Joan and Perry, Gyles and Sue, Christine and I. Christine and I found ourselves, after £7 or so per head had changed hands at the door, in a smallish club room, very full, but even so containing no more than fifty persons. When we entered, a stout red-faced man, trousers undone, was lying prone on a small stage being stimulated in one way or another by a nice-looking blonde young woman. The fact that the whole operation ended in failure was treated as a particular reason for uproarious merriment. It became immediately obvious that what was required was audience participation. This was something I had not bargained for. I am not quite sure what disgusted me most. In a sense the audience were almost more horrifying than the performers. To join in 'the fun' even by remaining there at all seemed to be sharing the humiliation to which the girl was subjected. The fact that she appeared not to realise her own degradation increased rather than diminished one's sense of revulsion from those who had brought her to this.

There are occasions in life when there are no hesitations about action at the time and none afterwards. This was such a one. I was moving out of the room before anyone quite knew that I was going. A small plump man, some form of manager, no doubt, expostulated with restraining hands misunderstanding my grievance. 'But you haven't seen any intercourse yet - I assure you it's coming,' he moaned plaintively. I was too upset to show him a reasonable civility.

The Times and *Telegraph* correspondents were quick to catch

He stands breast-high amid the alien porn
And notes excesses in his pocket diary.
Let Soho tremble. A purer day will dorn.
Longford the backlash has opened his inquiary.

Drawings by Dominic Poelsma, words by Angus McGill, from the *Evening Standard*

Top right and right:
Pocket cartoons by Osbert Lancaster from the *Daily Express*

SOME OF THE MEMBERS OF THE
LONGFORD COMMITTEE ON PORNOGRAPHY
Left to right, standing: Guinevere Tilney, Dr Dorothy Berridge,
Jeremy Murray-Brown, Martin Hughes, Professor Headlam-Morley,
Mary Miles, Sara Binney, Canon Sydney Evans, Lord Justice Edmund

Davies, the author, Archbishop of York, Richard Davies, Professor
Norman Anderson
Left to right, seated: Peregrine Worsthorne, Kingsley Amis, Elizabeth
Jane Howard, Dr Peter Scott, Dr Francis Camps, Sir Frederick
Catherwood, Bishop of Leicester, Sir Robert Lusty

A new beginning

up with me. 'I've seen enough for science and more than enough for enjoyment,' was my immediate summary of impressions. *Life* magazine later referred to this as one of the great British understatements. I still feel that it covered in a few words one or two necessary angles. The thought of my old master, Lord Beveridge, was never far from my mind. I persuade myself that he would have liked my statement.

On to another club where the scene was brighter and more excited. Here we were clearly expected, which was not the case at the earlier establishment. This time we found ourselves in a very prominent and exposed position - in a ringside seat round a small dancing-floor on which the performers cut their capers. Newspapers, cameras and television were this time much in evidence. The well-known expression so often heard at political meetings - the eyes of the world are upon us - was this time close to the truth. A tall rangy dynamic female, completely nude, soon emerged brandishing a whip which she offered to anyone who might wish to use it on her. One gentleman, who might charitably be described as paunchy, stepped forward goggling, accepted the loan of the whip and used it with uncertain strokes on her naked behind. His exertions commanded little applause and with no one following his example the lady adopted a new tactic of approach. Turning her whip into a kind of loop, she passed along our front row inviting any response that occurred to us. Christine Saville can look very sweet, but also very chilly. She now surveyed the performing female through her horn-topped glasses in a manner that could have mesmerised a stoat. I through my gold rims could only gape nervously. The lady took my measure. She strung the loop whip round my neck, vibrating me for a few seconds that seemed like minutes. Then as quickly withdrew it and passed to the next in line.

Expectancy was in the air; the demand for action was growing. I was becoming aware that no action which did not involve me visibly would satisfy. Now the lady was on my neighbour's lap, caressing him indescribably, amidst mounting response from the audience. The cameras were all too obviously getting ready for her next move. But my next move was still more obvious to me. At one moment, as seen through the eyes of one of the many newspapers that depicted the scene, I was sitting there like a stage professor in a house of ill-fame. The next my seat was empty. I had struck for home.

If I am asked why I left the two live shows, I explain it in this way. Both were, of course, utterly horrible, pornographic and unfit to be allowed in any well-conducted city, but I had known, admittedly, that they would deserve such labels before I came. And much the same could be said of a blue film which I visited on the following evening and saw to the end. The real reason for departure in the case of the live shows was that audience participation was required in a fashion totally unforeseen. In a general sense, the audience were joining uproariously in the alleged fun. One felt contaminated by sharing their mood, if only to the extent of sitting unprotestingly among them. But beyond that, it was clear that one would be expected to play an active part in the indecency. It might not have been quite impossible for some members of the audience to tuck themselves away unobserved, but that was out of the question for me, as the much-publicised visiting milord.

In the second live show, self-preservation was added to deep abhorrence. Another half-minute and a naked woman with a whip would have been inextricably linked with me before (ultimately) millions of viewers. Afterwards I was credibly informed that 'she' was in fact a man, but even if I had known that at the time, I would not have felt the danger diminished.

As so often in this part of my story, I do not seek to demonstrate that the course I took was perfect, or even the best in the situation prevailing. Except on the theory that all publicity is good publicity, the publicity I received on return was apparently damaging. The whole episode, and I myself as the central figure, were treated as ridiculous, and not only by those who were our committed opponents, though naturally it was grist to their mill. I was criticised for going to Denmark, for going to the shows and for walking out of them after a relatively short inspection. It was observed that my colleagues on the trip stayed to the end. This exaggerated any difference that there might be between us and at one moment raised

hopes in hostile breasts that we might be washed away al-
together in a mixture of absurdity and mutual recrimination.
It may well be described as the worst moment of the inquiry.
Yet in retrospect I cannot regret the total happening.

From then on the existence of our inquiry was known
throughout the length and breadth of the land. *The Times*, in
a most helpful leading article on our return, seemed, curiously
enough, to take us seriously for the first time. The Danes
shared the ridicule heaped on us and did not relish it.

A year later the *Daily Telegraph* headed an article from
Copenhagen: 'Danes curb Sex Clubs after Longford visit.'
According to the article: 'The visit of Lord Longford and his
committee investigating pornography and his walk-out from
a performance in one of the clubs received widespread publicity
in Denmark. Many Danes were angry that Copenhagen had
become known as the "porn capital of Europe".' The article
concluded: 'The Earl of Longford's visit to Denmark has led
to the closing of all but a handful of Copenhagen's sex clubs.'
Since then, I gather, some of the worst offenders have started
up again, but something at least was achieved.

Above all, I was grateful in my heart for the unrivalled
chance to offer testimony. I had been given strength to confront
evil and to repudiate it before the eyes of all. Up till then I
was never far from the innuendo that I was actually enjoying
the pornography I affected to detest. Once and for all, I felt
that I had nailed that falsehood in every honest mind.

The argument that if I were a really scientific investigator
I would have stayed on, would have had more point if a study
of live shows had been a main part of our purpose. But in fact
it was always peripheral or incidental. The real object of the
visit was to take part in discussions on the spot with experts.
In any case, the live shows themselves were so far beyond
anything that would be tolerated in this country that detailed
investigation would not have added any relevant knowledge.
As it was, I saw 'enough for science' and testified as only once
or twice in my lifetime to an irrepressible conviction.

*

The next year was spent on three overlapping processes: the

collection of evidence, the discussions in the full committee and the sub-committees, and the writing of the report.

The report was so completely *sui generis* that it is difficult to pass a comparative verdict. Of one or two things I am certain. In the time available it was impossible to conduct any systematic studies which would have passed in academic circles for research. No Government inquiry would have attempted research of that kind if we can take the Wolfenden Report as a fair example. When we began, I was under the impression that a good deal of research had already been carried out. But this proved quite wrong in regard to pornography, although violence had been academically studied for some time, without positive conclusions. Dr Peter Scott, our psychiatrist, wisely insisted that existing research should at least be described, even if the conclusions were not significant. It was well that this step was taken. Our critics would otherwise have leapt forward to say that we had not even studied what research there was.

We were indeed fortunate to find a research psychologist in Mr Yaffé to summarise and interpret the research that had been done, for the most part recently in America. One was not surprised by the time he had supplied his contribution to find that scientifically it was still an open question whether pornography did, or did not, do harm. It would, of course, be totally wrong, though even Lord Shackleton fell into this error in the House of Lords, to treat the scientific evidence as demonstrating that pornography in fact was harmless.

I may have been less surprised than most by the impotence of social science to produce coercive proofs from my experience in investigating the causes of crime for the Nuffield Foundation in the early 1950s. To mention only one appalling difficulty in tracing the influence of pornography: the cases where its influence could be isolated from other social factors were always bound to be few. We made use of an expert market research firm, but even if we had had more money and they had had more time, it never seemed they would get very far. If one can judge by the subsequent Lords' debate of November 1972, there seems no readiness on the part of the Government, or anyone on any side of the argument, to claim that a few more months, or a few more years, of well-endowed research would be likely to demonstrate in any scientific sense the harmfulness or innocuousness of pornography.

A larger and more official inquiry would probably have collected a greater number of individual cases of pornographic influence. We published some of those we received, but however many had been collected and published those who refuse to believe in the evils of pornography would never have accepted them as representative. A fair-minded person reading our report must concede that pornography *sometimes* does harm. How *often* it does harm and how *much* harm it does, and what *kind* of harm is done by particular kinds of pornography remain questions which are never likely to be finally disposed of. From the angle of practical policy they have, I believe, been much clarified by our exertions.

So, I hope, has the general character of the trade in pornography, where my old friend Matthew Oliver, a private detective, dug out all sorts of interesting things. The *People* demonstrated in a matter of this kind that a group of journalists can move more rapidly than one or two research workers. In this area we could have thrown a good deal more light on the murkier places with more help at our disposal, but the outcome would hardly have affected the argument.

We were criticised repeatedly, often unfairly but sometimes plausibly, about the composition of our committee. No one, as far as I am aware, attacked us for not casting our net wide enough in inviting evidence. I sympathised with the Marriage Guidance Council in feeling that we gave them and others an impossibly short time to complete our very thorough questionnaire. But subsequent experience suggested that the time factor did not make much difference to the value of the answers. It was hardly to be expected that various national organisations would have time to produce representative answers, but I am sure in my own mind that composite answers of that sort would not have amounted to much in practice.

The Arts Council Working Party had ceased to exist, but we received full evidence, written and oral, from the chairman, John Montgomery, and other leading members of the committee.

Inevitably questions to witnesses took on a fairly monotonous if logical pattern. If anyone told us, as quite a few did, that pornography did no harm, one naturally asked whether they believed that it should be made freely available to young persons and children, and in almost every case they said they did not. One pressed them naturally on their attitude to racial and anti-semitic propaganda; if they really believed in complete freedom of speech; were they or were they not prepared for unlimited propaganda of this kind, and where did they stand on violence? Many liberals are not unfriendly to sexual irregularities, but they rightly detest violence. Were our witnesses therefore ready to interfere with violent films, for example? On a different tack, if they disputed the moral *damage* done by pornography, they would surely not question the *offence* caused? Even in Denmark, still referred to, though decreasingly, as a libertarian Mecca, there are laws against offensive display. (The sale of pornography to children is also illegal.) How far were they ready for similar restrictions here? It would be broadly true to say that everyone drew the line somewhere, or for certain purposes. Even George Melly, who had stoutly defended *Oz* in court, was ready to maintain protection for children.

Perhaps our most extreme witness, and one of the most attractive personally, was Richard Neville. The trial of *Oz* was in many minds that autumn. Richard Neville had become something of a Dreyfus in quite a few enlightened quarters. Unlike almost all the other witnesses, he came flat out against the family. Somehow when he told us that he loved his father and mother, one hoped that his iconoclasm would not be lifelong. Inevitably no one who saw nothing wrong in sexual promiscuity could attach much importance to the notion of sexual corruption. But some of our witnesses did not wish this side of the argument to be pressed too hard, and one had to respect their position. Richard Neville appeared at first sight to have few such inhibitions, and indeed he could hardly have defended any such without repudiating past pronouncements. When confronted, however, with the ultimate question, whether he would like to see any moral check of any kind on promiscuity, he coined - perhaps not quite seriously - the phrase 'responsible promiscuity', which he claimed to stand for. After the discussions, he and a charming girl-friend came to lunch with Elizabeth and myself. The proprietor thanked him deadpan 'for all you are doing for us, sir'. For once Richard looked thoroughly nonplussed.

Pornography (III)

QUESTIONS AND ANSWERS

So much for our general approach to the evidence. Now for
rather more detail, though I can only mention a fraction of
those who helped us. We sent out a questionnaire to a large
number of organisations, religious, social and educational. The
public brought or sent enough to stock an extensive library,
which we kept under lock and key. This proved to be useful
when we were trying to discover where, if at all, one of our
witnesses proposed to draw any legal line. It was also invariably
an unpleasant eye-opener to serious inquirers who might have
pooh-poohed our concern. One of those who asked to see what
we were worried about was Mary Stott, the distinguished
Guardian writer. She at once wrote an article describing the
'wave of anger' and 'strong degree of repulsion' she had felt
when actually confronted with some of the hard porn that
had come into our hands.

Some of my colleagues, hardened by years in the courts,
were nevertheless shaken by the levels of sadistic and bestial
propaganda to which much of the stuff sold under the counter -
mostly imported from Scandinavia, West Germany or the
USA - had recently descended. A particularly hideous collection, for instance, was brought in by the psychiatrist who had
been called in to help some teenage boys at a boarding-school;
the headmaster had discovered a sales and protection network,
involving forced participation by 11-year-old new boys in various brutal and obscene practices, imitated from photographs.
Several had become seriously disturbed before the matter came
to light. In this, as in many other cases, it was of course necessary that the source of the evidence should remain entirely
confidential, and I was - not for the first time in my life - the
recipient of distressing personal case histories which had to
remain anonymous.

We spent a lot of time dealing with an enormous correspondence simply expressing concern, or volunteering personal
experiences with, for instance, unsolicited mail. It was equally
important, however, to find out the views of as many as
possible of those who were influential in the media or who had
professional experience of that unenviable task, 'drawing the
line'. We had to be arbitrary in some of these invitations,
because our time was limited. Even when we had set up sub-
committees for different areas, we were still faced with the
knowledge that some ground would be inadequately covered –
I regret, for instance, that we were unable to hear the views of
painters on whether, like so many writers, they are conscious
of commercial pressures to use pornographic appeal.

There is, of course, a fundamental problem in collecting the
views of a large number of individuals on a subject many see
as solely a matter of private morality: there is unlikely to be a
consensus on any collective action by society, because most
people are quite simply horrified at the thought of being called
priggish. One of the leaders of the national Press said precisely
this. Yet he and most of his colleagues were emphatic that they
would certainly apply a moral censorship to what was to appear
under their own imprint. They could not afford to shock
readers and, in most cases, they believed in the citizen's right
not to be confronted with offensive material. Regrettably I am
under an obligation not to reveal the contents of our discussions. Suffice it to say that, of those we saw, Michael Hartwell was the most discreet; Vere Harmsworth the most genial;
William Rees-Mogg the readiest to listen; Harold Evans the
most concerned with our actual task; David Astor the most
interested in the philosophical issues; Rupert Murdoch the
most surprising, and Max Aitken the most surprised by what
we told him of Rupert Murdoch's evidence. The editor of the
Guardian answered courteously on paper.

Obviously we had to see what those who were responsible
for publications that might cause legal or social offence felt
about the matter. I was not surprised to find that no one liked
being described as a pornographer – except, perhaps, for two
young men, now out of business, I understand, who seemed
proud of their mail order operations, although they were

eventually faced with more than fifty summonses. Many people we talked to who were enthusiastically involved in what might be called the sex trade were ready, when shown an example of someone else's product, to draw a line which often seemed to me curiously irrational. Paul Raymond, for example, told us he considered his magazines provided 'simple enjoyment at the sight of beautiful women'; he did not agree with publications such as *Forum*, because they were putting across value-judgments in the shape of sex education.

But the charming young editor of *In Depth* - first to follow the *Forum* idea - seemed sincerely convinced that she was helping lonely and ignorant people, some of them prisoners, who wrote for advice. She told me she had once intended to become a nun, and was very worried by an impending prosecution against her magazine. I ventured to hope she would soon put her obvious talents to other use. The publishers of *In Depth*, Ralph and David Gold, came for a consultation. They told us they believed so strongly in the help given by *In Depth* that it was now being subsidised by their successful range of children's books. I asked why they did not restrict their distribution to this innocuous and profitable field, but was told that retailers preferred 'a wide range'. They strongly disapproved - as did nearly everyone involved in this field - of displaying even 'soft porn' to attract children. They would welcome, they told us, some form of vetting board to tell them what went too far and some means of control by retailers to protect them from being pushed into competing with rivals. To them a live show was quite unacceptable, although they were happy to use photographic models for their magazine *New Direction*, which might to some people appear equally objectionable.

The particular hang-ups - as the sexual liberationists would say - continually surprised me: one witness would object to striptease but not to photographic poses, another found the printed article beyond his or her particular moral barrier. It had been suggested that we should try and follow up some of the names mentioned in the *People* series on what is known as the porn trade. Prepared to meet a lady whose career is devoted to promoting nude photographic models, I and my colleagues had not expected the shy frail young woman, looking half her age, entirely alone in her tiny attic office, with the walls papered by blown-up shots of her girls. I commented on one that seemed to me to cater for sadists, and she admitted that the model had very much disliked posing among so many whips and symbols of violence. Over lunch, she told us she had left home at 16 to pose for art students, only to find that Soho photographers were ready to offer more than twice the miserable rate she had been earning, and she had gradually built up her agency to protect the interests of others like herself. She could not understand why nudity could ever be offensive, but was prepared to refuse commissions if she suspected her clients' motives were unprofessional. She did not believe the law or society had any right to 'interfere' with any individual's personal morality or to mix what she saw as business with private lives.

Because so much pornography seemed to us to involve such exploitation of women by reducing them to sex objects, we also decided we should find out the views of some members of various Women's Liberation groups. Here I found that our discussions often came up against the conflict between abhorrence (which I shared) for the way magazines and advertisements commercialise women's sexuality and an equally strong abhorrence for any form of control by law, or by any group such as we were thought to represent, over the individual's freedom. The very mention of censorship was enough to provoke some of these eloquent young women to heated opposition. Some of them thought that advertising and the milder pin-up magazines did more to distort relationships than hard porn.

I think they thought that I and the study group were too much concerned with a mere symptom of society's ills and that control over the spread of pornography would not necessarily improve the status of women. (I have always been on the side of any measure to raise that status.) I remember that when Jill Tweedie, the vivid and talented *Guardian* columnist, came to see us, a lively argument took place between her and Perry Worsthorne - a member of our steering group - in which he maintained that he admired, was even envious of, the feminine role in our society, while Jill maintained that this role had always degraded and exploited women. She was also one of the few witnesses who were not worried by the idea of children being exposed to pornography, and the risk of indecent exposure was to her less disturbing than the traffic in London. In this she would have disagreed with George Steiner, a highly sophisticated and sympathetic figure, who opposed pornography on the grounds that, like indecent exposure, it intruded on personal privacy.

In the film world, many of those professionally involved whom we talked to found the increase of violence and explicit sex on the screen aesthetically and morally repugnant. Bryan Forbes, the film director, told us, for instance, that his wife, the actress Nanette Newman, had felt unable to accept many of the roles offered to her on these grounds. And the pressure on less well-known actresses is now very considerable, as we learned from one member of our committee, James Sharkey, who has first-hand experience as a theatrical and film agent. It was clear from our talks with both the British Board of Film Censors and the chairman of the Greater London Council Film Viewing Committee, Dr Patterson, that the responsibility for deciding what may be shown, and for protecting the young, is increasingly onerous. One or two critics we talked to, such as George Melly of the *Observer* and John Coleman of the *New Statesman*, were in favour of abolishing film censorship, but on the whole I found that most people agreed on society's duty to protect its most vulnerable members from damage. I sometimes wonder whether, as a result of our consultations and friendly arguments, the views of any of those who gave us their time were altered. I feel sure that some at least were startled by the kind of pornography now freely available. Their serious attention may have been focused anew on the true issues involved.

The report was signed on 31st July 1971. It ran to 435 pages with another 75 pages of appendices. No small feat in just over the year, in quantitative terms at least. There were 47 signatures and no minority report. The reservations were neither numerous nor prolonged, though I would not wish to minimise their significance. The only functioning member of the committee who refrained from signing was Eric Fletcher, eminent solicitor and former Labour Minister, although we had his strong support in the crucial legal recommendations and he was a tower of strength in the subsequent debate in the Lords. Eric Fletcher insisted that in seeking to describe pornography we ourselves became unintentionally but effectively pornographic. The difficulty he raised was not taken lightly. We were at great pains, for example, that no four-letter words should appear in our pages. Some of us were not very happy in retrospect about the cover featuring the single word 'pornography' in red but, on balance, we were satisfied that you could not explain to the public what we were talking about without going some way to describe it and that if our report was, in fact, a study of pornography, it would be misleading to describe it as anything else.

We defined pornography as 'that which exploits and which dehumanises sex, so that human beings are treated as things and women in particular as sex objects'. This definition on the whole seemed to provide general satisfaction – at least it encountered little criticism. I would not wish to improve on it now.

The connection between sexual exploitation and violence or, to use a better word, cruelty, was certainly not overlooked in our report. We devoted a special chapter to it, and David Holbrook dealt with it potently in his own contribution. But, looking back, I feel that we could have brought it out still more effectively.

In a sense the hard core of the whole report must be found in the legal proposals and the Draft Bill based on them. They are explained in full in the legal sub-committee's report and confirmed in the general conclusions. It will be appreciated that it was only the general conclusions, some 30 pages or so, for which the committee as a whole were asked to hold themselves responsible.

Briefly, we proposed a new three-pronged attack on pornography:

1. The basic law of obscenity would be totally remodelled. No longer would it be necessary to prove that a production was likely to deprave or corrupt. Instead, one would have to demon-

strate that it outraged contemporary standards of decency or humanity, accepted by the public at large.

It will be realised that not only the exploitation of sex, but also violence and drugs, would be covered by this definition.

2. The statutory defence of 'public good', so much abused recently in our eyes, would be eliminated.
3. The cinema, television and sound broadcasting would be brought within the purview of the Obscene Publications Act, 1959.
4. Penalties would be substantially increased.

That was the first prong. The second would be a new statutory provision for dealing with those who exploit or distribute in a public place material which, while falling short of being obscene, is 'indecent'. This would be the assault on display.

Putting the matter colloquially, one can say that purveyors of 'hard' or 'hard/soft' pornography would be found guilty if they sold it at all. Purveyors of 'soft' pornography if they displayed it in a public place, which in our view would certainly include newsagents and bookstalls.

Thirdly, we put forward a proposal to punish those who exploit performers in any obscene or indecent productions, or as models for photographs or films of a similar kind. This would be a new departure in dealing with obscenity, although not without analogies elsewhere.

In regard to films we not only demanded that the law of obscenity should be extended to cover them, but also that the Film Censorship Board should be drastically restructured to give supremacy to the public interest. Cinema clubs should be brought under much tighter control.

The legal sub-committee was strong by any standards, including a Lord Justice of Appeal, two first-rate academic lawyers, a leading Q.C., Lord Fletcher, already mentioned, Christine Saville (an active member of the New Horizon Council), with long experience of prisons, medicine and drugs, a former Lord Mayor of London - not to mention myself. With as little bitterness as possible, I observe that those who have criticised our report most vehemently have given few signs of having studied the work of the legal sub-committee. Professor Dworkin, in the *Listener*, spoke about our legal recommendations as though they had been drafted by ignorant schoolboys. The actual drafting of our Bill was, in fact, performed by the most distinguished draughtsman in this country.

We dispersed for August while Hodders pushed on rapidly and achieved almost miraculously a publication date of 21st September. I had felt confident by the end of 1971 that we had obtained the kind of evidence, starting with that of the BBC and ITA and the film censorship, that would make it impossible for serious people to ignore us. It was very encouraging quite early in 1972 that Hodders should give us such an excellent contract for producing it as a paperback. Not long after that the *Daily Mail* was ready to pay us £10,000 for serial rights before publication. Personally, left entirely to myself, I would have grabbed the offer before it ran away from us. On the whole, though I am still not quite certain, I think that I would have been wrong. At any rate our steering committee, then and later, was emphatically opposed to giving any one newspaper a preference over any other before the date of publication. They felt sure that such a course would destroy its prospects of really wide publicity, nor was it quite obvious what we would do with the £10,000 in question. We all assumed that we would cease to function as a committee when our work was done - a line that, in fact, we stuck to.

Other offers analogous to that of the *Daily Mail* were firmly turned down for the same reason. I could not, however, be unaware of the BBC's interest. When they discovered that the report was coming out on Thursday they developed the idea of producing a half-hour profile of myself on the Monday. This was manifestly good business for the report and presumably, in some unspecified sense, for me. During the summer Peter Cole, the producer, Francis Hope, Elizabeth's first cousin once removed, and their camera crew interviewed me and photographed me intermittently.

They were naturally anxious to discover as much action as possible in my sedentary existence. Starting from Brendan Behan's definition of an Anglo-Irishman as a Protestant on a horse, they arrived in Ireland and persuaded me to canter round against the background of Tullynally Castle. They succeeded, I hope, in making this operation as little phoney as possible. Two years before I had indeed hunted with the Bally-macad Hounds from Tullynally on Boxing Day. The local paper summed it up in words I am vain enough to reproduce. 'Lord Longford had his first day's hunting for forty years. He took a toss early but gallantly remounted and stayed with hounds all day. A good performance.' The toss on that occasion had occurred at a brook which I assumed, wrongly as it turned out, that my free-jumping Arab mount Salami had refused. On the contrary, after due deliberation she jumped it, leaving me behind. But on this BBC occasion there were no brooks to negotiate and Salami carried me with every consideration for my safety and dignity. Other scenes in the profile took place in New Horizon and round about the porn shops. Also in our small Catholic Church in Hurst Green. I had been rather nervous about the reception of such an idea, but Father Docherty, our parish priest, and the rest of our little com-munity seemed very happy with the way it was handled.

As 21st September drew near, the BBC, Independent Tele-vision and some of the newspapers began to nibble. In fact, however, the first publicity attending me during this period was totally different. By sheer coincidence a major argument developed in the public press about Myra Hindley - with myself figuring in it not a little - a week before our report was due to appear. I was rung up one night about eleven o'clock by the *Daily Express* and told that they had verified the fact that Myra Hindley had been taken for a walk that afternoon by the Governor, Mrs Wing. They had rung me somewhat earlier in the day when I suggested they got the story confirmed. Asked for my comments, I said without hesitation that I had no previous knowledge of it but it sounded an excellent idea. Then they rang off, but I was not left undisturbed for long.

There was a fine old hullabaloo next morning. The *Daily Express* carried a statement from a high official, presumably in the Prison Department, which explicitly approved Mrs Wing's action. But by the time I reached the office, coming up from Bernhurst, I learned that the Home Secretary, Mr Carr, had publicly reprimanded Mrs Wing and, for several days, the topic was front-page news. It was certainly not Fleet Street's finest

hour. No one knew better than myself when they read about
the public outcry in the morning papers that the public would
not have had time to be aware of the issue before the papers
were printed. No doubt the relatives of the tragic victims were
assailed from all quarters; no doubt there was very deep and
understandable public emotion waiting to be stirred up; but
on this occasion it was well and truly stirred up by the Press.

Not long afterwards Mrs Wing told me that she herself had
received 1,000 letters of support for her action, but one does
not remember seeing that alluded to in the newspapers, though
she did not lack defenders.

At the moment I am concerned with the autobiographical
issue. I got a good many letters denouncing me, most of them
too intemperate to be taken seriously, but one or two from
religious people who seemed to me to have a very Old Testament view of their religion. One gentleman, who recalled a
pleasant meeting we had had in the past, wrote as a Catholic
to say that if Myra Hindley were really penitent he would have
thought that she would wish to make expiation by remaining
in solitary confinement for the rest of her life. I ventured to
ring him up and discovered that he did not seriously mean that
at all. On reflection, he regretted writing in that fashion. He had
just felt so angry when he read about my attitude that he dashed
off a violent letter. I often wonder now how many people do
likewise. The Press had managed to create the impression that
I had said that she ought to be released on parole in the immediate future, when I had said no such thing.

There is a point I must make here at the risk of putting it
too crudely. In the week before our report came out I was in
the Garrick Club, to which I had been elected not long before,
and where I still regard myself, and am regarded, as a novice.
A senior member sitting with a group by the fireplace addressed
me consolingly: 'Don't worry,' he said, 'about the Press. We're
most of us on your side. Ninety per cent at least.' And I do not
think he was talking about pornography. In the following week
I sat beside John Calder for about an hour while we waited to
take part in the BBC programme 'Midweek'. On pornography
we were bound to be totally opposed. The Defence of Literature
and Arts' Society, of which he had long been a leading cham-

pion, had issued that morning a scathing attack on our report. That would be our issue when we got into the debate. But for the moment I asked him about his constituency and was interested to hear that he was still confronted with the demand for the return of hanging. There at least, I said to him, we can fight shoulder to shoulder. He replied cordially, 'You would be surprised what nice things the D.L.A.S. were saying about you this morning when they weren't condemning your report.'

The typical libertarian most opposed to the report would also be a penal reformer and sympathetic to what I appear to be trying to do for Myra Hindley. I would like to believe that the typical Christian would be favourable to both my attitudes, while he might regard me as imprudent or ineffective in one case or both. I had at least one letter (and other messages to the same effect) in which a woman actually wrote to ask me to forget her letter of the previous week denouncing me because of Myra Hindley. Now that she had read about our Pornography Report she realised, she said, that I was on the side of the angels and she was sorry that she had written.

A few words may be quoted from a letter received by me from Myra Hindley shortly afterwards. After referring to the 'two happiest and quickest hours' in her life, she went on: 'I can, albeit reluctantly, accept the fact that certain feelings towards me are more or less justified . . . much as I am loth to admit it, I can see the probably sound reasons which motivated the stand taken by Mr Carr . . . From his point of view I expect there was very little else he could have said under the circumstances . . . The only regrets that I have are that I feel wretched about the very unkind publicity which Mrs Wing has had to endure and that such a kind and thoughtful gesture has been so abused and strongly criticised.'

Pornography (IV)

CHEERS AND HISSES

The Press received their advance copies of the report about a week before publication, and whether or not as a result of what they read, there suddenly escalated a flattering interest in me. A long centre-page article was prepared for *The Times* after I had been interviewed more than once by Geoffrey Wansell. Similar features were arranged for the *Daily Express* and *Daily Mirror* after interviews with James Murray and Christopher Ward. An *Observer* profile, my first since 1947, appeared on Sunday, 17th; the three feature articles on the next day. These four essays could only be regarded as flattering to my self-esteem. They conveyed roughly the same impression of a sincere, rather eccentric Christian. The comic aspect was touched on more than once but in a friendly and not derisive spirit. One of the difficulties in getting our ideas across had lain in the ineluctable fact that sex is a comic subject, or at least arouses easy laughter. The opposition had three main options. To ignore us, to denounce us, or to ridicule us. It had proved impossible to ignore us and very hard to denounce an inquiry whose findings were still unknown. Ridicule, therefore, was the only weapon left to them and it had been applied to me in particular (but of course Mary Whitehouse had had the same treatment for years) with an unsparing hand.

But now the tune was changing. These four articles about myself, plus the 'Panorama' profile, represented a new attitude. The laughing had to stop. We watched the 'Panorama' programme *en famille* at Antonia's house and repaired for supper to a restaurant. Something, however, that I ate disagreed with me badly - I was not the only sufferer - and I was very sick when we went home. The next day I lay in bed eating nothing and reflecting on the rapid descent from the sublime of a 'Panorama' profile to the absurdity of a gastric prostration. In the afternoon things began to happen disconcertingly. It had been arranged by Hodders, our excellent publishers, with my approval that the report would be embargoed to the Press till publication day, Thursday the 21st. But television and radio were to be allowed to summarise and discuss it from nine o'clock Wednesday evening. I believe that such an arrangement is not uncommon. By Tuesday afternoon, however, the Press were demonstrating their resentment. My old friend Maurice Green, editor of the *Daily Telegraph*, rang me up, as did the Press Association, to describe the plans as totally unfair to the newspapers. Various attempts at compromise came to nothing. Maurice warned me that he intended to break the embargo, in other words, publish on the Wednesday morning. I told him that I could not object in the circumstances. He duly went ahead and on Wednesday morning the report received a massive coverage. The quantity and prominence of the publicity on the first morning exceeded anything I had ever expected. In view of the last-minute kerfuffle it was extraordinary how quickly the papers had made the drastic changes required, in some cases altering their entire front page.

Only the *Guardian* refrained from giving us full treatment. They had always been opposed to us in their leading and feature articles. News stories had varied from downright unfairness to fuller treatment of speeches by myself and Fred Catherwood than was found elsewhere. For whatever reason, their coverage on the Wednesday morning, and above all the headlines, were not in their highest tradition. Their main news story was headed: 'Longford alleges police corruption'. This was not even supported by the text that followed and as an indication of the general content of our report was a lamentable perversion. When I complained to the gracious lady news editor about this serious error, she expressed regret but pointed out that the headlines were not put on by the news staff. Some amends were made by a highly enjoyable account of the press conference that morning. The *Sun* did us proud on the front page. LORD PORN'S GOSPEL was the banner headline, and underneath the words: 'Send these filth pedlars to jail.' The leading article was undoubtedly against us, but on balance we could not complain. Jon Akass had written scathingly about me after the Denmark visit but now, or a little later, he said things which I certainly treasure – all too generous though they be. 'Lord Longford,' he wrote, 'is clearly a good man. If he is not actually a saint, he is certainly the most saintly member of the Upper Chamber, and I do not overlook the Bishops.'

The *Express*, *Mail* and *Mirror* were thoroughly cordial. *The Times* gave us extensive coverage. Marigold Johnson had been told by a high person there that ours was a magnificent report, so our hopes were raised. A little unduly as it turned out. When the leading article appeared on the Thursday it did not withhold praise but was cooler than we had expected. The *Daily Telegraph* leading article on the first day was perhaps the most significant of all the Press features. In the days that followed the *Telegraph* writers drew back a little, but nothing could detract in my eyes from certain things said in the leading article on the first morning. 'It may well prove,' they wrote, 'that the research by the Longford Committee investigating pornography is of more value than the actual recommendations which it makes. Few people will have any doubts, after reading the report, about accepting two things as established fact – one is that the commercial exploitation of pornography has expanded and is expanding vastly. The other is that in many cases pornography does lead to sexual attitudes which cause unhappiness and social malaise.'

Whatever view was to be taken of our precise legal proposals, our crucial points were accepted.

Summing up the morning's press, I was entitled to claim later in the day that the report had had a tremendous reception.

The happenings of that Wednesday need not be described in detail. Altogether I took part in nine programmes, plus one large and hectic press conference. I had prudently equipped myself with expert colleagues all round me. Norman Anderson and John Godfray Le Quesne to deal with legal points, Malcolm Muggeridge for broadcasting, Dennis Delderfield, advertising, and Fred Catherwood and David Holbrook, general. In some of the Press reports a leading figure in the audience was the 'Happy Hooker', and certainly in her own way she was a female personality as striking as Mary Whitehouse whom she sat

close to. 'The 29-year-old blonde,' said the *Express*, 'had written
a book describing her life as a brothel-keeper in New York.'
According to the headline, she was the girl who stole the
Longford show, but the staff reporter, Jill King, considered
that I was quick off the mark in dealing with her. The general
verdict of Jill King was that we 'maintained a humorous
dignity, above the hub-bub of questions at the crowded conference'.

In fact the bulk of the questions were thoroughly serious.
Some good laughs were had by all. I like to think that I supplied
a couple. A friendly journalist asked me anxiously whether I
did not mind being made a figure of fun by the Press. I replied
there were worse things than being a figure of fun. I worked
in a favourite memory of my own which no one there, except
Elizabeth, had probably heard. 'When I have trouble with a
journalist,' I told them, 'I always remember what Ernest
Bevin said when he came back from Moscow and people asked
him what Stalin was like. "He's just a working chap like you
and me," he replied, "trying to make his way in the world." '
This little anecdote got the best laughter of the day.

And so many hours and many programmes later I found
myself at the BBC television studios waiting to take part in
the 'Midweek' programme. I had a good deal of sympathy for
the position in which 'Midweek' found themselves. They had
taken great trouble to prepare a comprehensive programme on
our report. Suddenly their whole plan was wrecked by the Press
bursting the embargo and publishing very full extracts from
the report in the morning papers. Clearly the original programme could not go forward.

The full explanations of the report by myself and Norman
Anderson disappeared, and the BBC summarised it briefly
themselves. The charming chairman whom I had found highly
sympathetic when I met her with Joe McCulloch was now cast
for an unenviable role. Sitting beside her in a studio I had every
opportunity of reading off the teleprompter the script prepared
for her. One could only say, as one read it, 'some enemy has
done this'. It created the impression that the committee had
steadily fallen apart, though some at least had persevered to
the end. No one could possibly have grasped that we finished up

with more members than we began. It contained one gross inaccuracy and was altogether tendentious.

As the discussion proceeded, I became more and more conscious of what seemed to me the partisanship of the chairman, and finally I intervened, too roughly perhaps, with words which a good many viewers seem to have remembered. 'I thought you were supposed to be neutral, Madam chairman.' I pointed out inaccuracies in what she was saying and I am afraid talked her down. Norman Anderson dealt with our opponents just as sharply without being so insubordinate to the chairman, but his own strictures on the chairmanship were, in retrospect, even blunter than my own. 'You asked me,' he wrote to the BBC, 'what I thought of the chairmanship. I thought that it was absolutely appalling.'

Elizabeth was down at Bernhurst by the evening, though she had attended the press conference. When I rang her after the 'Midweek' programme she was quick to say that the press conference had been splendid but that I had perhaps seemed a little too angry in 'Midweek'. Similar comments were made by some of my friends. But most people who spoke to me or wrote about it were delighted that a Christian had for once spoken out so vigorously. In fact, our debate was allowed to run on an extra ten minutes, cutting out another item announced. So I suppose it was good television, whatever that might be.

If we visualise the struggle for and against the report as a tug-of-war, one could think of us heaving the other side a considerable distance by the end of the first day. Then came the turn of the others. Very hostile reviews appeared in the *Observer* by Bernard Levin, by Alan Brien in the *New Statesman*, by Professor Dworkin in the *Listener*, and an unknown scribe in *The Times Literary Supplement*. It is true that we received the praise I valued most. Cyril Connolly, a higher literary critic than any of these, wrote words which meant much to me in the *Sunday Times*. 'The Longford Report is perfectly respectworthy; it is reasonable, well documented, cool, unbiased, and in no sense an inquisition.'

The religious weeklies were enthusiastic. Bill Hewitt in *Smith's Trade News* described it as 'good reading all the way, socially valuable, cool-headed', Bill Hewitt's praise was of quite special significance. The author of the only first-class book in England about the obscenity laws, he had worked for their reform for years with A. P. Herbert and others. He had signed, reluctantly it now appears, the libertarian report of the Arts Council Working Party in 1969. He had been asked by *The Times Literary Supplement* to write the first of their series of articles on pornography in the first part of the year. He, if anyone, must be counted as a liberal expert on the subject.

Still, taking it for all in all, the literary establishment was adverse. One had been conscious, of course, of this antagonism from the very beginning. Fraser Harrison, our live and sensitive young editor in Sidgwick & Jackson, had asked me early on whether I thought that the interests of our firm would be damaged by my so-called 'campaign'. I had always reckoned with that possibility; indeed, with the danger to the prospects of the second volume of Elizabeth's book on Wellington. In fact, these dangers were averted. Her second volume was an even bigger success than the first.

I had, however, expected rather more fairness from intellectuals. The editor of *The Times Literary Supplement* had consulted me earlier in the year about their pornography series. Shortly before our report came out, he asked me for an early copy, so that it could receive serious attention. In the event, the review which appeared was at once contemptuous and hysterical: 'It is ill-written, repetitive, diffuse and unspecific. Its legal recommendations embody a mindless moral populism.' Bearing in mind what Cyril Connolly had said about us, and the high distinction of our legal sub-committee, one can only observe with resignation the depth of the prejudice.

I would distinguish among the harsher critics two sources of venom. One, a deep-rooted occupational bias in the world of the arts against any encroachment by the State that could be described, however inaccurately, as censorship. As soon as an issue such as the obscenity laws arise, they tend instinctively to take the libertarian side. Obviously this is not true of all writers and artists by any means, and it is in no way true of the educated classes generally. The *Bookseller* was obviously concerned with pornographic threats to literature and was on the whole favourable to us. But by and large the world of the literary editors as distinct from chief editors showed their hostility by the reviewers they selected. Professor Dworkin, who reviewed our report in the *Listener*, had given public evidence for *Oz* in its obscenity trial. Alan Brien, invited to handle it by the *New Statesman*, makes no secret in article after article of what Christians can only call a frivolous attitude to sexual morals. Bernard Levin in the *Observer* denounced us with genuine passion for insisting that sex and love must go together. He referred with disgust to 'the basic assumption on which the entire book rests which is that sexual pleasure is only obtainable, and certainly only permissible, when accompanied by love . . . The fact that the claim is not only untrue but manifestly ridiculous does not seem to have occurred to Lord Longford and his colleagues.' Nor it may be thought to most of the public, sophisticated or otherwise.

In short, we ran as might be expected into two deep-rooted psychological resistances – the wish of the professional writer to be left alone and the ideology of sexual liberation, or what used to be called 'free love'. To the exponents of this latter doctrine, the whole conception of sexual corruption was meaningless at the best and, at the worst, might lead to wholesale interference with happy goings-on. Taking the public generally, and I addressed many meetings before the end of the year, one found a clear majority in favour of the view that something ought to be done about pornography. Even the *Evening Standard*, whose editor has revealed himself in his own book as an out and out libertarian, discovered in a poll that two-thirds of the public wanted some action to be taken. A *Daily Mail* poll came to the same conclusion. On the other hand, the non-judgmental spirit of the age made it very uncertain how much support could be enlisted for any actual intervention.

Three weeks after our report came out, the Home Secretary, Mr Carr, gave an important indication of Government thinking. He told the Conservative Conference that he recognised the great and growing public concern about pornography. He was not, however, satisfied that a change in the Obscenity Law was desirable. He was considering actively the need for taking action against indecent displays. I welcomed the statement on the grounds that half a loaf was better than no bread and might lead on to the whole loaf later.

But a new spirit, at least as ardent as myself, packing in his own way a heavier individual punch, now injected himself into the proceedings. Raymond Blackburn had taken on Kings Norton constituency when Elizabeth gave it up during the war, as her family accumulated. Raymond won it by 12,000 votes in 1945. His maiden speech was hailed as a triumph, not least by Sir Winston Churchill, who took a keen interest in his progress. Whether this helped him or not is dubious. Raymond fell on evil days. His political career finished in shipwreck, but a few years ago he staged a creditable comeback with his attack on the operation of the Gaming Laws. Now he came right to the front with a demand that the existing Obscenity Law should be properly enforced. He was soon involved in a heroic one-man attempt to persuade the courts at every level, including the House of Lords, to compel the police to do their duty.

On 29th November the Bishop of Leicester, a key member of our committee, initiated a debate on our report in the House of Lords. He led off in a speech that was altogether admirable, solid, humorous at points, gently inflexible. There was certainly no question after he had finished of laughing us out of court. It was unfortunate for us that the first Labour speaker from the Opposition front bench was my successor as leader of the Labour peers - Lord Shackleton. He said that he spoke only for himself, but that kind of qualification is usually lost sight of in the Press. Eddy Shackleton has always been on the permissive side in these arguments. He strove hard to be fair; he in no way impugned the quality of the report; he indicated a readiness for steps to be taken against indecent display. But, by and large, he confirmed any governmental disposition to avoid interfering with the fundamental Law of Obscenity. Lord Beswick, Opposition Chief Whip, wound up strongly in our favour, also from the Opposition front bench. An intimate friend of mine since our partnership in civil aviation, he has emerged in these latter days as an intrepid champion of Christian morals.

The general balance of the debate was numerically favourable to us - nearly two to one in our favour on a rough count, but the main Government spokesman, Mark Colville, was able to refer to a sharp conflict of views on the correct definition of obscenity and to postpone any reform of the fundamental law. In certain respects, however, in regard to cinema clubs and indecent display generally, he gave the impression that action against the pornographers would be taken before long by the Government. In a broad sense, therefore, one could feel that real progress had been made since 21st April, 1971.

Only at one point did the debate become at all hot-blooded, though the House of Lords' mask of geniality was never long discarded. I had been put down to speak eighth and, when I arrived, found that Lord Goodman was due to follow me. Through no initiative of mine, Eric Fletcher asked to change places with me, owing to an engagement elsewhere, so that when Lord Goodman rose to his feet he found himself speaking before, instead of after, me. Rather naïvely, he began by saying that he had intended to speak *after* me, which led to a lot of humorous but rather irritated questioning. 'How had this been arranged?' and 'Who did he think he was to make these arrangements?' etc. All this he took with his usual air of benevolence, but the slight mystery surrounding the arrangements for his speech was helpful to our side rather than his. Arnold Goodman is probably the most amusing speaker in the House of Lords at the present time, which makes him additionally formidable. He managed to describe me as totally unqualified to conduct a social inquiry of this kind, without implying any personal animus - itself no mean parliamentary feat. My friend Lord Barrington asked a Law Lord afterwards: 'Was Goodman's speech as bad as it seemed to me?' He replied, 'Worse,' but the House indubitably enjoyed it. When I rose to reply, I had an easy task on this personal level. I dwelt, I hope not tediously, on the various major inquiries with which I had been associated, whereas Lord Goodman, to the best of my belief, was wholly unversed in social investigation. 'In these fields,' I ventured to conclude, 'he is a total ignoramus.' I would go to him in legal or, indeed, human problems, but when it came to social inquiries I could only quote the words of Chesterton's poem: 'Chuck it, Smith!' (Loud and happy laughter, in my imagination at least.)

No praise was more welcome than that of Norman Shrapnel,

parliamentary correspondent of the *Guardian*, next morning.
At the beginning of our inquiry I had predicted that the
Guardian was pretty hopeless from our point of view and been
rebuked by Trevor Huddleston: 'Do not despair,' he had said,
'of the *Guardian*.' Now Norman Shrapnel's article was headed
'Winner of Porn Stakes', and he referred to me as 'striding
through, alone to the end, knees lifting high and stylishly,
breaking the tape with a smile and a final speech. It rather
looked,' he concluded, 'Lord Longford first, the others no-
where.' But I was well aware that the real battle was only
just beginning and that it would last for my lifetime at least.
Our report had been a truly collective effort, but outside our
committee Mary Whitehouse, the Festival of Light and many
others were just as dedicated to the cause.

*

I cannot close the chapter without attempting a few words
about Malcolm Muggeridge, chairman of our Broadcasting
Committee, among many other things.

For fifteen years or so I have seen more of Malcolm Muggeridge in his home than anyone else, and with each year that
passes we have grown closer and closer in personal affection
and community of moral purpose. Malcolm lives in the next
village to us, Robertsbridge as against Hurst Green. When he
is in England (and he travels to America or Australia as readily
as to Kent or Surrey) a weekend seldom passes when Elizabeth
and I do not sit down to a meal with him and Kitty, serene and
spiritual, in their house or ours. There is a special link between
Malcolm and my daughter Rachel - he literally brought her
and her husband Kevin together. But all the children treat him
as something of a guru, though not one whose word must be
obeyed.

In my eyes he has changed more fundamentally in the years
that I have known him than any one of my generation. At the
risk of discourtesy to his former persona - he was always a
delightful and exhilarating companion - the change seems to
me to have been entirely for the better. He is now in public a
Christian prophet. No layman exercises a comparable influence.
The old Adam, it is true, comes out not infrequently in over-

sharp judgments, but that is surely the way of prophets, even
Christian ones. In private he is the most understanding,
buoyant and considerate of friends. He has become, as is well
known, a genuine ascetic. Drink has long since been rejected,
along with other recognised weaknesses of the flesh. Smoking,
of course, is 'out', though a few years ago an interview with
Lord Chandos was obliterated by the clouds of Malcolm's
cigarette smoke. Meat and fish are similarly proscribed. Yet
his astonishing vitality seems to have increased, if anything,
his cheeks pinker and more glowing than ever, his blue eyes
still more electric, his white hair suggestive of anything but
old age. The writing in his memoirs and in his heartfelt tribute
to Mother Teresa reveals a command of the English language
unsurpassed by any contemporary.

We must wait for the next volumes of his autobiography to
learn 'the reason why' all this came about (to exploit the title
of his recent television series). He has told us a certain amount
already, but some of the main points are still mysterious. In
his introduction to Mary Whitehouse's book (May 1971) he
distinguishes interestingly between his emphasis and hers.
'Mrs Whitehouse,' he writes, 'is more inclined than I am to
lean on censorship and the operations of the Director of Public
Prosecutions. My own disposition is to regard them both as
broken reeds.' It is at this point that the professional public
man like myself begins to demand of Malcolm what concrete
steps he would himself take to deal with mounting evil. But
you don't catch out prophets so easily.

Malcolm struck a characteristic note at the end of his great
sermon in the High Church of St Giles, Edinburgh, when he
resigned from the Rectorship:

As my friend and I walked along, [he said], like Cleopas and his friend,
we recalled as they did the events of the Crucifixion and its after-
math in the light of our utterly different and yet similar world.
Nor was it a fancy that we, too, were joined by a third presence.
And I tell you that wherever the walk, and whoever the wayfarers,
there is always this third presence ready to emerge from the shadows
and fall in step along the dusty, stony way.

No one who does not perceive his Christian absorption can

begin to understand the source of his strength and influence.

*

I will not prolong the argument about pornography here. There is a school of what I have called sexual liberation, some of its members highly gifted, many of them potently articulate, who condone total promiscuity and stand in fact for total sexual selfishness, for 'doing one's thing' in whatever way is most pleasant. Leaving them aside, I should say that almost everyone agrees that a line should be drawn somewhere in the interests of all, but especially of children, and that beyond this line pornography should not be permitted. It will never be easy to decide how that line should be drawn in principle, or applied in practice, but as mentioned elsewhere we apply throughout the field of criminal law a human justice which is always far from perfect. Pornography corrupts and degrades those who take part in it and those who come under its influence. I hope and believe that it will be tackled with increasing vigour as the issue is squarely faced. I have said that I condemn the offence and seek to help the offender in the field of crime generally. We set out to apply the same Christian philosophy to the pornographer and his victims.

PART FIVE

Books in my World

There was an apocryphal story before the war at Oxford that a certain respected don had got seven 'seconds'; that he had seven times achieved second class honours in the final schools. I myself can point to the rare distinction of having followed four main careers: don, politician, banker, publisher, and engaged in three major activities as social worker, social investigator, and author.

In none of my primary avocations have I challenged comparison with those who have reached the very top. I have in mind near contemporaries like Alan Bullock (academic life), Hugh Gaitskell (politics), Kim Cobbold (banking), Billy Collins (publishing), and others like them. Nor would anyone be illiterate enough to compare me as a writer with my wife. Still, the total variety offers some claim to uniqueness, though if Oliver Franks had held not only the great positions he actually occupied, but all those which he is understood to have turned down, he would have won such a competition easily.

My introduction to publishing came out of the blue at the end of 1968, about a year after I had resigned from the Cabinet. It arose entirely through the kindness and, perhaps I should add, the goodwill towards my other activities of Charles Forte, who had already built the great business of Forte's and who is now the effective head of the Trust Houses Forte combine. What passed through his mind at that time I have no means of knowing. No doubt he was aware that I had been a Minister for a good many years and chairman of a bank; that, like him, I was a Roman Catholic and that my family and I between us had written a large number of books. Whatever the reasoning, he asked me to become a director of Sidgwick & Jackson from 1st January, 1970, with a view to becoming chairman on 1st May. The job would be essentially part-time, the salary acceptable but moderate; one great attraction would be that I would be provided with a first-class private secretary, Gwen Keeble, and that she and the office facilities would be available to help me in my variegated social work. I accepted with alacrity.

I had had by this time no small experience of publishers. Books written by myself had been published (in chronological order) by Jonathan Cape, Weidenfeld & Nicolson, Geoffrey Chapman, Hutchinson, Collins (Fontana), Gill and Macmillan in Ireland, and Houghton Mifflin in America. Since then Hodders have produced our Pornography Report. My wife, my children and myself achieved a unique record in 1969 by producing five books in a single year, as I will explain in the next chapter. In the current twelve months Antonia is publishing *Cromwell*, Rachel her fourth novel, and I this autobiography, to which might be added *Edward the Fourth* by my sister Mary, *Ivy Compton-Burnett* by my sister Violet, and the latest volume of his superlative *Music of Time* by my brother-in-law Anthony Powell. That adds up to six, if I am allowed to commit the audacity of including Tony. My sister Pansy and my nephew Ferdie Mount are also talented authors. In addition to the publishers already mentioned, Rachel has published her books with Heinemann, and my sisters and sister-in-law Christine with Gollancz, Macmillan, Duckworth, and Faber. The blasphemous Frank Harris once felt called upon to compare himself with Christ. 'Christ,' he said, 'went deeper, but I have had wider experience.' There are authors who know more about publishers than I do, and publishers who know more about authors, not to mention their own trade; but directly and indirectly, I know as much as most people about the relationship between the two.

It is an invidious task for a publisher to pick out a number of books he is most proud to have published. Still more so, to define his own contribution. I find it easier to wear an author's hat and acknowledge at least some of the help that I have received from publishers. For purposes of illustration I will run quickly through the origins of my own books. The chance to write *Peace by Ordeal*, my history of the Irish Treaty, came through Eleanor Smith, the romantic novelist and sister of Freddy Birkenhead. Her father had been one of the signatories of the Treaty and his family had always been fascinated by the stories of Michael Collins and the other characters. The publishers, Peter Davies, had asked her who could undertake the work and she had suggested me, knowing that I was already beginning to be fascinated also. Eventually Jonathan Cape took the book over from Peter Davies.

As the Attlee Government drew to a close in 1951, I discussed with Jack McDougall of Chapman & Hall's the possibility of writing a book about the last hundred years of British foreign policy, but just about then Jonathan Cape made me a princely offer for my memoirs. He still remembered with pleasure his publication of *Peace by Ordeal.* A favourite author of his at that time was Peter Fleming. Jonathan told me that Ian had also written a book (*Casino Royale*), which he was going to publish, but he had told Ian he would have to do a lot better in future. From the absorbing life of Jonathan Cape by Michael S. Howard, it appears that the proceeds from Ian Fleming's books for the next eight years just about corresponded to Cape's profits for the period.

My first volume of memoirs is described in the same (Cape) biography as one of the mainstays of Cape's publications in 1953, but at the time Cape was somewhat disappointed. It did not in theory earn the large advance paid (£2,000 - very good money in those days), which illustrates the different meanings that publishers can attach to 'profitability'. I always remember that after the book had been out about three weeks, Jonathan Cape gravely told me: 'I have a feeling that your book is about to take off. I am usually right.' But not altogether on this occasion, although the first edition of five thousand copies was disposed of, plus a good sale to the Catholic Book Club.

The origin of my next book, *Causes of Crime*, was quite different. On my own initiative, I had persuaded the Nuffield Foundation to finance me with expert help in a two-year Inquiry into this subject. By the time it was finished, I was starting the New Bridge for ex-prisoners, with much help from Sonia Orwell, among others including Edward Montagu, who gave the society its name. Sonia asked to see my report on 'The Causes of Crime' and insisted that it must see the light of day somehow. She was at that time a key figure in Weidenfelds, who duly published it as a book.

A little later, Geoffrey Chapman, who was coming forward

rapidly at that time, asked me straight out to write a short book on the Idea of Punishment, which I gladly did for them.

Then Harold Harris, of Hutchinsons, came into my life. He suggested that I should write a book called *A Socialist in the City*, and certainly I was and am the only Socialist who had been chairman of a bank. I did not feel that without unworthy indiscretions there was a whole book to be extracted from that title. So we worked out between us the plan for a second volume of autobiography, in which the City was only one of the *Five Lives* referred to in the title.

Now came a literary break, while I was a member of the Wilson Government. Ministers often gather material during their time in office, but by and large they leave their books till afterwards. Joan Woods looked at me on one occasion with her mysterious, affectionate smile and said, 'You ought to write religious criticism.' I could not quite pluck up the courage. Soon after I left the Labour Government, however, I sat down to write a book on *Humility*, published by Fontana (Collins) in 1968. Who suggested Humility? I suppose I did, but am not quite sure even of that. I had already begun to be conscious of the extraordinary achievements of Pierre Collins in religious publishing. She regularly sent me the works of Teilhard de Chardin, of which perhaps only *Le Milieu Divin* came fully home to me. More than once we had discussed the idea of my one day doing a religious book for Collins. I have little doubt that it was I who spoke of such a project first. I have just as little doubt that Pierre's almost hypnotic sympathy encouraged me to make the proposal - a classic example, in a small way, of one kind of creative publishing.

I go into all this to suggest, in all humility, that you can no more separate a publisher from an author in the origination of a book than you can separate the rider and the horse who, between them, win the Grand National.

When I drew up the list of spiritual writers who were to figure in *Humility*, some at least were suggested by Pierre; others - Teilhard de Chardin, Gerald Vann - were suggested to me in the consciousness that they appealed to her strongly. When I brought her the first draft of the book she looked at me gravely. 'Frank,' she said, 'it's not right yet.' All sorts of amendments were suggested. Some of them I accepted, some I didn't. A Professor of Theology gave a warm imprimatur. A publicity manager of the famous firm impressed me profoundly: 'The public for a book is a wall of sludge. You take a book and throw it as hard as you can. Very often it sticks, but every now and then it goes right through the wall of sludge and becomes a big seller. I shall throw your book' - suiting the gesture to the word - 'against the wall as hard as I can. You can rely on me for that.' Indeed I did till next day, when I heard that he had moved to another firm. But even without him the selling machinery of Collins is incomparable and the book seems to have given a lot of pleasure, not least in prisons, as John Vassall has written recently.

After that I began to prepare for a companion book on *Suffering*, again in full co-operation with Pierre; but pornography overtook it.

I have jumped ahead of events. Early in 1965, Harold Harris consulted me about a partner for Tom O'Neill of the National Library of Ireland, in a full-length biography of Mr de Valera. This eventually appeared in 1970. By that time something like ten years had passed since Bob Lusty, managing director of Hutchinsons, had tried to persuade Mr de Valera to write his own autobiography and, failing that, to nominate a biographer. In the later stages of the book, contact was somewhat tenuous between the principals. Tom O'Neill, with the help of a considerable advance from Hutchinsons, worked for three years on Mr de Valera's papers in a room in his house, but by the finish he had taken up an important post in Galway University and, with him in Galway, the President in Dublin, and myself in London, liaison was maintained with indomitable energy by Harold. At one point, an emissary from Hutchinsons descended on Tom O'Neill in the West of Ireland, worked on the proofs with him on a late train back to Dublin, and dropped him at Athlone at midnight, reaching Dublin in the small hours. Another day, or a night, in the life of a publisher!

Once I begin to bring in the experience of my family, I shall not stop easily. The idea of Wellington was suggested by my wife's most imaginative publisher - George Weidenfeld.

But Queen Victoria was suggested to her by Graham Watson (senior partner of Curtis Brown, known to my family as 'the Head') at a time when she had got as far as deciding to write about a nineteenth-century woman - possibly Mrs Sidney Webb. Incidentally, Graham Watson suggested the present book, as soon as I told him I was beginning to feel the old urge to write something.

*

Why be a publisher? In our own firm, Sidgwick & Jackson, I am the only leading person who came into publishing because he was brought there by fortune rather than deliberate design. I was happy to arrive there during my middle sixties, but I cannot pretend that it was my selection from other alternatives. In the nature of things (and this is important), I could not expect to be in charge for many years. One of the supreme joys of the publisher - the discovery and building up of young talent - was inevitably denied me. It is no good asking me therefore why I chose publishing. Publishing, through the voice of Sir Charles Forte, chose me. But with the rest of our staff it was quite different. One, Stephen du Sautoy, son of the chairman of Fabers, had been brought up in publishing, but the others had come to it without any predisposition. I was moved when a member of our staff, trained as a printer, explained to me the romantic inspiration that publishing had come to offer him. 'As a result,' he tells me, 'of my total experience, I find great satisfaction from receiving an author's manuscript, reading it, putting right some errors (however small), visualising the finished book, discussing it with the author, designing the book, planning and following through the production (which means meeting people of all sorts due to the varied number of suppliers).' He refers finally to the satisfaction of actually handling the finished book. 'All very good for one's ego,' he says, 'but one remembers with humility at all times that one is dependent on the skill and goodwill of many people, who often become one's friends.' He makes a reference to humility, but anyone who has himself written a book must surely feel rather humble when he realises what glamour a book can hold for the man who produces it.

My colleagues, young ardent publishers by choice, seem to agree that what appeals to them most in publishing is the creative role. But they use the word with caution. Publishing, I feel, after talking to them and sharing their labours, provides an ideal opportunity for collective creativity; for creativity in concert. It does not carry the risks and discomforts of isolated creation - of actually writing your own book. It allows one to fulfil a creative role in the company of like-minded persons. 'Publishing,' agrees William Armstrong, our managing director, 'is an intensely personal business - inasmuch as a publisher's own attitude to a book can make or mar it.' All this I can confirm from both sides of the fence.

The economics of publishing are not in principle different from business economics in general. As chairman of a bank for eight years it was my duty to scrutinise the efficiency of many varied undertakings. There are certain qualities necessary anywhere. I take honesty for granted, with the addition of hard work, initiative, persistent drive, a flair for public relations, and the assurance that resources are fully used and that there is no waste of manpower or material.

In publishing, often thought of as a cultural or gentlemanly occupation, the need for commercial shrewdness is maximal. It has been said that anyone who can succeed commercially in publishing could make a million in any other business. There are certainly pickings to be had in publishing, but the publisher must scratch hard for them. If a publisher lacks the necessary commercial qualities, he will certainly fail to realise the full potential of a book. He *must* have the technical knowledge of production processes to make sure that the book is priced and presented in the most effective way. He *must* also have a thorough understanding of the market which is many-tiered and painfully complex for such a small industry. The priceless gift of estimating how many copies a first or later edition will sell is partly God-given, partly based on endless experience and reflection.

A small or new firm is tempted to conclude that the most successful publishers are large and relatively old. But there is no need to be discouraged. When I became chairman of the National Bank, I was told by wiseacres that we could not hope to compete with the Big Five. We were at that time ninth out of the eleven clearing banks, but in fact during my eight years our progress in England was much faster than that of any other bank. We claimed to provide a quicker and more human service, and whether that was true or not, the old slogan that a good big 'un will always beat a good littl 'un was certainly disproved in our case. In Sidgwick & Jackson our expansion during my three years has been exceptionally fast, but that in itself is no proof of efficiency.

Any energetic fool can expand a publishing business as fast as he wishes, if he has the necessary resources behind him. In publishing, there is no difficulty about finding books to publish. The difficulty is to find the right ones, whether in terms of profit or more ultimate values. It is too early to say how profitable Sidgwick & Jackson will prove eventually, although on that side also the progress has been satisfactory. Mr Anthony Blond, in his *Publishing Game*, tells us that 'of the eight significant publishers who set up in England since the war, six were refugees (and at least three went bankrupt)'. My family are specially interested in one of the newcomers, Weidenfeld & Nicolson, whose association with Elizabeth and Antonia has been so beneficial to everyone. I recently asked George Weidenfeld how long it had taken him to break through. He replied 'about four years'. My own impression is that it took a good deal longer, but we have not even had four years since I entered Sidgwick & Jackson.

Sidgwick & Jackson has a continuous history going back to the nineteenth century, although it did not become known as Sidgwick & Jackson until 1913. Jackson was killed in the First World War and Frank Sidgwick died in 1939, when Jimmy Knapp-Fisher took over as chairman. He continued in this office until I became chairman in 1970 - a wonderful record in face of many anxieties. With characteristic generosity he has remained on the Board and made his unique knowledge available to us at all times.

Thus, as well as a long-established reputation, we had something solid to build on. Yet we were still a small publisher. The decision we took at the outset was to transform Sidgwick & Jackson from a small into a medium-sized publisher. In pursuing this objective, we have more than quadrupled our turn-over in the three years I have been chairman.

Obviously a firm that is expanding must publish more and more books and, at the same time, the publisher must ensure that the books he publishes are profitable and bring back the money quickly. At first, authors and literary agents were not going to think of us initially if they had a book of this nature; so we had to go to them with suggestions. We proposed to Margaret Laing, for instance, that she should write a biography for us of Edward Heath. The result exhibits in my eyes a width and depth of understanding. Also at our suggestion, Claud Cockburn has written a book on the 1930s (*The Devil's Decade*); John Pearson, the biographer of Ian Fleming, an imaginary biography of James Bond; Douglas Bader the history of the Spitfire and Hurricane. And I could give many other examples from the present year alone.

Not long ago, one of our advisers suggested to William Armstrong that we ought to do a picture-book called *The History of Royal Horsewomen*. William was fired with enthusiasm. In a trice the idea had become *Royalty on Horseback*. By chance I met a great friend of Elizabeth and mine, Michael Adeane, so long private secretary to the Queen, and found that the subject appealed to him enormously. Himself the possessor of a first class degree in History, he was soon pouring out information about the equestrian exploits of all our Kings and Queens from Queen Elizabeth onwards. It seems that William IV, the sailor King, was the only one who could not be counted. What is more, he put us in touch forthwith with the perfect author for such a book, Judith Campbell, whose book on Elizabeth and Philip was much admired by my wife and who had written several books on royalty and horses. By the time these lines appear her book, *Royalty on Horseback*, should itself be just about appearing. I give the above little account of how a book is, so to speak, created out of the air. Every publisher can multiply it many times over.

Naturally we paid close attention to any manuscripts submitted to us. Elizabeth brought us Molly Gillen's *The Prince and his Lady* which had run into trouble elsewhere, but was much praised when we produced it. Two of our more successful books had both been rejected by nine or ten other publishers before we took them on. They were Margery Forrester's *Michael Collins*, the highest seller of its year in Ireland, and the Ranee of Sarawak's *Queen of the Headhunters*, which has already gone through five printings. Neither of these can be compared with a major best-seller such as Elizabeth's *Queen Victoria* or the two volumes of *Wellington*, or Antonia's *Mary Queen of Scots*, both published by Weidenfeld. We expect one of those any time now.

Sidgwick & Jackson have begun to expand beyond their traditional areas. We have already produced a number of illustrated books in the field of history. We have published our own mass market paperbacks, getting another paperback publisher, the New English Library, to distribute them for us. Children's books are another development. My daughter Antonia helped us by providing two books she had written some time ago, *Robin Hood* and *King Arthur*, which her daughter Rebecca, then twelve to thirteen, illustrated. Another children's book, *William the Dragon*, was written and illustrated by Polly Donnison when she was 11 years old. We have just appointed a Children's Editor.

In production and design a firm like Sidgwick & Jackson does not appear to labour under a handicap. And on the editorial side the boot may even be on the other foot. Just as in banking, so here. The speed and personal touch may be more easily provided in the smaller firm. Many of our authors tell us so. But sales are a different matter. Here the small man feels oppressed by a vicious circle, with too much application of the biblical motto, 'To him that hath shall be given'.

Other things being equal, which of course they often are not, the larger the firm, the larger the advance. But that is far from everything. Early in my publishing career I was warned by Graham Watson, wisest of literary agents, that it was impossible to achieve a real eminence as a publisher until one had attracted to one's firm a fair proportion of the most-sought-after writers. He warned me that these writers, unlike the great majority of those who turned out books, had either at first hand or through their agent become extremely conscious of the precise amount of their sales and of the efficiency or otherwise of the sales machinery of their publishers. This is a sobering thought for the small firm, whose sales representatives in sheer numbers must fall far short of those of the largest houses. Yet anyone who has listened to Sir William Collins describe the enormous progress made under his auspices in the last fifty years from just a small office in London should feel that what has been done once can be done again. Nevertheless it takes time and, in the meanwhile, all sorts of permutations and combinations have to be studied or attempted to overcome the handicap of size in distribution and selling.

No small or medium-sized firm can afford to have the same widespread and complex organisation as Collins or Hutchinsons or Hodders, for example. At the same time, we have to compete with these giants and win a reasonable proportion of the most desirable authors. Our own solution to this problem up till now is to keep our own representative in the most important areas, such as London and the industrial Midlands, and to employ a larger firm - David & Charles - to carry our books in the rest of the country. Who knows what the future holds?

To turn to a different aspect: the ethical standards to be applied in publishing. The business as a whole must pay if it is not to go bankrupt or be permanently subsidised. Temporary subsidies are all very well, particularly for small firms when starting up, but they are no basis for a healthy life over a period. Graham Watson told me that the wide extent of subsidisation in publishing resulted in a large number of uneconomic firms remaining in business. This in turn had a direct bearing on the financial bearing of the book trade. Be that as it may, I assume that our ideal publisher is going to make reasonable profits without publishing anything of which he could remotely feel ashamed.

He will stop a long way short of what is likely to be prosecuted. At least so I would think, and it is clearly the case with the publishers that I most admire. But supposing one happens to think - which I certainly do not - that the present law of obscenity, for example, or sedition, or blasphemy or, for that matter, libel, is much too restrictive, one may regard it as one's sacred duty to break through the existing rules and, if necessary, go to prison oneself. In my limited experience problems of pornography and problems of publishing overlap only at the margin. Problems of pornography or obscenity play little part in the lives of reputable publishers, although every now and then an awkward issue crops up. We have hitherto published so few novels in Sidgwick & Jackson that we have been spared, I suppose, the more difficult items, but I have inquired into the experience of others. One book only has caused me any embarrassment from this point of view. We published in hardback, and later in paperback, a book called *The Professionals*, a serious study in depth of five selected prostitutes. On the cover of the hardback were a pair of mini-skirted legs which, taken with the theme of the book, aroused some adverse comment. The fact that I - the so-called anti-pornographer-royal - was the chairman of the publishing firm, assisted the critics. When too late I looked again at the cover, I concluded that I would not have passed it a few months earlier. From that moment onwards, when people asked me whether I had been corrupted by my investigation into pornography, I gave a different answer from previously. I still said that my appetite had not been increased. If anything it had been diminished; but I realised that I was in danger of being deadened in my sensibilities, so that in a sense pornography was even more menacing than I had supposed. By the time we came to the paperback, we had learned discretion.

That, however, is a very rare class of case. There is a broader question which publishers never seem to me to be happy with. Perhaps they believe that no abstract answer is possible. Let us agree that a publisher wishes to publish a collection of books of which he can be justly proud, but does that mean that he would publish no book that he cannot approve of? And, if so, what can approval mean? No one would expect a Catholic firm to produce the same list as a Communist firm. Yet even a Catholic firm might consider that its educational list was incomplete without something at least from Karl Marx, and possibly *Mein Kampf* as well. My great friend, Victor Gollancz, was an ideological publisher, but one would hardly say that about any of the leading publishers today. They are not inclined to propound, either directly or indirectly, a propagandist message. The best publishers indubitably stand for certain moral and aesthetic values, but I have never found yet any publisher of a non-ideological kind who could put those values into convincing words.

I have given one example of an embarrassment in the field of sex. A very different case will illustrate the wider problem. We were proud and happy to play some part in building up Cecil King's literary reputation. He was already a most distinguished figure in the world of newspapers and public business. He would, I am sure, be the first to give William Armstrong much credit for help in editing his *War Diaries*, which we published in 1970. We were also very happy with his collected essays published the following year. He was then kind enough to let us read his diaries of the Wilson period, which were splendidly vivid. William gave some further help in editing, and the moment of publication drew near. But the more I studied these diaries, the more my uncertainties accumulated. They did not, and do not, seem to me to give a remotely fair impression of Harold Wilson and his colleagues of whom, after all, I was one. I certainly was not influenced against publication by the discovery, quoted earlier, that Harold Wilson had apparently attributed to me a mental age of 12. Quite the contrary, in fact. That was in summer 1965. I remained in the Cabinet for another two and a half years and left on my own initiative. So perhaps I matured in the meanwhile. I reckoned that if we did publish the book, this particular reference to myself would make it easier to persuade colleagues that they had got off lightly.

But let us take this as a test case of a publisher who considers that a book is all wrong, not in intention, nor in any hard facts, but in general impression. There was here the additional question of whether it would have been loyal for me personally to have published a book of this kind. The dilemma was beginning to be poignant. Luckily the legal advice received at that time would have rendered it unwise for a firm of our size to have taken the risks involved. Not without our help, the book was serialised in a big way and published by a first-class firm, with excellent commercial results. So everyone was happy in the end.

Publishers are probably right in shirking a doctrinaire approach to moral problems of this order.

What image comes to mind when I hear the words 'great publisher'? In Mr Michael Howard's fascinating life of Jonathan Cape, we are told that Dame Veronica Wedgwood still recalls the moment when she was ushered into his spacious room: 'The majestic figure with iron-grey hair rose to greet me. He must already have been in his fifties, and I was impressed by his splendid presence: he was absolutely my idea of a distinguished publisher.' He had certainly a formidable persona. I remember his returning a play that I had written with the single comment: 'You should remember that there was once a man called Charles Dickens.' I was left to guess his meaning.

Most of us cannot hope to live up to the Jonathan Cape standard of appearance, although Billy Collins still looks prepared to renew his captaincy of the Harrow Cricket XI at any moment. Victor Gollancz used to be referred to in his younger days as 'impressive, with his cigar and pince-nez'. For years he exerted more influence on me than any other layman (I have always assumed that he invented the word 'unputdownable'), but for me he was always still more of a prophet than a publisher.

George Weidenfeld creates an atmosphere wherever he goes of mental excitement, distilling books in the air from any more or less literate companion. I myself, when I go out to dinner, with a physiognomy increasingly compared to that of Alistair Sim, my gold-rimmed glasses and velvet bow-tie given me by Rachel and worn *en peintre*, am more readily mistaken, Elizabeth tells me, for the director of an art gallery. As she is herself a trustee of the National Portrait Gallery and a member of the Advisory Board of the Victoria and Albert Museum, she ought to know. So like most other publishers, it seems that I do not quite look the part.

Those who desire an authoritative analysis of publishing as a trade or art form, or way of life, should turn to the pronouncements of Sir Robert Lusty and others of high ability, who have devoted to it their working life. Sir Robert, in a memorable phrase reproduced in *The Bookseller*, insisted that 'a total readjustment was necessary'. He may well be right, but some fundamentals are unlikely to alter. Publishing is certain to remain a profession where the commercial side is indispensable, but where the joy of achievement lies elsewhere. Anthony Blond, in his striking book, is primarily interested in what he calls 'the entrepreneur, the owner, the big vegetable' and less in anyone employed. But such a distinction does not help us to categorise a 'hired hand' like Sir Robert, to use his own phrase about himself, and it has no meaning in a firm like our own. The real creativity springs there from William Armstrong and those who assist him. But the chairman has also his role. Once a tutor, always a tutor. When I was a don, I did not personally answer the examination questions, but I gloried (sometimes) in the published class lists. From my chairman's seat in Sidgwick & Jackson, I gain untold pleasure from the achievements of those I preside over. In the here and now and in the foreseeable future.

The great publisher is a man of great faith - faith in his authors, faith in himself, faith in his colleagues - faith, it may be, in his proprietor.

Close at Home

'But,' I may be asked at this point, 'did you never relax, did you never tear yourself away from your no doubt estimable causes to savour the marvellous variety of human existence? Did you have no pleasures, no hobbies, no friends?' Readers of earlier volumes will have been provided with partial answers to these questions, though my entry in *Who's Who* has always been blank under the heading of 'Recreations'.

In fact, I have all my life been a fanatical reader, with biography (political and literary) and theology figuring most strongly in recent years. My interest in sports of all kinds, both as spectator and participant, has been just as obsessional, and in my later sixties might be deemed extravagant. I could not swim until ten years ago, but now in summer Elizabeth and I swim four times daily at the weekend in the pool in our Sussex garden, which she has created with her earnings from *Victoria R.I.* My regular golf at Rye has been suspended regrettably. Two of my companions died on the links, one left the district and one, my great friend (Dr) Chris Maxwell, has been afflicted with ill-health and forced on to his couch from which he distils every Sunday a flow of Christian wisdom. When I go over to see him, or take an alternative trek of perhaps four and a half miles, I try to maintain a rate of progress of nearly five miles an hour, running or, more accurately, jogging down the hills. I still do regular exercises, some of them taught me by Martin Charteris on the Canadian pattern. I am still prepared to take on my children at tennis, though with some show of reason my sons do not now admit that I am their equal.

Friends are always a problem for the autobiographer. You cause them pain by leaving them out and irritation to the reader by putting them in. Personally I cannot imagine anyone being luckier in this respect than I have been. Certainly no joy outside my family is more intense than paying a visit to an old friend in his lair; Freddy Birkenhead it may be at Charlton, David

Astor at Sutton Courtney, Douglas Woodruff at Marcham,
Philip Toynbee at Chepstow, David Cecil in Dorset, or Nicko
Henderson in one of his exalted embassies. But this happens all
too seldom, for me at least. And I have left out those who live
in London, for instance, the Oxford paladins and others already
mentioned. I am on record as saying that the women who
appeal to me most are blue stockings, holy women, female
athletes, Irish women and Jewesses. But again that excludes
Sheila Birkenhead, Pam Hartwell, Virginia Crawley, Ann
Martelli, Bice Fawcett and other friends of long standing.

I used to make a pilgrimage once a year to Evelyn Waugh at
his country houses. He despised all politicians, Socialists
particularly, but not Socialists alone. The Conservative's ideas
were better, or less evil, but were regularly betrayed by their
nominal exponents. When I became a Cabinet Minister in 1964,
he expressed relief to Frankie Donaldson that at least I was not
going to the Home Office. 'We should all,' he wrote to her,
'have been murdered in our beds.' I come off fairly lightly in
his published diaries. The formula for arranging my visits was
stereotyped. I would telephone the great man and inquire
diffidently, 'Would it, by any chance, be possible to come to
you for a night in the fairly near future?' He would reply,
firmly and convincingly, 'I wish you would.' From him it
seemed to mean more than from most people. A more unusual
exchange took place on the telephone when my brother Edward
died, and I succeeded to the title. I rang up Evelyn to ask if he
would write something for a Sunday paper. When he reached
the telephone, his first two words to me were: 'Hello, Longford.'
He never called my brother anything but 'Edward', nor me
before and afterwards anything but 'Frank'. However, it was
his way of observing the formalities. The tribute when it came
was full of flavour.

Of course I enjoyed the visits and so, I think, did he. When I
learnt of his death I realised that it was more than a year since
I had seen him and it had been a period for him of much sad-
ness. I might conceivably have cheered him slightly and shall
always regret that I allowed the business of the Cabinet to
prevent my going.

Auberon Waugh is my godson, a fact which he discloses from

time to time in kindly, if satirical, vein. I am probably more proud of the fact than he is. Elizabeth often refers to him as 'the best contemporary novel reviewer'. In spite of, or because of, his highly original talent, Bron reminds me every day more and more of his father. It is to him, I presume, that I owe my special relationships with *Private Eye*. They will knock you, I am assured, but they will never knock you out. So far, it has worked that way.

But, naturally, everything yields pride of place to the family.

I have no theory of family life except to believe that a happy family is the greatest blessing that can come the way of human beings. I am not one of those who consider any failure in the relationship between a parent and a child as invariably and exclusively the fault of the parent. But I go a long way in that direction. There is no limit to the love that should be expected of a parent. If one is fortunate, as Elizabeth and I, and an infinite number of others have been, the natural affection makes a sense of obligation unnecessary.

When I wrote *Five Lives* nine years ago, I had eight children and four grandchildren. I have now seventeen grandchildren, but only seven children. I will explain this in a moment. But first of all I will say a few words about the achievements of Elizabeth and the seven children who survive. The short chapter on Elizabeth in the earlier book was written and published before the appearance of her noble *Victoria R.I.*, though not before I had read it. I hailed her as a literary star of the highest quality, but at that time I had little except my love and intuition to guide me. Have I not since been abundantly justified? Her *Victoria R.I.* (1964) was an exceptional bestseller, so has been her *Wellington* (Vol. I, 1969, Vol. II, 1972). Her books have been saluted with generous consistency by the reviewers, whether old friends like Alan Taylor and Robert Blake, or distinguished Americans hitherto unknown to us.

So I am quite certain will be her next book on the *House of Windsor*. So will its successor, if it be a life of Byron, or indeed a life of anyone. My part in these creations has been minimal. Elizabeth possesess two particular qualities, hardly ever in my experience found in the same person. She has a great love and aptitude for research (doing, incidentally, virtually all her own). But she also has a great love and aptitude for the actual process of writing, encouraged no doubt by her fine calligraphy. She could not write a dull sentence if she tried, or produce a slack piece of scholarship. Her only weakness is that her soaring interest in her subject sometimes leads to a scale of output that frightens even her adoring publishers. It was with some reluctance that they agreed to her expanding *Wellington* into two volumes. I cannot help her much there, as Winston Churchill once said of his inability to assist Asquith, as he pored over Greek inscriptions. If I render any service, it is that of providing some additional political background and heart-felt encouragement. But her literary urge, once her blood is up, is far too strong to depend on external aid.

Readers can put her works in their own order of merit. I myself place them in an ascending scale. In writing *Victoria R.I.* she was still teaching herself her biographical method, opera-ting in a field where there were no official canons. Her own slogan that the spotlight must never stray far from the central figure is not unique to her, but one which she worked out for herself. She has never been slow to learn from writers she admires, and in early days paid much attention to what Mrs Woodham-Smith told me about the necessity for narrative momentum.

The first volume of her *Wellington* demonstrated her capacity, starting without knowledge of, or interest in, military affairs, to describe and interpret a long string of battles, with Waterloo a superb culmination. She has ever since been involved in intricate correspondence with retired brigadiers and colonels, who had not previously been part of her scene. The second volume covering the years 1815-52 dealt with subjects more familiar to her - politics, the Court, Oxford University, and family life, or lack of it. Her friend, Field-Marshal Templer, told me at the outset that he had no doubt about her ability to deal with the military side of Wellington, but did not believe that any woman would, or could, describe his multitudinous relations with women. All that, however, has been accom-plished, to what seems general satisfaction, and the second volume turned into a story as absorbing as the first. Bernard Levin, as generous as he is on occasion deadly, wrote to salute her as one whose heroes continued to be interesting, even when they were not doing interesting things.

Each book works up to a crescendo at the finish.

'She would be judged along with the humblest of her people. The most that she and any of them could hope to say was that they had tried to be good.' (*Victoria R.I.*)

'I ought to have somebody behind me to remind me that I am but a man.' (Wellington - *The Years of the Sword*.)

'Sometimes mistakenly, always selflessly, he continued to serve.' (Wellington - *Pillar of State*.)

Her parting words reflect with equal fidelity her final estimates of her heroine and hero, and unselfconsciously but surely the unchanging values of her own nature.

I persuaded myself that I had become somewhat identified with Prince Albert in her life of Queen Victoria. It will be recalled that he died of insufficient medical attention when he was in his early forties. I thought that I detected a new solicitude in her concern over my own health. I was more fortunate than my City friend, Cyril Ansley, whose wife identified him with de Gaulle, with many consequent tribulations. None with any knowledge of Wellington or myself could conceivably identify him and me, but he did at least marry my great-great-aunt, the long-suffering Kitty, of whom a portrait, on the whole rehabilitative, is given by Elizabeth. So that I was not entirely left out on that occasion either.

Antonia has taken by storm the reading public in England and America with her *Mary Queen of Scots* (her *Cromwell: Our Chief of Men* will have appeared before these words are in print). Thomas, with his *Year of Liberty* (the rebellion of 1798), has made an important addition to Irish historical literature, and is now deep in the Boer War. Rachel will have published her fourth novel this year. These three and Elizabeth and myself made 1969 in a literary sense our *annus mirabilis*. Judith has published two Jackdaw books on *The Gordon Riots* and *Women in Revolt*. According to one plausible view, she is the best natural writer of all the children, but so far she has not exactly put the matter to proof. At the moment she is preoccupied with painting.

In regard to the 'literary Longfords', Thomas writes as follows:

I expect you remember the time, a few years ago, when some journalist coined that flattering phrase, 'The Longford literary family'. It was the time when we fairly bombarded the public with books; out they came, month after month, pouring forth 'like hot rolls', as someone said of Joe Chamberlain's interminable Blue Books. (Ours, I hope, were more like hot cakes.) Anyway, the solemn question was then raised: why five authors in one family?

At the time I thought I knew the answer. That cheerful, optimistic temperament we have inherited from you must have its darker side: at any rate, a taste for melancholy. It is this – a streak of melancholy – that must be common to most authors. How else to explain the self-exile; the 'long, tranquil, lonely days' as Evelyn Waugh called them, facing an endless supply of blank paper; the writing and non-writing; the wrestling with the devil for the soul of one's narrative.

But recently it occurred to me, after a visit home, when I had to battle for an hour to get a word in edgeways at the dinner table, that there is a much simpler explanation for our literary impulses. We are not writers at all. We are talkers disguised as writers. Ten talkers in one family, and no listener: it was inevitable that half at least – the weaker half, perhaps – should be driven to take refuge in authorship in order to try to find an audience.

Paddy has achieved a vigorous practice at the Criminal Bar. Michael has moved on extremely fast in the Diplomatic Service. Kevin, at the age of 25, has become Senior Economist at Rothschild Intercontinental Bank. At just about that age, I was hoping to turn myself into a professional economist with City interests, till discouraged by no less a pundit than J. M. Keynes. Antonia has six children, Thomas four, Paddy three, Judith two, Rachel three. Kevin has recently married.

And Catherine? Writing in 1963, I quoted of her what Scott Fitzgerald says of Dick Diver in *Tender is the Night*. I said that 'she was awaiting her intricate destiny'. But her destiny was one that was mercifully unforeseen. On the morning of Monday, 11th August, 1969, Catherine and her close friend Gina Richardson, being driven to London by another friend, were killed in a car crash. In the words of the *Daily Telegraph*, for whose Supplement she was working, 'this wasteful, arbitrary, irrevocable tragedy, among many grievous consequences, robbed Fleet Street of two of its most promising young writers'. It robbed her army of friends of a dearly loved companion and her family of one who held, and will always hold, a quite special place in their hearts. In her memory was established the Catherine Pakenham Memorial Prize for young women journalists, which has already been three times awarded. When she died, she was 23 years old, tall, with long brown hair, dark hazel eyes and a round laughing face.

Soon after her death, Antonia and Judith wrote poems:

ANTONIA

The Harvest

At first in the green bewilderment
Of fertile August
I could not understand.
A mistake must
Have been made: this was not the season to be spent
Why should she die
When the corn still waved
And the holiday sun still shone in the high-summer sky?

But in September when the stooks
Made abstract shapes
Of what had once lived –
So the mind gropes –
This practicality out of all that remembered richness
Made me see
For us, granaries and diligent storehouses,
This was the remainers' destiny.

But for her always the golden moment
The eve of the harvest
Our corn still waves above her garnered head
And we must turn its memory into bread.

JUDITH

Oh Catherine, my darling sister whom
I did not know,

Speak to me from
Heaven.
Tell me you're all right –
Life goes on without you
I don't want it to
But what can I do?

These lines of Hugh's can fittingly go with them:

All life she questioned and those verities
Threadbare, those hand-me-downs of convent schooling
Her time a pilgrimage, through fustian fooling
She dragged forth truth, battled uncertainties,
Broke images and yet some likeness ruling
Shaped up the débris, valiant, gruelling.
Her dented armour caught those rays of light
Her lover sought; and found. And we in night.

A little later, a tablet commemorating her was put up in
our small Catholic church in Hurst Green. Paddy composed
and spoke the following prayer at the dedication:

Dear God,
It is so difficult to understand why you took Catherine away
from us. But Your Will in that as in everything else be done.
Thank you for having given Catherine to us for twenty-
three years – a marvellous girl whom none of us will ever
forget.
We remember her gaiety, her enthusiasm, and the real
love she felt for each one of us. For her we ask everlasting
life in Heaven with You.
When we die, we look forward eagerly to being with her
again.
May she rest in peace.

Amen

The fullest account of her was set down at the time by Kevin,
with whom her affinity was notable. Only one or two passages
can be quoted here. She was, it should be mentioned, the only
one of the children who did not go to a university. No one who
knew her doubted her intelligence, but to use Kevin's phrase,
'the choice she took was not to be education-obsessed like the

rest of us', yet by the time of her death 'she believed in education and pure knowledge more than any of us . . . She found her morality and a burning desire to know things when she was old enough to understand'. He tells an anecdote to illustrate the new confidence she had acquired in her relationship with her parents. She was staying with us in our flat and after an exhilarating party which we had all three attended, was apparently saying she didn't intend to go to work. 'Mummy,' goes on Kevin, 'was saying that Catherine looked ghastly. Catherine, of course, returned the compliment. Then suddenly Mummy said to Dada and, at this point, Catherine's face lit up with real glee, as she mimicked the words. "As for you, Frank, you look about a hundred and eight" . . . To Catherine it was fantastically important, because she suddenly saw Mummy and Dada as suffering people whom she knew adored each other, and yet Mummy could say this. She told me this story,' says Kevin, 'about six times, to show that they were really human and loving.' And he concludes: 'When I heard of her death, I couldn't help feeling that she was probably more ready to die than any of us. I think that she was dedicated and that was why she was ready to die.'

All this is confirmed by my own experience. Not long before her death, she was asked by Malcolm Muggeridge to take part in a big television programme, in a series 'The Reason Why'. It was immediately concerned with the Papal announcement '*Humanae Vitae*' on birth control. She read the long document with extraordinary care. Neither I nor any of the other children would have taken so much trouble. She cross-examined me closely, almost line by line, and stimulated me to show her passages in St Thomas Aquinas. She remained unconvinced at the end, but expressed an opinion that she afterwards repeated in the programme: 'I think it is a very loving document.' Her mind was still fresh and eager. In a sense the loss was all the greater, because her powers were only just beginning to blossom. But I agree with Kevin that she had already in the deepest sense found herself, and that she had nothing to fear in this life or the next one.

Letters, wonderful affectionate and compassionate letters, poured in from countless friends and many strangers. I will select from two, for reasons that may occur to readers:

'I know,' wrote Lord Salisbury, my predecessor as Leader of the House of Lords, 'that nothing really helps much at a time of very great sorrow like yours. Only time can ease the pain. But I *can* understand something of what Elizabeth and you must be suffering; for, as you know, we have had the same experience with two of our children. It is the cruellest of all griefs; for as one gets older, one lives more and more in them, and when they die before one, they leave a gap that nothing can fill. I do feel for you more than I can say, and pray that you may be comforted.'

The other letter came from a prisoner whom I was visiting at the time in Maidstone. He wrote to ask me to disregard a previous letter requesting my help because, in his own words, 'my own troubles are so very, very small', and enclosed a copy of his letter to his wife, which left me in no doubt as to the depth of his feeling:

'Darling Mo,' he wrote, 'tonight I have heard some tragic news, which you also will have heard – that of the death of Lord Longford's youngest daughter. I know I don't have to ask you to send some flowers.'

After some kind words about Elizabeth and myself and our devotion to our children, he went on to his wife:

'What I felt straight away was "And I think I have got troubles." Our troubles are as nothing compared with this tragic loss, and I am so very thankful that even if I am in prison, I know or feel that you have a protecting shield round our two children.'

After a visit to Parkhurst I was asked the other day whether I thought I ever did prisoners any good by visiting them. That I cannot be sure of, but I know what some of them have done for me.

It was assumed by many who wrote to us that our Christian faith would prove a large consolation, and they were right. But such relief may not be automatic or immediate. Those who believe in immortality, in any sense, can cherish an expectation of seeing their loved ones again, which is inevitably denied to those for whom the grave is final. But it is, I think, a fairly common experience that an abstract belief in resurrection can remain unshaken without diminishing for a while the ghastly shock of personal deprivation. The terrible question, 'Why should God have done this, or allowed this to happen to me?' may even place on believers an additional agony which agnostics and atheists are spared. Ultimately, Christian hope and faith assert themselves. When I visited Mr de Valera in connection with his biography, he told me that Mrs de Valera wished to have a private word with me. When she received me, she clasped my hands in hers and asked me to carry a special message to my wife. I was aware, of course, that they had lost their beloved son Brian in a riding accident in Phoenix Park in 1936. 'I want you to tell your wife,' she said to me earnestly, 'that when I lost Brian I cried every day for a year. But now, for a long time, I wouldn't have him back.' Her message meant a lot to Elizabeth when I brought it back to her, and still more as time went on and she came to realise its truth.

Elizabeth and I, in our usual studious way, did much reading that autumn about the after-life. Frank Soskice has more than once urged me to write a book on that subject. But I doubt if I shall ever be qualified.

Agnes Headlam-Morley, unfailingly kind to all the children in their life at Oxford, sent us a handsome edition of Dante's *Divine Comedy*. Elizabeth composed and circulated a little Mass Card in memory of Catherine, in which these lines were included:

From Dante's *Purgatorio*:

'This mountain is always hard at the start and the higher one goes it is less difficult; therefore when going up seems to you as pleasant and easy as going down-stream in a boat, then you will be at the end of this path.'

(Last lines of the *Purgatorio*)

'From the most holy waters I came forth again remade, like new plants renewed with new leaves, pure and ready to mount to the stars.'

Two of the other texts cannot be omitted:
Gospel for 11th August, Feast of Saint Susanna, Virgin Martyr. Matthew 25, 1-13:

'And at midnight the cry was raised, Behold, the Bridegroom is on his way; go out to meet him. Thereupon all the virgins awoke and fell to trimming their lamps . . . Be on the watch then: the day of it and the hour of it are unknown to you.'

Tract for 30th April, St Catherine of Siena. Psalm 44, 11-12:

'Listen, my daughter, and consider my words attentively, thy beauty now is all for the King's delight.'

Gervase Mathew had baptised Catherine in February 1946 at the same time as he received Elizabeth into the Catholic Church at St Aloysius, Oxford. He and his brother David, the Archbishop and historian, had helped our family in many varied connections. Now, to the great comfort of Elizabeth, he preached at the Requiem Mass, using words that went home to every one. 'That is why,' he ended, 'we do not believe that Catherine is dead. She is alive and will live for ever. We will grow old as a garment, but she will be the self-same. And we do not believe that she is far away from us, for she is present in God and God is all around us. And always she will be closest to those who love her and to those she loves.'

Much later, Rachel set down some of her own thoughts:

In February 1946 my sister Catherine Rose was born. In February 1973 my daughter Catherine Rose was born. My sister was the sort of person one enjoys remembering.

After Catherine's funeral, I and one of her close friends went along to her flat to sort through her things and decide what to keep. Most of her clothes and girlish clutter of make-up, scents and powder seemed too painfully intimate a memory; some we gave to charity, others filled a dank dustbin. But the books, jewellery, notes for stories, articles, letters, we packed to bring away. At the time, I felt curiously guilty, as if she might come in at any time and accuse us of prying. Death makes a person's privacy public so suddenly.

Yet we only found what made her seem a better person than she showed herself to the world – someone who was trying hard to be better. So I treasure the Sweetheart plant with leaves shaped like hearts which I found on her table and which now grows rampantly in my Dorset kitchen. All the same, I am aware that this was not her, only my earthly instinct to provide the isolation of death with the friendly furniture of the living.

I had a dream on the second anniversary of her death. Catherine was doing what I had done three years before, going to seek her fortune in America. I, as elder sister, was filled with anxieties for her happiness, going away so far, alone. I knew she hated loneliness above all, and this had continued to haunt me about her dying. We were at the airport, her cases packed, and it was a nightmare of parting. Then, suddenly, I was struck by the realisation that this journey to America was nothing to Catherine. For she had braved the supremely difficult journey about which I knew nothing; Catherine had died.

After that dream, I felt confident that the qualities of courage and honesty which had made her in life so special had also conquered death.

'One short sleep past, we wake eternally,
And death shall be no more; death thou shalt die.'

Catherine's death brought home to me something that I should have understood much earlier in life, but have only grasped intermittently at times, during the war, for example. Try as we will, we cannot control our own destiny. There is a large element in our fate which has no perceptible relationship to our own merits or demerits. Anyone who has worked as hard as Elizabeth and I for objects generally considered worthwhile, acquires the habit of looking on results as the product of their own exertions, successful or otherwise. Luck, one is aware, enters in, but tragedy in one's own case is not catered for. Tragedies occur to other people all over the world, at all times. One may devote quite a large part of one's life to relieving them. But in one's own plan of the universe, one acquires the habit of suppressing the possibility that they may occur to oneself. When they crash down on one out of a clear sky, an ancient question that has puzzled mankind since the beginning of recorded history emerges with new force, and far more urgent application: Why does an all-powerful and all-loving God allow such innocent suffering?

From then on, it was inevitable that, for me suffering should occupy a central role.

To Live is to Suffer

How do we explain suffering? How do we *bear* suffering? How do we relieve suffering? There is much overlapping here. The explanation of suffering is likely to be mingled with one's fundamental beliefs, religious or otherwise. It cannot be separated from one's own suffering. Both explanation and acceptance are relevant to one's ability to relieve the sufferings of others.

C. S. Lewis has set out the eternal dilemma as clearly as anyone:

If God were good, He would wish to make His creatures perfectly happy, and if God were almighty, He would be able to do what He wished. But the creatures are not happy, therefore God lacks either goodness or power, or both.

But at this point I must blend the narrative form with something closer to reflection.

When I was preparing my book on *Suffering*, I studied the great religions of the world quite thoroughly. Seneca and the other Stoics were not neglected. It would be an impertinence, however, to try to dispose of the faiths outside the Judao-Christian religion in a passing commentary. Coming to Judaism one moves on to better-known ground. The more profound became the Jewish understanding of God, the more acute the problem not merely of the fact of suffering but of the distribution of it. For a long time the idea was accepted that suffering was a punishment for sin, but unfortunately as Dr Bowker points out in his classic treatise, 'this idea was open to an important objection; it was not true'. Hence arose the special poignancy of the situation of Job, who was essentially defined as innocent. The alternative notion of suffering as a test of faith was also deeply embedded in the Jewish tradition, passing over in later times into the conception of suffering as an ennobling force.

The claim, however, that suffering is or can be ennobling arouses strong conflicting emotions. In November 1970 I participated in a television programme on suffering led by Malcolm Muggeridge. Mr Frank Spath, speaking from a wheelchair on behalf of the Cheshire Homes, described how permanent disablement led on in his own case to permanent studies and ultimately Christian belief. A young Polish student gave a moving account of how he was cured at Lourdes, but the opposite testimony was also given. 'Mrs Peake,' said Malcolm Muggeridge, 'you had to watch over the terrible tragic end of your enormously gifted husband, whom I admired so much. What feeling has it left with you?' Mrs Mervyn Peake replied: 'It is a very sad experience for everybody around to see a man losing every facet of a human being . . . his mind going. I can't see that if I were God, I would let that happen to my child . . . I don't think suffering is ennobling at all.' Yet it is notable that she added: 'I think that we, as a family, are far more compassionate now.' Muggeridge: 'That's something, isn't it?' 'Yes. At a very great price to another man.'

At the other end of the scale came Malcolm Muggeridge himself. 'I tell you, in utter seriousness and truthfulness, that the only thing I have ever learned anything at all from is from suffering - the only thing . . . If I were to subtract that from my life, I would subtract everything that was of any worth.'

On that occasion there was no consensus as to whether suffering ennobles often or very seldom. Few would claim - certainly Malcolm Muggeridge did not claim - that it always ennobles, but just as few would surely claim that no one ever emerges a nobler person after affliction, whether or not one likes to say that the affliction is the cause of the ennoblement.

To judge by the television debate, there is an underlying fear that if one admits that suffering can ennoble, one is weakening the motive for defeating it. But the opposite has been proved by countless saints and healers, from St Vincent de Paul downwards.

But to return to suffering in Judaism. The supreme contribution of Israel lies in their growing awareness that suffering could be made redemptive - that a man's suffering is capable not only of ennobling him if properly accepted, but of redeeming others. This concept appears almost casually in Job - in Deutero-Isaiah it emerges as a superb vision and, of course, the vision was to be vastly deepened and widened through the Passion of Christ.

As regards modern writers, I have space here to quote only from three whom I keep returning to: Kierkegaard, Dostoevsky and Bonhoeffer. Kierkegaard quotes St Matthew (11:30), 'My yoke is good (sic) and my burden is light,' and asks the question: 'How can the burden indeed be light, since suffering is heavy?' He provides a confident answer; the proposition that suffering is good has to be *believed*. It cannot be *seen*. One must have faith that the yoke is good for us. The yoke is indeed Christ's yoke, but only that yoke is Christ's yoke which a sufferer believes is good for him.

No one has ever put the eternal dilemma more vividly than Dostoevsky:

'Tell me frankly, Aloysha,' continues Ivan, 'imagine that it is you yourself who are erecting the edifice of human destiny with the aim of making men happy in the end, of giving them peace and contentment at last, but that to do that it is absolutely necessary, and indeed quite inevitable, to torture to death only one tiny creature, the little girl who beat her breast with her little fist, and to found the edifice on her unavenged tears - would you consent to be the architect on those conditions? Tell me and do not lie!' 'No, I wouldn't,' says Aloysha softly. (Game, set and match, it would appear, to Ivan.) 'You said just now, is there a being in the whole world who could or had the right to forgive? But there is such a Being and He can forgive everything, every one and every thing and FOR EVERY THING, because He gave his innocent blood for all and for every thing. You've forgotten Him, but it is on Him that the edifice is founded, and it is to Him that they will cry aloud: "Thou art just, O Lord, for Thy ways are revealed!" Thus, and thus only, is an ultimate consolation offered by Christianity. Thus only are God's ways, including the extremities of suffering, justified to Christian believers.'

Finally, Bonhoeffer, theologian, hero and martyr of our own time. On 21st July, 1944, the day after he had heard of the

263

failure of the anti-Hitler conspiracy and the crash of all his hopes, he wrote one of his most arresting letters from prison, using language that must at first sight seem surprising: 'During the last year,' he wrote, 'I have come to appreciate the *worldliness* of Christianity . . . I am still discovering up to this very moment that it is only by living completely in this world that one learns to believe.' This, at a moment when worldly hopes of rescuing his country from total catastrophe and, incidentally, of saving himself from a horrible death had just received a mortal blow. 'For a long time,' he continues, 'I thought that I could acquire faith by trying to live a holy life or something like it.' But he had come to feel that his purpose contained an element of selfishness; he embraced a worldliness, a deeper involvement in humanity, and a new approach to suffering.

By *worldliness* he had come to mean abandoning every attempt to make something special of himself. He now meant 'taking life in one's stride with all its duties and problems, its successes and failures, its experiences and helplessness. How could success,' he wrote, 'make us arrogant, or failure lead us astray, when we participate in the *sufferings of God* by living in this world?' And with these words on his lips and this spirit in his heart, he was taken to his execution by the Gestapo to what he called 'not the end, but the beginning of Life'.

Kierkegaard, Dostoevsky and Bonhoeffer were permeated with Christian thought and feeling. We must turn back briefly to their source. No one can deny that the Christian religion is related in a special way to the theory and practice of suffering, or that the Christian doctrine of suffering is different from any other. Since the Crucifixion, the whole subject has been carried on to a different plane. Christian teaching is shot through and through with the fact that God became Man and died for mankind in great agony on the Cross.

It is not only that Jesus Christ came on earth to proclaim a new and far higher ethic and was executed horribly for doing so. It was not only that he exhibited under extreme suffering a sublime charity in such words as those from the Cross: 'Father, forgive them, for they know not what they do.' There is a further, all-important aspect. No one who accepts the Gospel story can doubt that Christ underwent his sufferings on the Cross deliberately. They were the culmination of His life's plan. 'The Son of Man has not come to have service done to Him, but to serve others and to give His life a ransom for many.' It is clear that Christ set a supreme example of self-sacrifice and of readiness to endure intolerable suffering. In some sense at least, whoever calls himself a Christian is under an obligation to copy Him.

Passing for the moment from the example of Christ's life and death, what doctrine of suffering is actually spelt out in the Gospel? The explicit passages are very few, they can be counted on the fingers of one hand (allowing for repetition as between the synoptics. There is no spelt-out directive in St John). We read in Matthew 10:38: 'He is not worthy of Me that does not take up his cross and follow Me.' (Knox translation.) The thought continues: 'He who secures his own life will lose it; it is the man who loses his life for My sake that will secure it.'

We are taken a little further in Matthew 16:24: 'If any man hath a mind to come My way, let him renounce self and take up his cross and follow Me.'

There is a different kind of reference to suffering in the Sermon on the Mount (Matthew 5:4): 'Blessed are those who mourn, for they shall be comforted.' The doctrine quoted from Chapters 10 and 16 is rounded off in 20 and 21: 'Jesus asked them: "Have you strength to drink of the cup I am to drink of?"' They said: 'We have.' And He told them: 'You shall indeed drink of My cup.' The central message is unequivocal. To follow Christ involves self-sacrifice and suffering, faithfulness to death in spirit if not in the physical happening.

And that is virtually all the direct instructions in the Gospel about the duty of suffering, apart from the special duty to face persecution. Apart also from the aforementioned, 'Blessed are those who mourn, for they shall be comforted.' Here, it is true, we are not told we *ought* to mourn; we are instead consoled by the prospect of future bliss, if we should find ourselves afflicted in this life.

We have not mentioned so far the references made by Jesus to His own suffering, which have provided such abundant food for spiritual meditations. Of these perhaps the cries from Gethsemane and from the Cross itself are the most famous of all. 'Father, if it pleases Thee take away this chalice from Me . . . only as Thy will is, not as Mine is . . .' 'My God, My God, why hast Thou forsaken Me?' although the latter can never be quoted without the last word of all from the Cross, resignation overcoming agony: 'Father, into Thy hands I commend My spirit.'

Two further passages from St Luke cannot be omitted - 24:26 (on the road to Emmaus): 'Was it not to be expected that the Christ should undergo these sufferings and enter into His glory?' And on the same evening when He appeared in the midst of the disciples: 24:46: 'So it was written, He told them, and so it was fitting that Christ should suffer and should rise again from the dead on the third day . . .' These passages could admittedly be understood to carry a reference limited to Christ's own mission, viz. that His own crucifixion represented a task which only He could effectively perform. Or it could convey a universal message and universal duty to all of us men and women, and this is how I believe it should be understood.

So far, then, the Gospel, easy to follow in thought, if not in deed. The Christian must never cease to seek perfection; in that life-long search suffering is an ineluctable element while the natural man is being fought and overcome. Be it noted that this is not the same as saying that *all* suffering is helpful to perfection. It does not detract for a moment from the overwhelming duty to relieve suffering wherever possible. Suffering and self-sacrifice are not, of course, identical. Self-sacrifice is a moral act on our part, suffering itself is neither moral nor immoral. It is our attitude towards it, towards its infliction, relief or acceptance that exhibits moral value or the opposite.

*

Again and again we have found the Christian answer to suffering expressed in terms of acceptance; whether sheer stoical endurance, welcome to the manifest will of God, or union through suffering to Christ crucified on behalf of the world. The Reverend Hugh Hopkins, in *The Mystery of Suffering*, quotes a moving poem by Amy Carmichael, written after the loss of a close personal friend and indispensable colleague in missionary work in South India. The last lines of each verse bring before us a whole wealth of meaning and range of attitude.

'Not in forgetting lieth peace . . .
Not in endeavour lieth peace . . .
Not in aloofness lieth peace . . .
Not in submission lieth peace . . .
For in acceptance lieth peace.'

For her, acceptance meant not any certainty as to the meaning of particular sufferings, but 'contentment with the unexplained due to a deep-seated faith in the loving providence of God'. No doubt, in one form or another, that will always be the attitude of believing Christians in the face of inexplicable suffering, but there are logical problems which should at least be clarified, if faith is not to be opposed to reason.

The Reverend Hugh Hopkins devotes a chapter to the question, 'Can suffering ever be God's will?' He found in his hospital visiting many sick persons who bravely told him, 'I think this must be my cross.' But this language he is at pains to repudiate. We should say with confidence about our troubles, not 'this *is* the will of God', but rather 'it is certainly *within* the will of God'. He puts the answer this way: 'The important thing to notice is that whenever the ideal will of God is frustrated and His permissive plans begin to operate, it is certain that a degree of pain and suffering are involved.' In other words, the ideal will is the will of God as it would operate if it were not interfered with by man's sinfulness. The permissive will is the will as it actually operates in the sinful world we live in.

This distinction between the ideal will and the permissive will makes logical sense at ordinary levels of discussion. There is, however, no escaping from many expressions in spiritual books which seem to imply that God's will is carried out as He intends it to be carried out in everything that happens. If we turn for a moment to de Caussade's great treatise on self-abandonment to Divine Providence, we find this almost at random: 'Divine activity floods the whole universe, it pervades all creatures, it flows over them. We have but to allow ourselves to be carried forward on the crest of its waves . . . What happens to us each moment by God's design is for us the holiest, best and most divine thing.'

But put the other side of the argument, at its most extreme. Can anybody say that the Nazi massacres of the Jews were in any meaningful sense designed by God? The thought is so repulsive that surely it has only to be mentioned to be rejected. Could any of us in Catherine's little world believe that God designed her death in that way, and at that age? And yet de Caussade's doctrine has had appeal to many massive intellects and sensitive souls for two hundred and fifty years. There must be some explanation which disposes of so obvious and crude a difficulty. Perhaps it can be found, again picking on a sentence almost at random, in phraseology of this kind: 'It was enough for those who led a spiritual life to see that each moment brought with it a duty to be faithfully fulfilled.'

When he writes that 'passive fidelity consists in the loving acceptance of all that God sends us at every moment', the thought is surely the same, and it fits in with the more prosaic language quoted from the Reverend Hugh Hopkins. I suppose that the more religious a man or woman, the more imbued he or she has been with the feeling described by de Caussade, that Divine activity floods the whole universe. God is everywhere and in everything and in everybody. But how far and how often, and in what precise fashion He is intervening day by day to correct the distortion introduced by the sins and errors of men, this no one can say; no profound believer is in the slightest degree disturbed at the limitation of human understanding at this point.

We have most of us had enough experience by now to know that out of great suffering, or even injustice, still greater good can be achieved by God, with or without the activity of men; but in face of any particular distress or evil, we cannot and must not take it on ourselves to announce that we can see the hand of the Lord at work. What we believe, and clearly it needs faith to believe it, is that God intervenes in the world process sufficiently to make sure that whatever the evil or tragedy for each one of us, a duty of the successive moment emerges. In that sense, the duties that flow from the events of the world are sent to us directly by God. And, of course, there is the ultimate conviction that *in the end* the will of God will prevail. In that sense, the supremacy of God's providence can never be challenged.

I began by distinguishing three questions - How do we explain suffering? How do we bear suffering? How do we relieve suffering? I have touched on Christian answers, not, I hope, unhelpful to others. But a fourth question is clearly inseparable. How does one *use* suffering? - for one's own benefit and that of humanity. The first answer must be that one should use it to purify oneself, in the interests of oneself and others. And the second that one must use it with a redemptive purpose. The purification may take a very active form. I had the very honourable task of introducing into the House of Lords, in 1970, the Disablement Bill, which will always be associated with its creator, Alf Morris, M.P. Suffering, I declared, in my Second Reading speech, while it sometimes degrades, can also ennoble. It was not difficult to perceive illustrations of the latter proposition on the floor of the House - Sue Masham, Davina d'Arcy de Knayth, Mike Crawshaw and Martin Ingleby - all crippled for life, all speaking from wheelchairs, a unique phenomenon, one would imagine, in the legislative chambers of the world. But they would be the first to point out that they had been granted opportunities of making public use of their suffering in a fashion denied to the disabled generally. Not only in my connection with the disabled, but as chairman for a number of years of the National Society for the Mentally Handicapped, I know well the quiet heroism in the face of suffering which is exhibited by countless ordinary people. I can pay ample tribute to the purifying use that is made of it.

Christianity, however, is not only a code of ethics but a theology. The idea of redemptive suffering is certainly not confined to Christianity and owes much, as already pointed out, to the Old Testament. But the Christian story by its very nature places redemptive suffering at the centre of its whole doctrine, alike in theory and in practice. There is here much that is mysterious. I have not, so far, undergone much physical suffering, but no father of a large family can avoid his share of mental anxieties, not to mention those which spring from his own frailty. Like all instructed Christians, I try to offer up my personal sufferings for the benefit of others, often uncertain as to whether I would do better to put them out of mind as far as possible. Yet I cling feebly, at an immense distance, to the example of the Saints. Men and women that I have known, of real spirituality, achieve redemptive suffering far less self-consciously.

I stand, shall we say, in front of someone totally paralysed, who accepts his affliction sublimely. I note the ennobling effect of his example on those around, but a Christian must surely believe that even if their example were known to no one, the mystic power of his redemptive acceptance would reach out and benefit humanity. If I am told that this is to impute a miraculous influence to suffering, I would accept the term only if one intends to use it of all prayer offered for others and all love that operates from afar.

A Single Thread

Then with a rush the intolerable craving
Shivers throughout me like a trumpet call
Oh! to save these, to perish for their saving,
Die for their life, be offered for them all.
              F. W. H. MYERS – St Paul

What does it all add up to? At 67, one must begin to take stock.
Cicero was only 62 when he wrote his treatise on old age, *De
Senectute*. Sir Walter Scott was 54 when he forecast as a finale,
'Good night Sir Walter about 60!' In fact, he died at 61. It's
true that Gladstone formed his last Ministry at 82, Disraeli at
69, and Churchill at 76. Simone de Beauvoir tells us that among
human beings old age is hard to define, which is perhaps
obvious. But whether one calls oneself ageing, elderly or, more
simply and honestly, old, one is well aware that one's natural
force is well past its maximum. One must expect to operate
with a diminishing stimulus of public attention and to be
steadily overhauled by young and vigorous spirits. 'The crown-
ing glory of old age,' said Cicero, 'is influence.' One knows of
cases where this is still true, but not as many as we older ones
could wish. He said also, 'I am profoundly grateful to old age
which has increased my eagerness for conversation and taken
away that for food and drink.' I concur happily with the first
part but not so readily with the second part of that statement.

It is disconcerting to find that the love of fame dies harder
than one cares to admit. In a different context, Simone Weil
described 'the unsatisfied appetite, the desire to keep on increasing one's circle', as due to 'a desire for contact with universal beauty'. I wish that I could think that it was always so.
For my part I strive to bear in mind continuously the intima-
tion that the first will be the last, and even if one has not been
exactly among the first, to make preparations accordingly.

If one is wise and reasonably fortunate, and content to live
increasingly in the lives of one's children and others, one can

still have confidence that 'the best is yet to be'. Certainly the obligation to help one's fellow-men does not diminish with one's range of usefulness. One's duty to 'make one's soul' increases as the years hasten on, though in my case a short burst of notoriety has not been helpful. It would be prudent for me to assume that in any sense known to the public, my main contribution has now been offered. They are entitled to form their assessment on what they have seen hitherto.

My son Paddy asked me the other day whether I had been a success or a failure. Robin Day, with his usual penetrating gaze, asked me a similar question. In the sight of God the question is, of course, unanswerable. (One need not necessarily agree with Kevin that success is human, while failure is Divine.) Even by a mundane standard, the answer is bound to be relative. I asked Paddy whom he regarded as a successful man, and he replied at once, 'Lord Hailsham.' A very fair answer, when one thinks of Quintin's long string of brilliant performances, from his triumphs at Eton and Oxford to his present eminence on the Woolsack. But when Quintin missed the Premiership in 1963, after leaving the House of Lords to win it, one would have said the opposite, and I have no idea how he would answer the question in his own heart today. In the same way, Lord Curzon goes down in history as a brilliant failure for losing the Premiership to Baldwin. Yet he was otherwise loaded with every kind of honour. Most Prime Ministers come to unhappy ends, Chamberlain and Baldwin being two of the most notable examples. Do we call this latter pair successes or failures?

Starting, so to speak, at the other end, one pictures literally millions of people, the majority of the population in fact, who have no reason to regard their lives as failures and, in old age, look back contentedly on success in their own vocations.

For myself, I have pointed out earlier that I have not reached the highest level in any one occupation. It seems safest therefore to leave my performance situated somewhere between the heights and the depths, nearer perhaps the first than the second. The question of success or failure in the worldly sense will obviously not be the crucial one in front of St Peter. Nor will it be totally irrelevant. He will surely want to know how far we have used the talents given us. I have been very fortunate in more ways than one. A hereditary title, even if it has ruled out the highest posts of all which, in any case, I would not have attained, has given me a much better than average chance of influence. A first class degree may be attributed to my good work at Oxford, but just as readily to a natural academic talent which was apparent by the time I was nine. I have been happily married for forty years to someone who was the most remarkable girl of her time at Oxford and, quite independently of me, has won widespread renown. When I think of all that has been bestowed on me, beyond my personal merits, I am humbled and abashed in front of the limited outcome.

What, then, have been my governing ideas and motives? My son Michael has recorded for my benefit what he calls my 'obsessions'. My obsession with sport; with the Press, with the maintenance of what he calls a moral stance and the exercise of political power. He reminds me, as readers of this book have been reminded, that there has never been a time when I was not proud to call myself an Irishman. This is something, says Michael, which comes close to being the 'perfect motto' for me. I am happy to think he is right. But it is, I suppose, a beginning rather than a finish.

Much was written about me in 1971 and 1972, and a good many interviews short and long were published. Most of them concentrated on my connection with pornography, though this was certainly not true of some very generous writing by Harold Hobson, Susan Barnes and others, in this country and abroad. Two articles appearing on the eve of the Pornography Report's publication tried to put my latest so-called crusade in the perspective of my life's activities. The *Observer* profile, under the heading 'Anti-pornographer Royal', was written, I understand, by one old and dear friend, Philip Toynbee, with some assistance from another, the editor, David Astor. *The Times'* centre page article was headed 'The Many Paths to Glory', with a reference on page one to 'the Humble Peer'. The author was Geoffrey Wansell, a young and highly intelligent reporter, whom I did not know previously, but who had interviewed me intensively. If by some odd chance a foreigner had arrived in England at that moment and wished to know about me, he could have got a very fair picture from these two articles.

Philip I would always regard as one of my half-dozen true intimates. Grandson of Gilbert and Lady Mary Murray, son of Arnold Toynbee, he was a scholar of Christ Church and a Communist president of the Oxford Union (he has long since renounced Communism), while I was finding my feet in the highly Marxist atmosphere of the Oxford Labour Party in the thirties. Apart from an occasional raid on his fastness near Chepstow, I see him, alas, very seldom nowadays. I feel entitled, therefore, to remedy some gaps in his knowledge. After reciting the facts of my conversion to Socialism and Catholicism, he continued: 'It is harder to say what set him on the course that he has increasingly followed, of devoting himself to serving the interests of those in greatest need.' As regards pornography, he comments: 'Some would say that there must be a neurotic basis to Longford's campaign against what he often calls by the unscientific term of "filth", on screen, stage and in the printed word.' I should add that the article is more than generous to anything I have tried to do for prisoners and young people in difficulties. What I respectfully point out is that no central clue is offered, though personally I believe one to be available. Putting down this article one gets, I should imagine, a vivid impression of the type of man who would take the many heterogeneous steps referred to. But it all seems to be attributed to feeling, mostly humane feeling, rather than thought. Whereas I see myself a compound of the two. The fact is barely mentioned in the article that I was a tutor at Christ Church. But in my own eyes at least I am a person of strong academic bent, with an endless determination to work out general ideas and apply them in practice. The late John Strachey comes into my mind as a natural comparison.

Geoffrey Wansell remains closer to the surface than Philip, but in one sense he was more up-to-date, as he had the chance to question me. He quotes me as saying in conclusion: 'If you suggest that my life is a series of paradoxes - in favour of prison reform and against pornography; a Socialist and a banker - I would say that the thread is my Christianity. My main purpose in life is to try to give effect to Christian principles, particularly the Gospels.' I am glad he finished in that way.

Philip's 'Profile' in an overwhelmingly flattering comparison with the later Tolstoy, records the final judgment: 'He remains essentially paradoxical.' The question arises whether anyone who tried to base a public life on the Gospels, in the Britain of 1972, must incur this epithet, or whether the paradoxical flavour is something peculiar to me.

Let me take the latter point first. Years ago in the House of Lords, Lord Jowitt was sharply attacking Lord Beveridge and, pointing his finger at him, asserted: 'The noble Lord looks confused.' 'I am not confused,' insisted my old master, Lord Beveridge, half rising and blushing violently. 'The noble Lord looks confused,' repeated Jowitt, forensically remorseless, and by this time there was no disputing his statement. In that respect I am like Beveridge. If anyone chooses to call me eccentric, genially or otherwise, I cannot resist them. In costume I never deliberately set out to flout convention, or arouse unnecessary comment, but I must admit to having achieved some surprising effects without intending to. When I was asked, at the age of 66, to join in a game of football for charity, in company with Bobby Moore and other heroes, I could not resist the fun of participation. If Bunny Girls playing in the previous match wished to be photographed obtaining my autograph – well, who was any the worse off? And, after all, who knows, it might even have humanised my image, at a time when our opponents were out to present me as a senile tyrant. Still, it must have seemed rather unusual conduct.

What has not been urged against me recently, although it has never quite ceased to worry me, is that my comfortable way of life is in conflict with Socialist principles. I am not, in fact, in my own right, at all a rich man. I would not be able to maintain our flat in London and our small place in the country without the large literary earnings of my wife in recent years. Still, on any fair reckoning, my standard of life is far above the average. I can only plead that since I became a Socialist in the middle thirties, I have at all times acted in total disregard of my economic interests. I very much regretted the failure of the Labour Cabinet to reduce their own salaries along with the other cuts in 1968. But at that very moment I was resigning, so my standing in the argument was weak. I have always been prepared to give up all economic advantages, if necessary, but large sacrifices have never been called for. Long before my brother died, I had stepped out of the family inheritance and, later, tried to give up my seat in the House of Lords. I have nothing in this area to be proud of, but equally nothing to hide.

Philip, in his 'Profile', did not deal with this sordid topic. But he put his finger on something much more fundamentally disquieting. He quotes the view that 'Longford has never entirely managed to shed that touch of inner arrogance that seems to be fed to the aristocracy with their mother's milk'. I don't think that this kind of arrogance is confined to the aristocracy - but let that pass. The trouble about it is that it seems to be so deeply rooted, affecting even one's physical aspect, that one cannot recognise it in oneself and has no idea of how to diminish its effect on others. Years ago, Tony Crosland told me that I would have had much more influence on his generation if I had not shown such arrogance towards the waiters in the George Café, Oxford. I admired Tony's gifts enormously, as a writer and social thinker, but in this particular sphere I felt that it was a case of the pot calling the kettle black. Still, I have never forgotten his criticism and ever since have set out to be positively obsequious to waiters.

In previous writings I have mentioned jealousy as the weakness I was most conscious of in myself. Since my official career ended, and in some indeterminate sense I retired, I am, in the nature of things, less thrown into direct competition. Today I am more conscious of arrogance than jealousy, although aware that the first may well breed the second. The arrogance I have in mind probably springs from an inflated idea of what I am entitled to expect from life, and this, I fear, is a fault that is very common among the children of privilege. If one's mental empire is illegitimately expanded one tends to be apprehensive about potential invaders who do not share one's own view of one's importance. I admittedly find it hardest to love those, including colleagues, who would diminish my self-esteem, but surely that is common enough. I am usually at ease with the weak or rejected. At any rate, if I am to be convicted of arrogance, let me add in self-defence that I have proved myself aware of this defect, which was, consciously or subconsciously, very much in my mind when I wrote my small book on *Humility* (1969), after no little study of spiritual theory and political practice. The man who wrote that book did not see himself as 'the humble Peer' referred to by *The Times*, but as one who knew his need of humility.

There are other aspects of my character, or temperament, which would, no doubt, be of some interest to the psychiatrist. Am I more or less insecure than the average? More or less obsessional? More or less aggressive? More or less ambitious, in any sense of the word? No man can be his own best judge in these matters. In respect of the qualities mentioned, I do not feel that I differ much from my political contemporaries. After all the pornography bally-hoo I have been accused, not surprisingly, of an undue taste for publicity. More than most politicians, I wonder? What was called by *The Times* after our Danish visit a 'flair for public relations' has been referred to elsewhere as disastrous. In any case, as I once heard Lord Chandos say on television, 'the best men in public life are primarily concerned to put over their ideas, and if one is not in an official position how else but by publicity?' But one cannot be unaware of the spiritual dangers. As I draw towards an end let me relate my ideas to basic Christian conceptions.

For Christians, the overriding priority belongs to the two commandments: Thou shalt love the Lord thy God with all thy heart and with all thy mind and with all thy soul and with all thy strength. And thou shalt love thy neighbour as thyself. A Christian will be judged in the last resort by the extent to which he lives up to these two injunctions. I include his prayers, his spiritual reading, his devotion to his Church and to the Sacraments. But the second commandment, in so far as it inculcates a general benevolence, is not unique to Christianity, and in one formula or another is pursued by all altruistic people. What is more clearly distinguishable in Christianity is, in the first place, the doctrine of humility, and in the second place that of forgiveness.

In my book on *Humility*, I distinguished five main meanings of humility:

1. Knowledge of oneself as one is.
2. The opposite of pride.

3. Meekness in conduct.
4. Obedience (where I found myself particularly weak).
5. Service.

But at all points I went back to the Gospels. Christian humility, I insisted, begins with Christ. In a sense it ends there. The whole life and death of Christ are, of course, a stupendous example of the virtue. The point has been put on endless occasions, but never more effectively than in Philippians 2:6-8, where we are told that Jesus Christ 'emptied himself, taking the form of a servant, being made in the likeness of men and in habit found as a man. He humbled himself, becoming obedient unto death, even to the death of the cross.'

The explicit instructions in regard to our own humility are limited to a few passages, although the conception is everywhere prevalent. If only one text can be quoted here, let us take Matthew 18:3-4:

'Unless you turn and become like children you will never enter the kingdom of heaven. Whoever humbles himself like this child he is the greatest in the kingdom of heaven.'

If anyone asks me whether one of the highest persons in the land is truly great, I begin to apply this test to them. It may well be a counsel of perfection, but all the same a good criterion. Wellington's 'I am but a man' already quoted is a classic example of a humble attitude in circumstances of earthly glory.

Lord Attlee and Field-Marshal Lord Alexander of Tunis can be cited as outstanding examples of humility and even, as we say in the House of Lords, 'at this late hour', it is worth pausing on this comparison for a moment. Only the humble man, as I see it, is capable of treating every human being as of equal and infinite worth. Nothing less can satisfy anyone who aspires to be called a Christian. At the risk of being misunderstood, I must record that my idea of Christian humility leads straight to Socialism, admittedly in some vague sense, as no doubt did Lord Attlee's. Yet I have just said that Lord Alexander was equally humble, and while he was certainly no political partisan, he served in Sir Winston Churchill's Conservative Government. It comes down therefore to this: Some of us trying to apply Christian ideas of humility find them incompatible with any system that does not seek to produce the equality of man on this earth, treating all men as potential brothers - black, white, yellow or brown. Other Christians, equally humble in personal life and aspiration, do not believe that such an equality can be realised here below. For my part I belong to the former school and ever more ardently.

All this is a long way from support for any particular social or economic policy, and still farther from an assessment of the effectiveness of rival parties.

There is no substitute for hard unremitting (factual) work on the great issues of the day where the technical and moral elements are inseparable - world peace, racial justice, riches and poverty among the nations, inflation and industrial relations at home. The last two issues dominate British thought as I write these words. But Christian humanism supplies a starting point, an unfailing inspiration and an inflexible criterion of merit.

Whatever else has been discouraging in the history of the last ten years, there has been one front at least on which we have seen triumphant progress. A Catholic priest said to me recently: 'Today, if you meet anyone who tells you that he is a Christian you feel at once a bond, a bridge, a warmth between you. Fifteen years ago, your first instinct was to ask yourself, "Is he my sort of Christian?" Your first reaction was one of prudence, of wariness.' All that has wonderfully diminished since the Vatican Council and, on the Anglican side, the historic visit of the Archbishop of Canterbury to Rome. Cardinal Heenan, the present Archbishop of Canterbury and the free church leaders have never wavered in their ecumenical purpose.

Father Heenan, Father John as he allows his friends to call him, remains at heart a parish priest; pre-eminently, in spite of all his successes in the pulpit and on television, a pastor of souls. In my own religious life, I owe most in these years to Father Docherty in Hurst Green, Father de Zulueta in Chelsea, and Father d'Arcy and Father Corbishley elsewhere.

Have I provided an answer to the question how I came to be involved with the rejected of men? If not I have pointed towards one. If one is a committed Socialist in my sense one does not confine oneself to seeking to aid the British working class, or even underdeveloped countries and underprivileged races. One reads and re-reads Matthew 18 - verses 12-13:

12: Suppose a man has a hundred sheep and one of them goes astray, what do you think he will do? Will he not leave the ninety-nine on the mountain side and go after the one that strayed?

13: And if he is lucky enough to find it, believe me, he rejoices more over it than over the ninety-nine that did not stray.

One strives harder to identify and rescue those outcasts whose plight is most compelling. Sometimes, but not always, for often there is no question of blame, one needs to draw on Christian depths of forgiveness. A famous American prisoner serving a sentence of 'life plus ninety-nine years' was helped in many ways by many people often in the face of much opprobrium. In his book he passionately asks himself what justification there was for all this noble exertion on his behalf. What was there in him that drew it forth? And he replies unhesitatingly: 'Only my great need. But that apparently is enough for real champions.' These words have echoed and re-echoed throughout my brain. They sum up the motivation that led to the New Bridge for ex-prisoners and the New Horizon for young people with urgent problems; to my chairmanship for several years of the National Association for the Mentally Handicapped and my intense preoccupation with the mentally troubled.

I should be proud indeed if anyone applied to me the words I used of the unforgettable Dick Stokes, the outstandingly Catholic politician of my period - 'He was always the prophet of the neglected cause.' But that is a large pretension.

So I finish by offering a limited but, I hope, coherent system of Christianity in action, with emphasis falling again and yet again on charity, humility and forgiveness. In a not very satisfactory book by Freud and Bullett about President Wilson, the authors said of him - 'Wilson, after all, stood for human decency. He stood weakly for human decency, but he stood where it was an honour to stand.' It has been an honour to have the opportunity of speaking as a Christian here and elsewhere. If the practice followed is far inferior to the ideals propounded, let not the blame fall on the source of the message.

Index

Abbott, Joan, 161
Abse, Leo, 179
Adams, Miss J, 157
Adeane, Sir Michael, 241
Adenauer, Konrad, 94
Aitken, Sir Max, 209
Akass, Jon, 220-1
Albemarle, Countess of, 154
Alexander of Tunis, 'Alex' (1st Earl of), 278
Alexander of Hillsborough, Albert (1st Earl of), 22-3, 28-9, 41
Alexandra, Princess, 137
Anderson, Professor Norman, 188, 191, 221, 222, 223
Ansley, Cyril, 252
Armstrong, William, 239, 241 passim to 247
Arran, 'Boofy' (8th Earl of), 41, 179
Astor, the Hon. David, 130, 209, 249, 273
Attlee, Clement (1st Earl), 21, 28, 29, 53, 64, 69, 71, 94, 278
Ayer, Sir Alfred, 19

Bacon, Alice, 131
Bader, Group Captain Douglas, 241
Barnes, Susan, 273
Barrington, Patrick (11th Viscount), 185, 227
Beetson, The Rev. Trevor, 192
Beswick, Frank (Baron), 189, 226
Beveridge, William (Baron), 21, 188, 201, 275
Bevan, Aneurin, 62, 66, 71
Bevin, Ernest, 37, 55, 222
Biggs, Norman, 45
Billington, Kevin, 69, 228

Billington, Lady Rachel, 69, 228, 234, 246, 252, 253, 259
Birkenhead, Freddy (2nd Earl of), 248, 249
Birkenhead, Countess of, 249
Blackburn, Raymond, 15, 226
Blake, Robert, 250
Blond, Anthony, 240, 247
Bluck, Judith, 67
Bodkin, Professor, 91
Boland, Fred, 87
Bonham-Carter, Lady Violet, 68
Boothby, Robert (Baron), 179
Bottomley, Arthur, 56
Bourne, Joan, 131, 154, 197
Boyle, Edward (Baron), 153
Boyle, Kevin, 104
Bradford, Roy, 104
Brady, Ian, 126, 140-52
Brandreth, Gyles, 198-9
Brien, Alan, 223, 225
Brockway, Fenner (Baron), 68
Brodie, Peter, Asst. Commissioner, 119, 120, 221-2
Brooke, Henry (Baron), 14, 15
Bullock, Sir Alan, 233
Burrows, Henry, 34-5, 39

Calder, John, 217
Callaghan, James, 44-5, 49, 57, 65, 107, 184
Campbell, Judith, 241
Cape, Jonathan, 235, 246
Carr, Peter, 50, 216, 218, 225
Carrington, Peter (6th Baron), 34, 38-9, 40
Castle, Barbara, 59, 72, 74
Catherwood, Sir Frederick, 191, 220, 221
Cecil, Lord David, 249

Champion, Joseph (Baron), 32, 40
Chandos, Oliver Lyttelton (1st (Viscount), 229, 277
Chichester-Clark, James, 103, 104
Churchill, Randolph, 29, 86
Churchill, Sir Winston, 86, 92, 95
Clive, Lady Mary, 234
Cobbold, Cameron (1st Baron), 233
Cockburn, Claud, 241
Cole, Dr Martin, 189
Cole, Peter, 215
Coleman, John, 212
Collins, Pierre (Lady), 236-7
Collins, Sir William, 233, 243, 246
Colville, Mark (4th Viscount), 226
Compton, S. D., Miss, 157
Connolly, Cyril, 223, 224
Conway, Cardinal, 105-6, 108, 112
Cooper, Lady Diana (Diana, Viscountess Norwich), 15
Corbishley, Thomas (Rev.), Father, 115, 279
Cosgrave, Liam, 113
Cousins, Frank, 56, 62
Craig, Christopher, 135-6
Craig, Niven, 135-6
Craig, William, 100-1, 102
Crawley, Virginia, 249
Crawshaw, William (4th Baron), 269
Cripps Sir Stafford, 57
Croft, Michael Page (2nd Baron), 137
Crosland, Anthony, 32, 46, 53, 57, 60, 65, 74, 154, 276
Crossman, Richard, 36, 38, 39, 40, 48 57, 74
Cupitt, Don, the Rev., 119, 121

Dalton, Cardinal, 91
Dalton, Hugh, 15, 56
D'Arcy, de Knayth, Davina (Baroness), 269
D'Arcy, Very Rev. Martin Cyril, 19, 279

Davies, Lord Justice Edmund, 128, 191
Davies, Rev. Meredith, 159
Day, Robin, 119, 192, 272
Deeney, Finnoula, 97, 102
De Gaulle, General Charles, 94
Delderfield, Dennis, 221
Denniston, Robin, 97
De Valera, Eamon, 16, 83, 86-7, 91, 92-94, 237, 258
De Valera, Mrs, 93, 258
De Zulueta, Alfonso, Father, 279
Devlin, Bernadette, 86, 102
Devlin, Paddy, 102, 103
Docherty, Father, 216, 279
Donaldson, Frankie (Lady), 249
Donaldson, Jack (Baron), 129
Donnison, Polly, 242
Dufferin and Ava, Sheridan Frederick (5th Marquess), 85
Dulanty, John, 88
Durbin, Evan, 13, 16, 86
Du Sautoy, Stephen, 238
Dworkin, Professor Ronald, 214, 223, 225

Eccles, David (1st Viscount), 189, 190
Elizabeth II, 195-6, 241
Evans, Harold, 209

Faulkner, Brian, 103
Ferguson, Richard, 104
Fisher, Most Rev. Geoffrey (Baron), 115
Fitt, Gerry, 103
Fitzgerald, Desmond, 113
Fitzgerald, Garret, 113
Fleming, Ian, 235
Fleming, Peter, 235
Fletcher, Eric (Baron), 212-13, 214, 227
Foot, Michael, 35
Forbes, Bryan, 212
Forester, Margery, 242

Forte, Sir Charles, 233, 238
Franks, Sir Oliver, 233
Fraser, Lady Antonia, 28, 188, 219, 234, 242, 252, 253, 254
Fraser, Hugh, 28, 39, 86, 187, 255
Fraser, Rebecca, 242
Fraser, Tom, 56
Freeman, John, 71

Gage, Henry (6th Viscount), 67
Gaitskell, Hugh, 23-4, 53, 58, 59, 73, 233
Gaitskell, Dora (Baroness), 76, 189
Gallagher, Rev. Eric, 102
Gardiner, Gerald (Baron), 30-1, 33, 35, 39, 57, 66, 67, 108, 131
George VI, 16
George-Brown, George (Baron), 44-5, 53, 54-6, 57, 62, 65, 66
Gibson, Ashton, 156
Gold, Ralph and David, 210
Gollancz, Sir Victor, 244, 246
Goodman, Arnold (Baron), 189, 191, 192, 227
Gordon Walker, Patrick, 32, 37, 64, 65, 67, 68
Grant, Alec, 156, 157
Green, Maurice, 220
Greenwood, Anthony (Baron), 30
Griffiths, James, 68
Gummer, John Selwyn, 197
Gunter, Ray, 56, 62, 65, 154

Hailsham, Quintin (Baron), 30, 33, 272
Hair, Gilbert, 122
Hardcastle, William, 192
Harris, Harold, 92, 236-7
Hartwell, Michael Berry (Baron), 209
Hartwell, Lady, 249
Headlam-Morley, Agnes, 258
Healey, Denis, 74
Heath, Edward, 27, 50, 57, 60, 71, 111

Heenan, John, Cardinal, Archbishop of Westminster, 58, 69, 279
Henderson, Sir Nicholas, 249
Herbert, Sir Alan, 182, 187, 224
Herbison, Margaret, 62, 76
Hertford, Hugh (8th Marquess of), 137
Hewitt, W. R. (C. H. Rolph), 129, 223-4
Hindley, Myra, 126, 140-1, 147-8, 216, 217, 218
Hobson, Harold, 273
Holbrook, David, 213, 221
Home, Sir Alec Douglas-, 57, 99
Hope, Francis, 215
Hopkins, Rev. Hugh, 267-8
Howard, Anthony, 40
Howard, Michael, 246
Howell, Dennis, 154
Huddleston, Rt. Rev. Trevor, Bishop of Stepney, 57, 228
Hume, John, 104
Hunt, John (Baron), 68, 107, 132
Hunt, Nikki, 160 passim to 164

Ingleby, Martin (2nd Viscount), 269

Jagger, Mick, 193
Jay, Douglas, 45, 54, 74
Jay, Peggy, 131
Jellicoe, George Patrick (2nd Earl), 33, 34, 39
Jenkins, Roy, 30, 31-2, 43, 53, 58-61, 64, 74, 75, 76, 99, 154, 184
Johnson, Marigold, 191, 221

Kaufmann, Gerald, 52
Kazantzis, Alec, 156
Kazantzis, Judith, 252, 253, 254
Kee, Robert, 192
Keeble, Gwen, 191, 233
King, Cecil Harmsworth, 70, 245
King, Jill, 222

Knapp-Fisher, James, 240
Kray, Charles, 126
Kray, Reginald, 125-7
Kray, Ronald, 125-7
Kray, Violet, 125
Kutchinsky, Professor, 197

Laing, Margaret, 241
Lambert, Angela, 160
Lee, Jennie (Baroness), 66, 189
Leicester, Bishop of (Rt. Rev. Ronald Ralph Williams), 226
Lemass, Sean, 99
Le Quesne, Godfray, 221
Levin, Bernard, 223, 225, 251
Levy, Ben, 189
Listowel, William Francis (5th Earl of), 34, 56
Longford, Christine (Countess of), 93
Longford, Edward (6th Earl of), 93, 226
Longford, Elizabeth (Countess of), 14-15, 16, 17, 24, 187, 195, 198, 223, 224, 241, 242, 246, 248, 250-2, 258, 260, 261 passim
Longford, Francis Aungier (7th Earl of), origins and upbringing, 12-13; works for Conservative Party, 14; marriage, 14-15; post-war political career, 21; bank chairman and prison worker, 22; political position in 1964, 22-4; Leader of House of Lords in Harold Wilson's Government, 27-33; Lords' Reform, 33-40; Abortion Bill, 1967, 41-2; Cabinet policy issues, 43-53; going into Europe, 53-4; Labour politicians, class and religion, 55-61; resignation from Government, 1968 62-8; dissatisfaction ith Wilson's Government, 68-77; Ireland: early connections, 81-4; the war, 84-6; Ireland leaves Commonwealth, 87-9; collaboration on

Life of de Valera, 92-5; involvement with Northern Ireland, 97-116. Prisoners, 119-52; helps start the New Bridge, and co-author of the Pakenham-Thompson Report, 129-30; Chairman of report to Harold Wilson on treatment and prevention of crime, 131-2; the New Bridge, 137-9; correspondence with Ian Brady and Myra Hindley, 140-52; Chairman of National Youth Employment Council, 154-6; chairs inquiry into I.L.E.A. Youth Service, 156-8; starts New Horizon Youth Centre, 159-73. Views on the permissive society, 177-85; sets up pornography inquiry, 190-94; made Knight of the Garter, 195; visits Copenhagen sex clubs, 197-203; collects evidence for the report, 203-12; report comes out, 212-25; Government and parliamentary reaction, 225-8; becomes director of Sidgwick & Jackson, publishers, 233; publishing experiences, 238-47; family, 248-61; Christian idea of suffering, 261-70; personal reflections, 271-80
Lusty, Sir Robert, 237, 246
Lynch, Jack 92, 99, 113

MacBride, Sean, 87-8
Macmillan, Harold, 91
Margesson, Francis Vere (2nd Viscount), 195
Martelli, Ann, 249
Masham of Ilton, Susan (Baroness), 110, 269
Mathew, Most Rev. David, Archbishop of Apamea, 259
Mathew, Rev. Anthony Gervase 259
Maudling, Reginald, 119, 120, 121 124
Maxwell, Dr Chris, 248

Mayhew, Christopher Paget, 62, 67
McBride, William John, 115
McCulloch, The Rev. Joseph, 222
McDougall, Jack, 235
McKie, David, 58
McKie, John, 177
McKenzie, Robert, 193
McWhirter, Ross, 178
Mellish, Bob, 31
Melly, George, 206, 212
Montague, Edward, 129, 235
Montgomery, John, 205
Morris, Alf, 269
Morrison, Herbert (Baron), 55
Moseley, Sir Oswald, 18
Mother Teresa, 229
Moyne, Bryan (2nd Baron), 91
Muggeridge, Malcolm, 221, 228-30, 256, 262
Murdoch, Rupert, 209
Murphy, Noel, 115
Murray, James, 219

Napley, David, 119, 120
Neville, Richard, 206-7
Newman, Nanette, 212
Noel-Baker, Philip, 87-8

O'Neill, Tom, 85, 87, 92-4, 237
O'Neill, Phelim, 103-4
O'Neill, Terence (Baron), 95, 97-100, 102, 103, 104
Oliver, Matthew, 205
Orwell, Sonia, 235

Paisley, Ian, 102, 104-5
Pakenham, Lady Catherine, 93, 253-60, 268
Pakenham, Kevin, 253, 255-6
Pakenham, Michael, 253, 273
Pakenham, Paddy, 253, 255, 272
Pakenham, Thomas, 252, 253
Parkinson, Michael, 192, 193
Patterson, Dr Eric, 212

Peake, Mrs Mervyn, 262
Pearson, John, 241
Pegden, Sue, 197-8
Phillips, Norah (Baroness), 67
Powell, Anthony, 234
Powell, Enoch, 39, 71
Powell, Lady Violet, 234
Prince, Leslie, 160
Probyn, Walter, 133-4
Profumo, Jack, 160
Profumo, Valerie, 160

Ranée of Sarawak, 242
Raymond, Paul, 210
Reading, Stella (Marchioness), 160
Rees-Mogg, William, 209
Richardson, Charles, 124
Richardson, Edward, 124
Richardson, Gina, 253
Robbins, Lionel (Baron), 91

Salisbury, Bobbety (5th Marquess), 41, 62, 257
Savile, Jimmy, 193
Saville, Dr Christine, 197, 201, 214
Scott, Dr Peter, 204
Serota, Bee (Baroness), 131
Shackleton, Edward (Baron), 29-30, 31, 33, 39, 40, 41, 67, 226
Sharkey, James, 212
Shepherd, Malcolm, (2nd Baron), 28, 34
Shrapnel, Norman, 228
Silkin, Lewis (1st Baron), 185
Sim, Alastair, 246
Slattery, Sir Matthew, 160
Smith, Lady Eleanor, 85, 234
Smith, Ian, 51
Snow, Jon, 164 passim to 173
Soper, Rev. Donald (Baron), 57-8
Soskice, Sir Frank, 131, 136, 260
Spath, Frank, 262
Stansgate, Wedgwood Benn (1st Viscount), 33
Steiner, George, 212

Stewart, Michael, 32, 48, 53, 74
Stockwood, Right Rev. Mervyn,
  Bishop of Southwark, 58
Stokes, Donald (Baron), 280
Stonham, Victor (Baron), 132
Storr, Anthony, 119 *passim* to 124
Stott, Mary, 208
Stride, Rev. Eddie, 188

Taylor, Sir Alan, 250
Templer, Field-Marshal Sir Gerald,
  251
Thatcher, Margaret, 28
Thompson, Peter, 129-30
Thorneycroft, Peter (Baron), 62
Toynbee, Philip, 249, 273-4, 276
Trench, Sally, 160
Turner, Merfyn, 133
Tuzo, Lt.-General Sir Harry, 108
Tweedie, Jill, 130, 192, 193, 211-12

Villiers, Arthur, 153

Walker, Martin, 159, 161 *passim* to
  167
Wansell, Geoffrey, 273-4
Ward, Christopher, 219
Warner, Esmond, 23
Warnoch, Mary, 120

Watson, Graham, 238, 242, 243
Waugh, Auberon, 250
Waugh, Evelyn, 11, 32, 249
Wedgwood, Dame Veronica, 246
Weidenfeld, Sir George, 237, 240,
  246
Wheeler-Bennett, Sir John, 94
Whitehouse, Mary, 188, 194, 198,
  219, 221, 228
Whitelaw, William, 111-12
Williams, Marcia, 52
Willis, Ted (Baron), 189
Wilson, Harold, 24, 27 *passim* to 33,
  35 *passim* to 40, 43-4, 46 *passim* to
  52, 54, 56, 58, 60, 62-3, 66, 68-73,
  91-3, 95, 136, 160, 184, 189, 245
  and *passim*
Winchester, Simon, 108
Wing, D. M., 142, 148, 216
Winter, Patricia, 191, 197
Wolfenden, Sir John, 184 (Wolfen-
  den Report *passim*)
Woodham-Smith, Cecil, 251
Woodruff, Douglas, 249
Woods, Joan, 236
Wootton, Barbara (Baroness), 56,
  131, 133 (Wootton Report *passim*)
Worsthorne, Peregrine, 197, 211
Wright, Martin, 138

Yaffé, Maurice, 204